THE HISTORY OF CHRISTMAS FOOD AND FEASTS

Also by the same author for Remember When
The History of Tea

Other books by Remember When include:
Classic Playground Games – From Hopscotch to Simon Says by Susan
  Brewer
Christmas Collectables by Tracy Martin
Food through the Ages by Anna Selby
Great British Fictional Detectives by Russell James
Great British Fictional Villains by Russell James
History of Men's Fashion by Nicholas Storey
Mary Gilliatt's Fabulous Food and Friends – Entertaining Princess Margaret,
  Spike Milligan and Other Friends by Mary Gilliatt
The Pocket Guide to Plays and Playwrights by Maureen Hughes
The Private Diaries of Alison Uttley, Author of Little Grey Rabbit Edited
  by Denis Judd
The Victorian Christmas by Anna Selby

Coming soon
Old Farmhouse Recipes by Alison Uttley
The Pocket Guide to the Classics by Maureen Hughes
Victorian Health Remedies by Thomas Allinson, edited by Anna Selby

Please contact us via any of the methods below for more information or
a catalogue.

REMEMBER WHEN
47 Church Street – Barnsley – South Yorkshire – S70 2AS
Tel: 01226 734555 – 734222 Fax: 01226 – 734438
E-mail: enquiries@pen-and-sword.co.uk
Website: www.rememberwhen.co.uk

THE HISTORY OF CHRISTMAS FOOD AND FEASTS

by

CLAIRE HOPLEY

First published in Great Britain in 2009 by
Remember When
an imprint of
Pen & Sword Books Ltd
47 Church Street
Barnsley
South Yorkshire
S70 2AS

ISBN 978 1 8446 680 658

Typeset in 11/13pt Plantin by
Mac Style, Beverley, East Yorkshire

Printed and bound in the UK by
by CPI

Pen & Sword Books Ltd incorporates the imprints of Pen & Sword Aviation,
Pen & Sword Maritime, Pen & Sword Military, Wharncliffe Local History, Pen
and Sword Select, Pen and Sword Military Classics and
Leo Cooper.

For a complete list of Pen & Sword titles please contact
PEN & SWORD BOOKS LIMITED
47 Church Street, Barnsley, South Yorkshire, S70 2AS, England
E-mail: enquiries@pen-and-sword.co.uk
Website: www.pen-and-sword.co.uk

Contents

Acknowledgements

THIS BOOK would not have been possible without help. First, I want to thank all the following people and organisations for their generosity in providing images. Wendy Watson, Curator of the Mount Holyoke College Art Museum, located Orazio Sammachini's drawing of the nativity in Chapter One and the Adoration of the Magi by Jean de Montlucon, which is among the colour plates. I greatly appreciate her help and the kindness of Mount Holyoke College. Similarly, I thank Sebastian Wormell, who generously allowed me to use four images from the archives of Harrods, Limited: the pictures of the Meat Hall and the 1935 advertisement in Chapter Seven, and the wonderful Santa in ARP uniform and 1908 certificate among the colour plates. The QUALITY STREET ® name and image is reproduced with kind permission of Société des Produits Nestlé S.A. I also thank Phyllis Mitchell, of Walker's Shortbread Limited in Aberlour, who provided the image of the Walker's shortbread tin. David Sejrup of Chester Marketing generously shared his photographs of the Chester Mystery Plays and Christmas Lantern Parade, and Jonathan Briggs of Mistletoe Matters in Tenbury Wells shared his expertise about mistletoe, and kindly gave permission to use his photographs. My thanks to both of them, and to Joanna Hanna of the Michele and Donald D'Amour Museum of Fine Arts, Springfield, Massachusetts, who arranged for me to reproduce the museum's portrait of Charles Dickens' *Boz* by Nathaniel Currier, which is in the museum's Currier and Ives collection donated by Lenore B. and Sidney A. Alpert. The Renaissance Center of the University of Massachusetts has kindly allowed me to use pictures from volumes in its library, including the portraits of Ben Jonson and Robert Herrick, and fruit and vegetable pictures from Gerard's *Great Herball, or General Historie of Plantes*. Ann Fitzpatrick Brown generously welcomed me to use the photograph of her stupendous Christmas tree at Blantyre, Lenox, Massachusetts. She also allowed me to photograph the cribs and Santas with which she decorates Blantyre at Christmas. For this and many other kindnesses, she has my heartfelt appreciation. My thanks also to the Vicar and Parochial Church Council of All Saint's Church, Daresbury, Cheshire for kindly allowing me to use the photograph of the *Alice in Wonderland* nativity window, which commemorates the birth of Charles Dodgson, better known as Lewis Carroll, in the village in 1832. I also want to thank my husband Bob for endless patience in taking photographs, assembling all the images, and for his help in numerous other ways.

Publishers and writers' agents have also been generous in permitting me to quote from copyrighted work. Tom Jaine of Prospect Books kindly welcomed me to use images from the facsimile editions of the old culinary books that his company has published, in particular the pie shapes from Robert May's *The Accomplish't Cook*. I deeply appreciate Tom Jaine's long commitment to expanding and sharing knowledge of how our ancestors ate and cooked; without it, a book such as this would be impossible. I also thank Bruce Hunter of David Higham for granting permission to quote from *In Search of a Character* by Graham Greene and published by The Bodley Head in 1961, and also from *A Child's Christmas in Wales* by Dylan Thomas, published by New Directions in 1954. The Christopher Little Literary Agency generously granted permission to quote from *Harry Potter and the Philosopher's Stone* © J.K. Rowling, 1997. Aitken Alexander Associates kindly gave permission for me to quote from *Bridget Jones's Diary* © Helen Fielding, 1996.

I want to thank Five Colleges, Inc. for their continuing support; my friends, Susan Roy for making the wreaths shown in this book and Anne Rylestone for bringing Wordsworth's poems to my attention; and Maxwell Hopley, who told me about Harry Potter's Christmas. Finally, my thanks to Pen and Sword editor Fiona Shoop for commissioning this book and sharing her collection of Christmas cards, and to copy-editor Pamela Covey, not only for her expert work on the text but for her many helpful comments as it progressed through production.

CHAPTER 1

Introduction: Traditions and Transformations

In the bleak midwinter
Frosty wind made moan,
Earth stood hard as iron,
Water like a stone;
Snow had fallen, snow on snow,
Snow on snow,
In the bleak midwinter,
Long ago.

Christina Rossetti,
In the Bleak Midwinter, 1872

MORE THAN any other holiday, Christmas brings back special memories: of stockings bulging with toys, trees sparkling with lights, the turkey or a goose reigning over the table, and afterwards the pudding, the mince pies and the marzipanned cake under its carapace of icing. Memory's trawl also brings up pictures of Christmas outings, such as carol-singing or shopping for gifts in brilliantly lit streets and shops. And who can forget the family get-togethers, the pantomimes, and, of course, the parties where things perhaps get a bit out of hand?

We bundle all these and other festivities together as 'Christmas traditions'. They shape Christmas with customs, revelry and foods that must be repeated each year so that every Christmas is 'a proper Christmas', like all those that have gone before.

Mixing old and new traditions

However, Christmas in fact plays fast and loose with tradition. It creates new frolics, picks new foods as must-haves, and incorporates charming customs from other countries. Equally, Christmas can be cavalier about the past: it forgets or abandons old customs, then, perhaps, later revives them. Today, we have Christmas trees and Christmas stockings, but not the Bean King, Lord of Misrule or the Twelfth Night characters who held sway over medieval and Renaissance Christmas – an era when Christmas trees and stockings were unknown. We have Christmas carollers, but rarely Christmas mummers; Christmas pantomimes, but not Christmas masques. Indeed, the Christmas festivities that developed in the Nineteenth Century and now reign supreme differ radically from the ones created by early Christians, which were celebrated with gusto until the Renaissance, and still influence Christmas today.

What, then, are the really *real* Christmas traditions? Are they old customs that we no longer follow: mumming for example? What about the 'real' foods of Christmas? Are they such antique delights as boars' heads, roast peacock and the fantastical spun-sugar confections called subtleties? Are such newcomers as beribboned boxes of chocolates and bright tins of biscuits true Christmas traditions?

The answer is that Christmas foods have always included anything that was luxurious. In earlier eras they highlighted specialities we now take for granted, such as dried fruits from the Mediterranean, oranges from Spain, spices from the East – all of which were expensive. Adding even small amounts of spice or dried fruit to bread dough was a way of transforming the everyday loaf into something special for Christmas. This is why many traditional Christmas foods feature currants, raisins, and spices – Christmas cake, Christmas pudding and mince pies being extreme English examples of a common European tradition. Today, such ingredients have lost their *de luxe* status, but others have replaced them: a tin of caviar, perhaps, or a toothsome pâté, or box of plump marrons glacés.

The other Christmas staple is seasonal foods. In the past, many animals were slaughtered in late autumn because farmers could not feed all their stock through the winter. Thomas Tusser reminded farmers to get on with this November work in his manual *A Hundred Good Pointes of Husbandrie*, first printed in 1557:

> *At Hallowtide slaughter time entreth in*
> *And then doth the husbandmen's feasting begin.*

Autumn and winter were the seasons for hunting, too, making Christmas the one time of year when meat was plentiful – hence the emphasis on large birds or big joints as centrepieces of the Christmas meal. In the Eighteenth Century this was energetically spelled out by Martha Bradley in her *British Housewife or the Cook, Housekeeper's and Gardiner's Companion* (1756). It is organised with sections for every month, and she begins December with:

> *Butcher's Meat in general is never in better season than at this Time of Year, and Beef in particular may appear in the largest Pieces at the best Tables: the French Fashions have carried it a great way against us but they are not arrived yet so far as to banish the Sirloin of Beef from a Christmas dinner.*

As well as beef, she notes 'Mutton never is in better Season … Lamb is now in prime Season … Veal is in as good Season as at any Time … This is the time of year when Pork is most of all in Season … After Pork it is necessary we mention Ham, for there is no Season of the Year when it comes more properly to Table … A Haunch of Venison boiled, with Garden-stuff, is also a very good December dish.' She is equally enthusiastic about fish and poultry. 'Nature seems to have intended that in this cold dark Season Mankind should indulge themselves in the Variety of Good Things,' she enthuses.

Autumn crops such as nuts and apples have always played a part in Christmas baking and desserts, though even Martha Bradley noted 'If there is a Season in which Fruits are more deficient than any other, it is this and the two or three succeeding months.' Apples and pears, which keep well, were highly valued. Town-dwellers would also have been well supplied with oranges, which began arriving from Spain in the Sixteenth Century, and were hawked in the streets. Vegetables were more plentiful: as well as hardy cabbages, carrots and parsnips, the gardeners of large houses maintained hotbeds to ensure a supply of lettuce, cress, radish and asparagus. Brussels sprouts didn't arrive on the British scene until the early Nineteenth Century, but their convenient habit of tasting better after December frosts have nipped them has made them a Christmas fixture.

Our opportunistic attitude to Christmas food illustrates the way Christmas evolves. It hangs on to good things from the past, though often adapts them to new times. Christmas cake descends from Twelfth Night cakes of old; Christmas crackers capture some of the themes of Christmas jests of old; pantomimes feature the same disrespectful humour as the foolery organised by the Medieval and Renaissance Lords of Misrule.

Yet while Christmas retains or transforms the past, it is also ever ready to clasp new delights to its heart. Not all new things, of course, just those that fit in with the Christmas spirit of fun and plenty – even excess. Underlying both the old and the new traditions of Christmas is the urge to kick over the traces of everyday concerns: to eat lots of lovely rich food rather than watch waistlines, to splurge on presents rather than shop for bargains, to stay at home rather than work. We enjoy good times with others rather than focus on private matters, getting together with family and friends, even sending cards to keep in touch with many who have gone long unseen. In these ways, we are like our ancestors who ate meagrely for most of the year, but could be assured of a feast and a good time at Christmas.

Fundamentally, then, Christmas is about transforming the humdrum of everyday into the thrill of festivity. It's about holiday rather than work, feast rather than fast, abundance rather than scarcity, excess rather than restraint, social bonds rather than privacy, life rather than death – though death is sometimes surprisingly close in Christmas stories.

Roman origins

Talk about the eating, drinking, shopping and the general excess of the Christmas season often rouses grumbles about the commercialisation of the holiday. The grumblers are undoubtedly correct. Retailers know that the financial success of the business year depends on turning hard-headed customers into Christmas spendthrifts. Yet commercialisation is only the modern manifestation of the spirit of excess that has always underpinned Christmas celebrations. Unlike our ancestors, most of us can't go hunting deer and wildfowl, but we can buy a new party dress and sparkly shoes or go to the supermarket and pick out the best it has to offer. The bright array of Christmas foods rouses appetites; perhaps it even calls us back to ancient days when the one sure thing about abundance was that it wasn't going to last, so feasting was always justified when the opportunity arose.

Such explanations notwithstanding, there's no doubt that the long-enduring habit of Christmas consumption and Christmas frolic is not in tune with the biblical story of the Nativity. Implicitly or explicitly, those who complain about commercialisation suggest that shops, restaurants and other businesses have shanghaied Christmas, changing it from a celebration of Christ's birth into a festival of greed. However, scholars agree that things happened the other way around: that when the Fourth-

Century Christian church decided to celebrate Christ's birth on 25 December it drew from riotous, heavy-eating, hard-drinking Roman holidays that existed before the birth of Christ and continued for many centuries beyond.

One of these Roman holidays was Saturnalia. The high point of the Roman year, it honoured the god Saturn as the patron of agriculture and of Latium, the region surrounding Rome. At first Saturnalia was a one-day mid-December holiday, but by the time of the earliest Christians it lasted a full week ending on 23 December. Temples and buildings were decorated with greenery. Masters and slaves feasted and drank together. In this spirit of equality, slaves couldn't be punished, so they would cast dice to choose one of their number as King for the day. He would then devise japes or invent ridiculous rules and insist that everyone follow them. This custom survived as the Lords of Misrule that governed English Christmases until the time of the Tudors.

Only a week after the end of Saturnalia came the New Year holiday of Kalends. Once again, work was abandoned along with normal rules of status and behaviour. On New Year's Day everyone exchanged generous gifts. Libanius, a Fourth-Century Greek commentator, compared the thousands of presents given at Kalends to the thousands of flowers that bloom in spring. He very much approved of the generous gift-giving, writing, 'It teaches men not to hold too fast to their money, but to part with it and let it pass into other hands' – a sentiment no doubt shared by modern marketers. The similarity between the lavish presents and open-handed expenditure of Kalends and today's Christmas is easy to see. On the following days the Romans entertained themselves with gambling – another tradition that was long continued and survives today in the board games and electronic games still popular as Christmas presents. Less obviously typical were the Roman masquerades of young men dressed in animal skins and horns, though parades in which Father Christmas arrives or the street lights are turned on still bring crowds into cities.

Saturnalia ended on 23 December and Kalends began on 1 January. Together they made a twin-peaked holiday like our Christmas and New Year festivities or Thanksgiving and Christmas in the USA. In the lull between Saturnalia and Kalends a third celebration developed. It focused on Sol Invictus, the Invincible Sun, and it fell on 25 December, the date of the Roman winter solstice. The cult of Sol Invictus originated in the eastern Mediterranean and in the Persian devotion to Mithras, the God of Light. It appealed initially to Roman soldiers and emperors, who

13

naturally liked to think of themselves as invincible. For Christians, too, it was a potent symbol of Christ as the bringer of spiritual light to the world. The early Christians who debated when to celebrate the Nativity

The Sun at Christmas

This sun-shaped lantern, which appeared in a children's parade to celebrate the start of late-night shopping in Chester, carries on a long tradition of sun symbols at Christmas.

With all its cornucopia of good things, Christmas lacks the most vital of all: the sun. Those days following the shortest day of the year on 21 December are the darkest we have, and the further north we live, the darker they are. Christmas takes much of its power and many of its symbols from this lack of sun. Ancient solstice festivals focused on charming the sun with symbols that recalled its memory and ceremonies that appealed for its return. The evergreens used at winter festivals such as Saturnalia and Christmas are one example. Twisted into wreaths, they have the shape of the sun that brings everything to life. In Scotland the traditional round golden Scottish shortbread mimics the sun, with its notched rim imitating its rays. The older oaten Yule bannock, from which shortbread may have developed, was pinched in points round the edge to make the rays stand out more dramatically. Traditionally the bannocks were made on Christmas morning, and marked with the sign of the cross to divide them into four farls. Each family member got one. The trick was to keep it intact until the evening feast. Anyone who succeeded could expect unbroken prosperity in the coming year.

could have picked any time they liked, because the Bible does not record the date of Christ's birth, nor even indicate the season. When the Fourth-Century fathers chose to celebrate it on the day devoted to Sol Invictus, they clearly hoped to tap into the emotional power of the day, and, perhaps, to divert converts from a rival religion. Increase Mather, a Seventeenth-Century Puritan clergyman opposed to Christmas because it lacked biblical authority, explained that those who picked 25 December as Christmas Day well knew that Christ was not born then: 'But the heathen Saturnalia was at that time kept in Rome, and they were willing to have those Pagan Holidays metamorphosed into Christian [holidays].' Subsequent historians agree with his analysis.

With so much to be gained from having Christmas at a time of year when Romans were already celebrating, taking on board some of the extravagance, revelry and symbolism of pagan holidays was a small price for Christians to pay. Then, too, early Christians shared that human need to relax and enjoy the fruits of their labour after the busiest time of the year. They must have wanted to enjoy the festivities of the Roman world they lived in. It would have been a bad strategy for any proselytising new religion such as Christianity to try to wean them away from traditional festivities. Much better to join in and subvert them to Christian ends.

Gospel stories

However, while many Christmas customs throughout Europe and much of the Christmas spirit can be traced back to ancient Rome, and also to other solstice festivals such as those of the Scandinavians and Celts, the Nativity chronicle of the gospels of Luke and Matthew has shaped the holiday for everyone, and explains the spiritual significance of Christmas to Christians.

St. Luke's gospel account of Jesus' birth focuses on the journey of Mary and Joseph to Bethlehem for the Roman census. When they arrive all the inns are full, and they must shelter in a stable. There Mary's baby, conceived while she was a virgin by the intervention of the Holy Ghost, is born, and for lack of anything better, he is cradled in a manger. A host of angels appears to the shepherds on the nearby hills with news of the birth, telling them to go to the stable and announce to the parents that their baby is the Saviour, Christ the Lord. The psychologically realistic end of Luke's version is 'Mary kept all these things, pondering them in her heart' – as well she might. The shepherds returned to their sheep,

Nativity scene with animals drawn by the Italian Orazio Sammachini around 1600. (Photograph courtesy of Mount Holyoke College Art Museum)

'glorifying God for all they had heard and seen and all that had been told them'.

Luke's account emphasises Joseph as a member of King David's line and Bethlehem as David's city, thus highlighting Christ's royal Jewish genealogy. Apart from this it describes the lowly elements in the Nativity – the stable, the manger, the poor shepherds. St. Matthew's gospel description is more political and more dramatic. He tells of the Three Kings (also called Magi or Wise Men) who arrive in Bethlehem guided by a star. Despite their benevolent wish to give gifts to the child they believe to be the future King of the Jews, their arrival precipitates a disaster. Before visiting the stable with their gold, frankincense and myrrh, they stop at King Herod's court and tell him about the newborn King-to-be. He immediately decides to eradicate this potential usurper by killing all the infant boys in Bethlehem as a way of making sure he gets the one who threatens his throne. An angel warns Mary and Joseph of the danger to their baby, and they escape to Egypt, and live there until after Herod's death. Other parents were not so lucky; their children were killed in a murderous rampage, later called the Slaughter of the Innocents.

Many cribs such as this white porcelain example show both the Three Kings and the shepherds worshipping the new-born Jesus. Gospel accounts suggest the shepherds arrived immediately after the birth, but the kings arrived many days later.

These two stories differ in many details, but they both focus on the nuclear family of parents and their baby. Perhaps because everyone can identify with this fundamental family group, the gospel stories often merge in popular imagination. Illustrations of the Nativity frequently show the kings and shepherds worshipping the baby together, though Luke suggests that the shepherds arrived immediately after the birth, while the kings had a journey, traditionally thought to have taken twelve days. These images of kings and other adults kneeling to the newborn child of poor parents tap the well of festive tradition that emphasises the community of strong and weak, rich and poor at the holiday season. Nativity scenes also include animals: the sheep that have followed their shepherds, the camels that carried the kings, the cows and donkeys and hens that live in the stable. Gazing at the child, their presence implies that the whole natural world has paused to acknowledge the new order that Christ has brought. English tradition long averred that as the clock struck midnight on Christmas Eve, the animals always fell to their knees as Thomas Hardy affirmed in his poem *The Oxen*:

> *Christmas Eve and twelve of the clock.*
> *'Now they are all on their knees,'*
> *An elder said as we sat in a flock*
> *By the embers in hearthside ease.*
>
> *We pictured the meek mild creatures where*
> *They dwelt in their strawy pen,*
> *Nor did it occur to one of us there*
> *To doubt they were kneeling then.*

The religious account of Christmas is fuelled by the same spirit of transformation from the ordinary to the extraordinary that inspires so many secular celebrations of the season.

The literary record

Historians, anthropologists and folklorists have mined the rich lodes of official records and local lore to reveal the origins of Christmas and the ways it has been celebrated in earlier times and different places. In Britain we know that until the Seventeenth Century Christmas was a twelve-day event because traditionally the Three Kings travelled for twelve days to Bethlehem. It lasted from Christmas Day to Twelfth Night on 6 January, the Feast of the Epiphany, which celebrates the kings' arrival. For many centuries Twelfth Night was the most ebullient of all the Christmas celebrations. Indeed, Christmas was a season rather than a brief holiday, with merriment beginning to stir after All Saints' Day on 1 November, the rich keeping open house at Christmas, and festivities not entirely fading until Candlemas on 2 February, which celebrates the Presentation at the Temple and the Purification of the Virgin. The pleasures of the season included games, jousting, processions, singing, dancing, gambling and, of course, eating and drinking. Status barriers were lowered at least a little, so that even the poorest could expect food and drink at Christmas; indeed they were licensed to ask for it, often by singing or dressing up to enact traditional dramas for which they expected payment.

The Reformation put a firm damper on much of the revelry of those distant Christmases, and it was not really until the Nineteenth Century that Christmas as we know it with stockings and trees and pantomimes emerged. When it did the male adults who gambled and got drunk and played wild games in earlier centuries were firmly sidelined.

Carols

The 'carol' comes from the *chorus* of ancient Greek drama, the role of which was to dance as well as sing. English carolling included dancing until the Sixteenth Century, and though carols were typical of Christmas, they were not exclusively Christmas songs nor solely religious. For example, *We Wish You a Merry Christmas* is a Sixteenth-Century wassailing carol from the West Country that encourages listeners to hand over figgy pudding, while the *Boar's Head Carol*, first printed in 1521, was sung as the boar's head was paraded into the hall for the Christmas feast. This carol includes Latin tags, and the first religious carols were Latin church songs sung by clergy from the Fourth Century onwards. Carols, both religious and secular, were sung all over Europe, and their tunes often migrated from one country to another. The first English collection of carols is that of John Audley of Haughmond Abbey in Shropshire, who prefaced it with the injunction 'I pray you sirs, both more and less, sing these carols in Christmas'. England's best-loved Eighteenth-Century carol, *O Come All Ye Faithful*, was written in France by John Wade at the Roman Catholic College in Douai in the 1740s. By the early Nineteenth Century few carols were in print; most were only known as folk songs. Inspired by the new interest in old Christmas customs, scholars began to collect them. The first collection was David Gilbert's *Collection of Christmas Carols* in 1822. Other collections followed throughout the century, and many new carols were written including Christina Rossetti's *In the Bleak Midwinter* and *Ding Dong Merrily on High*. In 1880 Bishop Edward Benson, then of Truro, arranged the first Ceremony of Nine Lessons and Carols. Other churches followed suit. Eric Milner-White, Dean of King's College Chapel in Cambridge, introduced it there in 1918. It has been broadcast since 1928, and televised since 1963, with *Once in Royal David's City* as the opening carol.

Children now took centre stage, with parents trying to provide gifts and entertainments that would make Christmas the happiest time of their year. This is yet another of the transformations typical of Christmas, and it was not complete until the middle of the Twentieth Century, when even working-class families had enough money to buy many toys for their children and plenty of food and drink for all.

The energetic way that Christmas renews itself by developing new aspects of its inheritance is its greatest glory. It can also be rather mystifying. Do we really know what Christmas felt like in other centuries? What would it have been like to spend Christmas in the court of a great lord of the Middle Ages? Did they really revel away twelve whole days and more? Why did the celebrations of those days disappear? Did people forget Christmas until the Nineteenth Century renewed it? If not, how did they celebrate it? And those Victorian or Dickensian Christmas events that nowadays lure visitors to tourist venues or restaurants, how authentic are they? Do they show us what Christmas was really like for Britons during the Industrial Revolution?

Nothing provides a better record of Christmas in earlier centuries than the glimpses we see of it in poems, novels, diaries and plays of other times because they often record details that fall below the radar of official church or legal documents. Equally significantly, they suggest the emotional power of Christmas, and capture the undercurrents and ambivalences that led to change, even in a holiday that foregrounds its age-old traditions. And literature does more than simply record how people used to celebrate: it has also actively shaped Christmas by presenting new facets and insisting on new interpretations of the holiday. Charles Dickens' *Christmas Carol* is only the best-known example of a tale that became so popular that its focus on deprivation in the midst of plenty, especially as it affects children, helped shape the way people thought – and still think – about Christmas.

The culinary record and note on recipes

Just as literary works transport us imaginatively back into earlier Christmases, so cooking and eating the dishes that used to star in Christmas feasts gives us the flavours of Christmas Past. Certainly, food has changed: our meat is tenderer; our bread is softer; our butter less salty; modern brewing and wine-making produce drinks that differ from those quaffed by our ancestors. Still, the closest we can come to the

Christmas feasts in medieval courts, Renaissance manors, or an Eighteenth-Century country house is by trying to recreate the dishes recorded in their cookery books and mentioned by the diarists, poets, playwrights and novelists of the period.

Some old dishes are hard to reproduce. Such ingredients as ox palates or heifers' udders are no longer available or appetising. Sometimes, too, old cooking methods such as spit-roasting in a wide fireplace have disappeared. We now roast meat in closed ovens, so there is usually little point in reprinting roasting recipes from earlier centuries. The aim in this book is to highlight old dishes that will appeal to modern tastes and can be made in modern kitchens. The innumerable pies that appeared on old Christmas tables, the baked dishes of meat and poultry, and the spiced drinks and puddings are well worth reviving for today's Christmas feasts. The pies are especially convenient because they can be baked ahead of time, making Christmas catering easier. Medieval pies of apples and pears with dried fruit are a lighter alternative to mince pies. The Eighteenth-Century Orange Pudding on page 141 is one of the many rich custard tarts of the era with an intriguing texture and flavour. Jane Austen and her mother entertained at Christmas with a tray of widgeon, preserved ginger and black butter. That black butter is actually a firm apple and berry preserve. It's easy to make in autumn, and looks jewel-like set among cheeses at Christmas, or served at a holiday season breakfast with muffins or croissants. The recipe is on page 181. Francatelli's Sweet Pudding Sauce on page 180, presented as economical for Nineteenth-Century working-class homes, is an unusual companion to Christmas pudding.

Even when we cannot be sure that a modern interpretation of an old dish captures the tastes and flavours of the original, reading classic literary texts and eating the dishes their authors would have enjoyed takes us into the culinary work and pleasures of the past, and brings us a few steps closer to what Christmas has been like since it was first celebrated in Fourth-Century Rome.

Dress the Halls

The Romans wreathed their buildings in greens for Saturnalia just as we do at Christmas. The symbolism is easy to see. In the darkest, coldest time of year, when the ground is too hard to produce a crop, trees that keep their leaves promise the return of spring, when everything will green up and grow again. Holly, ivy and mistletoe are especially beloved because they bear their berries when other plants have withered. 'Dress the halls with boughs of holly' begins the well-beloved Welsh carol. Another sings the symbolism of Christmas greens:

The holly and the ivy, when they are both full grown
Of all the trees that are in the wood, the holly bears the crown.

Here the prickles of the holly are reminders of Christ's crown of thorns, with its red berries symbolising droplets of blood. Bay was used in crowns for conquerors and poets, as well as at Christmas, to signify undying fame. Tottell's *Miscellany* of 1557 explained 'When other frutes and flowers decay, the bay yet grows full grene.' Ivy was also used in poets' crowns because its greenness betokened 'noble wit and sharp'. In the Seventeenth Century Robert Herrick cited rosemary, bay, mistletoe and holly as the greens of Christmas in his *Ceremonies for Candlemasse Eve.* A century later John Gay evoked the season with:

> *Now with bright Holly all your temples strow,*
> *With Laurel green and sacred Mistletoe.*

Despite its potent symbolism, Christmas greenery hasn't gone uncriticised. In the Sixth Century Christian authorities at the Council of Braga forbade their use because they were linked to Saturnalia. During the Reformation Puritans recalled the pagan origins of Christmas greenery. When they abolished traditional Christmas festivities in 1647, officers were sent to remove evergreens from St. Margaret's, Westminster and other London churches. Nevertheless, evergreens at Christmas have survived all attacks.

CHAPTER 2

Christmas in the Court of Camelot

For there the feast was the same for fifteen days
With all the meat and mirth that men could wish
Such gladness and glee, glorious to hear.

Anonymous, *Sir Gawain and the*
Green Knight, c.1390

SINCE THE mid-Nineteenth Century publishers have been harvesting an annual crop of Christmas books ranging from novels and short stories to anthologies, albums, children's books, and most recently, Christmas cookery books. Even before opening their glossy covers, we know that whatever the ostensible topic, all Christmas books focus on the joys of family, the comfort of home, the pleasures of food and the elation of wishes come true.

This is very different from the Fourteenth-Century poem *Sir Gawain and the Green Knight*, which is most definitely a Christmas tale, yet equally definitely, quite unlike the familiar Christmas stories of the last century or so. It introduces us to a Christmas world that has no Christmas trees, no Christmas stockings, no Father Christmas and no Christmas cribs with the kings and shepherds adoring Mary and her Child. Indeed, there are no children at all; adults – men in particular – dominate Christmas in Sir Gawain's world. They are Christians, yet their Christmas pleasures show them still in touch with the Saturnalian and other pagan sources of the holiday. Reading about them takes us back to a time when Christmas brought people together for games and feasts and whatever sport or chance betided. General revelry was the rule. The family togetherness we know today was not celebrated – at least not at a level that has reached historical or literary records. Yet the ancestors of customs that live on in today's Christmas peep out from Sir Gawain's world, and his encounter with the Green Knight reveals some of the most deeply buried underpinnings of our Christmas season.

A strange tale of a Christmas game

Sir Gawain and the Green Knight is one of the greatest poems in English, yet it's little known outside university classrooms. One reason is that though its author was Chaucer's contemporary, he writes in the North Midlands dialect, which is much harder to understand than Chaucer's English. Then, too, the author does not use rhyme or free verse, but writes in lines that alliterate like those of Old English poetry. The alliteration can seem odd, though it often packs stunning power in such scenes as the amazing arrival of the Green Knight in King Arthur's court, the vibrant detail of Sir Gawain's wintry journey and the throbbing pace of the hunting scenes. The story moves quickly in a series of dramatic and thrilling episodes, though at every point there are ambivalences or mysteries that suggest the way Christmas reaches into all corners of the psyche.

Christmas in Camelot

As the story begins King Arthur and his knights are enjoying the long medieval Christmas in Camelot. The court was filled with hubbub as the knights 'jousted full jollily' and danced with the 'loveliest ladies who ever lived'. They exchanged presents on New Year's Day rather than Christmas Day – a tradition long continued – then feasted with 'all the meat and mirth that men could wish':

> *Dainties came forth of delicious food*
> *Plenty of fresh meat on so many silver dishes*
> *That it was hard to find a place to set them in front of the people.*

King Arthur stood, following the custom rooted in Saturnalia and Kalends in which the lord of the feast defers to lowlier folks. More significantly:

> *Arthur would never eat on such a cherished day*
> *Until he was amused by some adventurous thing,*
> *A strange tale of some ancient marvel of arms or other adventure.*

Telling old stories, often with monsters or magic or ghosts, was long a favourite Christmas entertainment, but Arthur doesn't get an 'ancient marvel', he gets a real 'adventurous thing'.

The Green Knight and his game

Suddenly a huge man rides into the hall. In one hand he hefts a forbidding axe, in the other 'a holly spray that is greenest when the groves are bare'. This interloper is 'greenest' too: his face, his hair, beard, clothes, furs, belt, jewels – all green. His horse has a green saddle and bridle glimmering with green gems. Gold filaments interlace its green mane, and golden bells and more green jewels glitter its tail.

The 'green as the grass' visitor compliments Arthur on his knights: 'The wisest and worthiest in the world … sporting and courteous too.' Explaining that his holly branch shows he comes peacefully, he asks for 'a Christmas game for Yule and New Year' and offers his mighty axe as a prize to whoever withstands 'one stroke for another'. He will suffer the first blow, but whoever accepts the challenge must submit to a return blow a year and a day hence.

Arthur's knights are transfixed. Silently they consider this 'game' and the axe it is to be played with:

The length of an ell, made of green steel and gold
The bit burnished bright, with a broad edge as sharp as a razor
Engraved in green with lovely designs, and looped
  around with a tasselled cord.

On the one hand, no-one feels confident of prevailing against the mighty Green Knight, yet surely any blow he took from that mighty axe would kill him. What then to fear? With the Green Knight dispatched, there would be no question of having to withstand a return blow. Would there?

When Sir Gawain accepts the challenge, the Green Knight repeats the condition:

By thy troth, you shall seek me yourself, where you think I may be found
To fetch the same wages as you deal me today.

He moves back his green hair and exposes his neck. Gawain hefts the axe and takes a mighty swing:

He let it down swiftly on the naked neck
And the sharp blade shattered the bones
And cut through the flesh and severed it in two.
The bit stuck in the ground as the handsome head fell to the earth
Fellows found it rolling at their feet,
The blood pumping from the body: bright red on green.

The Green Knight rises, picks up his head – which Arthur's knights are booting round the floor – and holding it aloft by its green hair, mounts his green horse and gallops away, pausing only to remind Gawain to keep his bargain: next Christmas he must find the Green Chapel, ask for its Knight and there accept a return blow.

Arthur shrugs all this off as typical of Christmas:

Laughing, singing, lords and ladies dancing, watching interludes are
fitting fun for Christmas.

Yet chopping off heads seems an entirely other order of entertainment. The question fastens in the mind: how can Gawain hope to come away from next year's encounter alive?

Gawain's journey

The tale moves swiftly into its second phase. After the great feast on All Saints' Day (1 November) Gawain readies himself, dressing to impress in a coat of eastern silk, an ermine-edged cape, gilded armour and spurs, and a heavy helmet with a diamond-studded diadem and a jewelled band embroidered with parrots and lovebirds. His shield has a red pentangle – a star of lines 'that overlap and lock each other'. The five points characterise Gawain: he is faultless in his five senses, his five fingers never fail, his faith is in the five wounds of Christ and the five joys Mary had in her child. A picture of Mary on the inside of the shield may remind us of the Nativity, but *Sir Gawain and the Green Knight* focuses on Mary's role as Gawain's guardian – not on her connection to Christmas.

Gawain certainly needs help as he travels north on his horse Gringolet. They journey through drear forests and mountains, eventually coming to North Wales, and then fording the River Dee. On they go through the wilderness, fighting outlaws, battling dragons and wolves, but never hearing tell of the Green Chapel. On Christmas Eve, exhausted with hardship, Gawain prays to 'Mary that is mildest mother dear'. Soon, he spies a beautiful castle. Longing to see out Christmas in its sheltering walls, he's delighted when a friendly porter opens the gates and the Lord welcomes him, saying: 'All is your own here to have at your will.'

Feasts, hunts, temptations and the return blow

Now Gawain's story moves to its final phase. He is given a luxurious bedroom. Servants bring him clothes and furs, and set a table for him. In the Middle Ages Christmas Eve was kept as the last day of the Advent fast, which began early in December. Meat was forbidden. Fish was the rule, but on Christmas Eve in a great court, that translated into a veritable feast:

> *Soups and stews, all well-seasoned*
> *Double portions as is proper, many kinds of fish*
> *Some baked in bread, some grilled on the coals*
> *Some boiled, some cooked in stews savoury with spices*
> *And also sauces so well-made that Gawain savoured them*
> *Often proclaiming that this meal was a feast.*

The evening concludes with wine and convivial conversation about King Arthur's court with the Lord and Lady. Finally, his host takes off his hood, hangs it on a spear, and invites all to compete for it in a Christmas game.

On Christmas Day everyone briefly remembers 'the tiny lord whose destiny was to die for us' before heading for the Christmas feast, where Gawain sits with the beautiful Lady, while the Lord of the castle sits with her ugly, but obviously esteemed, attendant. After three more days of feasting, Gawain talks of departing but his host won't hear of it. The Green Chapel lies nearby, he says. Why doesn't Gawain keep his wife company until New Year's Day while he goes hunting? They can even have a friendly Christmas game:

> *Whatsoever I win in the woods will be yours,*
> *And what gains you get you will exchange with me.*

Gawain agrees. The Lord leaves before dawn, and is soon chasing deer into a valley 'with such ear-splitting cries as if the cliffs had cracked'. And what is Gawain up to? He's snug under warm covers until awakened by the Lady sidling into his room and settling herself on his bed. 'A sound sleeper you are!' she teases him. Threatening to tie him to the bed, she says:

> *Since I have in this house a man who everyone likes*
> *I shall use my time well while it lasts*
> *You are welcome to my body your own wish to meet*
> *It behoves me of force to be your servant.*

This alarms Gawain. As King Arthur's knight he cannot take advantage of another man's wife; equally, he must be courteous to a lady. So when she says that a true knight would demand a kiss, he says he can only kiss at her command. No sooner said than done. When her husband returns, Gawain has the kiss to exchange for his venison.

The next day proceeds in the same way. The hunters start off after a powerful boar. Many are injured chasing it, until finally the Lord of the castle slays him with a sword after a fierce fight in a river. Again, Gawain spends the day in bed, the Lady joins him, and again, Gawain accepts her kisses, which he later exchanges for the boar that the Lord presents. Together, they spend the evening in feasting and carols.

On the third day, the Lord hunts again, and yet again the lady appears in Gawain's room, now wearing robes that display her lovely décolletage. She chides him with not loving her – a fault she can justify only if he is in love with another woman. Gawain admits he has no other love. Now 'Great peril stood between them unless Mary thought of her knight.' Once again, Gawain seems to save himself by surrendering a kiss. He refuses a ring the Lady offers, saying he has nothing to give in return. 'If you decline my ring, I shall give you my girdle, which is worth less,' she responds. Again Gawain refuses.

To this point, Gawain has been the perfect knight. He accepted the Green Knight's challenge and travelled through difficulty and danger for the return bout. He has been a good guest, entertaining his newfound friends with tales of Arthur and his knights. Thrice he has resisted the Lady's wiles. Yet she repeats her offer:

> 'Do you reject this silk because it is simple?' then said the Lady.
> 'It may seem to be of little worth,
> But peradventure whoever knows the secrets knit therein
> Would prize it at more price.
> For whoever is girded with this green band
> While he has it about him no warrior under the heaven can hew him
> He cannot be slain through any sleight on earth.'

She has him! Gawain sees that the belt is 'a jewel for the jeopardy' he faces, promising safety from the Green Knight's deadly stroke. He agrees to take it and also to hide it from her husband. Later, Gawain gives him only the day's kisses, which his host accepts as fine payment because all he has to give is a fox pelt – not the luxury meats of the previous days.

Next day Gawain adds the Lady's girdle to his rich armour. Led by a servant, he rides through the snow to a hill where they look down on the frozen wasteland where the Green Chapel lies. The servant warns Gawain that this cold and desolate land is ruled by a monster 'bigger than the best four in Arthur's court', and eager to kill travellers. Nonetheless Gawain rides on, through hills and crags, until he hears the sound of blade on whetstone. Suddenly, the Green Knight leaps into sight, vaulting over a river with the help of a stupendous Danish axe and shouting alarming instructions:

> *Take your helmet from your head and have here your pay.*
> *Talk no more than I did*
> *When you whipped off my head with one whop.*

Gawain obeys and kneels with naked neck, apparently fearless.

> *Then the Warrior in Green got himself ready*
> *Gathered up his grim weapon to smite Gawain*
> *With all the strength in his body he lifted it on high.*
> *Had it driven down as hard as it seemed it would have injured,*
> *He would have been dead from the blow.*
> *But Gawain gave a glance at the weapon*
> *As it glided down to cut him,*
> *And his shoulders shrank a little from the sharp iron.*

The Green Knight holds back. 'You can't be Gawain,' he mocks. 'I have never heard such cowardice of him.' Reasonably enough, Gawain points out that he lacks the power to restore a chopped-off head to its proper place. Nevertheless, he says, 'I shall stand the stroke and flinch no more until your axe has hit me.' Shouting 'Have at thee then', the Knight takes another mighty swing, yet once more stays his arm. Gawain urges him to get it over, and finally he brings the blade down. It merely nicks Gawain's neck.

Why this mini cut? The Green Knight explains that he twice raised his axe without striking because Gawain twice kept the bargain and swapped the Lady's kisses for the spoils of the hunt. The third stroke cut the skin because Gawain broke faith: he kept the magic girdle. The Green Knight now reveals that he was the Lord, telling Gawain:

> *I know well your kisses and the costs also.*
> *I brought about my wife's wooing myself.*
> *I sent her to try you, and truly I think*
> *One of the most faultless men that ever trod on foot.*
> *As a pearl is prized higher than a white pea,*
> *So is Gawain, in good faith, by other gallant knights.*
> *But here you lacked a little sir: loyalty was lacking*
> *Not for any wicked purpose, nor for wooing either*
> *But because you loved your life, so I blame you the less.*

31

Asked for his name, the Green Knight says: 'Bertilak of Hautdesert, I rule in this land through the might of Morgan le Fay.'

Gawain knows Morgan as a sworn enemy to Arthur. Disguised as the Lady's ugly attendant, she has dreamed up the beheading challenge to test the mettle of Arthur's court. Mortified because he has brought shame on Camelot by concealing the girdle, Gawain now vows to wear it as a sign of the frailty of the flesh. When Arthur and his knights welcome him back, they are eager to hear his story, which is, of course, that tale of marvel and adventure that Arthur had wanted the Christmas before. Gawain describes the bargain with Bertilak, calling the green girdle 'the emblem of the blame'. Laughing off this punctiliousness, they say they will all wear identical baldrics in his honour. Thus, the green sash became a symbol of the Knights of the Round Table – though for Gawain it always signified a bargain betrayed.

Survival against the odds

The tale thus has two endings and both stay clearly in view: Gawain succeeded heroically against seemingly impossible odds to keep his first bargain with the Green Knight. Equally, he failed to keep the second bargain to trade winnings. Christmas also stays clearly in view. The poem starts with Christmas feasting and the Green Knight's challenge is made and accepted as a Christmas game. We move quickly from the first December to the next. Once Gawain arrives at the castle, Christmas revels take centre stage again with yet another Christmas game: the trade of the winnings of the day.

Yet *Sir Gawain and the Green Knight* has a tension that is different from the Christmas tales of the last couple of centuries with their focus on children and jollity. Instead of comfortable Christmas cheer, *Sir Gawain* is full of mystery and danger. The Green Knight's deadly Christmas game puts a conundrum at the centre of the tale: how can Gawain withstand the return blow? The answer comes with the revelation that the Green Knight and Bertilak are one and the same, and that the wicked Morgan le Fay masterminded his 'game' to undermine the prestige of Camelot.

This is an adult ending. Here is no sentimental resolution typical of later Christmas fiction. Yet *Sir Gawain and the Green Knight* sounds deep notes that reverberate through many later Christmas tales. At their heart they tell of transformations brought about by new understandings. In Gawain's case, it is the knowledge that brave man though he is, when it comes to possible death, terror shapes his actions. Indeed, death is rarely out of sight, entering the story with the Green Knight's frightening challenge and clearly in view as Gawain travels through the wilderness to offer his neck to the axe. Today, death seems alien to Christmas, yet it lurks everywhere in Christmas tales. Charles Dickens' Scrooge faces death when the ghost appears. After the Spirit of Christmas Yet to Come shows him his own deathbed, he votes with his feet and his wallet for life. Death from starvation haunts Dickens' next Christmas story, *The Chimes*. Hans Christian Andersen's Match Girl expires in the Christmas snow. In Tchaikovsky's *Nutcracker* Clara only travels to the wonderland where she meets the transformed Nutcracker Prince after the battle between the toy soldiers and the mice has left the stage littered with bodies. Dylan Thomas's *A Child's Christmas in Wales* begins with a fire at the Protheros' which apparently threatens disaster. The threat of death in Christmas tales creates anxiety; survival releases the tension, turning fear into the elation typical of the season.

The death of winter

Far from being out of place, death is the source of Christmas. The holiday comes at the darkest and coldest time of the northern year. Nothing is growing. In earlier centuries, any winter journey might bring death. Food could run low. Illness could strike while resistance was down. While Christmas traditions such as feasting celebrate the harvest recently gathered in, the energy powering many others is the battle against the death-dealing cold of winter. The main weapon is fire and light. From the torch-lit halls of the Middle Ages to the fairy-lit Christmas trees and flaming Christmas puddings of today, warmth and light are the most deeply rooted of Christmas customs because they counter the threats of cold and darkness.

Similarly, the bright colours of Christmas array themselves against the dun of bare trees and fields. Red is the colour of heat and warmth. Gold signals wealth and plenty. Green is the colour of life: of fattening buds and brightening grass; it's the colour of spring and a new year of growth and life. It's the colour of the Green Man – a familiar figure in medieval churches, carved in wood on choir stalls or in stone on pulpits and buttresses, and just as popular in garden ornaments today. He has leaves growing from his mouth or sometimes from every part of his head. Folklorists say the motif is ancient, found in many cultures, and certainly pagan in origin. They suggest that Puck and Robin Hood may be forms

Carved images of a Green Man with a head of leaves are common in Fourteenth and Fifteenth-Century churches, especially in the south-west and north-west of England.

of the Green Man, as may the Jack-in-the-Green figures who still lead traditional May Day processions in some villages. In Clun in Shropshire, for example, he comes on the old Whit Monday to battle the spirit of winter on Clun Bridge. The Green Man is especially common in churches in the west of England, where *Sir Gawain* was evidently written.

Like the Green Man, the Green Knight with his holly branch that is 'greenest when the groves are bare' is nothing if not full of life. Before he arrives at the Green Chapel nothing could be wintrier and more drear. The sound of the axe being sharpened is the sound of death in a cold land. Things change as soon as he comes bounding down the hillside, leaping over the river to stand emerald in the snow. In this manifestation, the Green Knight is like the Green Man – a warrior of the spring who triumphs over winter. He is just as potent when he manifests as Bertilak, appearing always at one with winter in the Christmas and hunting scenes. Winter and spring are thus equally powerful, but spring always puts an end to winter.

It is also possible to see Gawain, in a Christian light, as a vainglorious man tempted by evil. He needs help from Mary and redemption from 'the tiny Lord whose destiny was to die for us'. At the end he is ashamed of his dishonesty about the green girdle, and those who hear his story sympathise with him, so the complacency of King Arthur's court seems wrong. Morgan le Fay's elaborate trick has exposed a weakness in Camelot: it is too self-assured, too proud. However, the Christian and secular meanings of the poem do not contradict one another; they

34

coexist. Christmas synthesises the pagan with the Christian, the secular with the spiritual, to celebrate the joys of living, even when the world is dark and cold.

Pictures of a medieval Christmas: games and entertainment

Another way that *Sir Gawain and the Green Knight* illuminates Christmas is by painting a detailed picture of the long medieval and Renaissance holiday, revealing customs that survive today and those that have long gone or been transformed into something seemingly new.

One of the biggest differences between then and now is that Christmas lasted at least twelve days from Christmas Day to Epiphany or Twelfth Night, which celebrates the revelation of Jesus' divinity, and traditionally focuses on the Three Kings and their gifts. Though the days before Christmas were a fast, celebrations heralding Christmas could begin right after All Saints' Day on 1 November. The days immediately following Christmas were sacred to martyrs who lived at the time of Christ. St. Stephen's Day fell on 26 December and was the traditional day for giving alms. St. John's Day came on 27 December, and in many places was celebrated by drinking wine, Holy Innocents' Day fell on 28 December, and New Year's Day was the Feast of the Circumcision and the day for gift-giving. The spirit of revelry could continue even longer, with Candlemas on 2 February celebrating the Purification of the Virgin and Christ's Presentation at the Temple. As the name suggests, it was celebrated with candles in churches and sometimes with candlelit processions. The season of revelry only petered out with a final burst on Shrove Tuesday, the last day when animal foods could be eaten before the forty-day Lenten fast that preceded Easter.

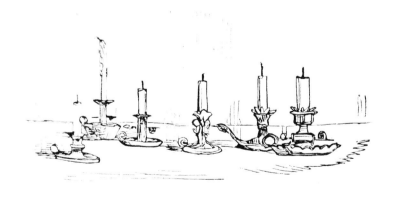

Little work could be done in the cold fields during Christmas, so it was one of the few times of year when people could spend long periods simply having fun. Christmas games were popular, but as *Sir Gawain and the Green Knight* shows, they were not the mild board or card games of today. For knights the games were jousting and tourneys; for poorer men they could be feats of strength such as wrestling. Games of chance, such as Sir Gawain's agreement to exchange winnings with his host, were also favourites. The prizes could be valuable: the Green Knight offers his axe to the man who will chop off his head, and in his role of Bertilak he offers his hood as a prize in a Christmas game. The games and prizes have changed. Soccer, rugby and Boxing Day dips in the icy sea or Serpentine replace medieval feats of arms, but Christmas has always been a season of competition.

It has also always been a season of music, dancing and other entertainments. King Arthur's knights danced and watched plays called interludes. In Bertilak's castle, too, the evenings were spent in pleasure:

> *Around the fire and in many ways*
> *At supper and afterwards, were sung noble songs of Christmas and new*
> *   carols*
> *With all fine mirth that man can tell of.*

Carols during this era were circle dances as well as songs, and the Lady of the castle keeps casting glances at Gawain, perhaps in the hope that he will ask her to dance. Most significantly, both Arthur's and Bertilak's castles seem filled with the Christmas merriment entirely like our own in spirit.

Christmas food and feasting

Most importantly, Christmas has always been a season of feasting. Christmas meals would have been even more welcome than they are today in earlier centuries, when food could be scarce and fasts were frequent. The pre-Christmas Advent fast may not have mattered much to poorer people, who got little meat at the best of times, but for the wealthier denizens of the courts described in *Sir Gawain and the Green Knight* the lack of meat, butter and cheese was monotonous. Cooks alleviated this by inventing dishes in which chopped fish was substituted for chopped meat. They also dreamed up splendid ways of spicing fast-day foods, as in the multitude of fish dishes served on

Christmas Eve at Bertilak's castle. Gawain has fish cooked in bread, probably mortrews of fish, a medieval dish that resembles a Portuguese *açorda* thickened with crumbs. He also has both grilled and boiled fish, and a spiced fish stew. The Christmas Eve feast of fish survives in Roman Catholic countries such as Poland and Italy, where it is the most special meal of the Christmas season.

Though such a fasting meal was enjoyable, the Advent fast heightened the pleasure in the meat feasts of Christmas, as did the knowledge that the six weeks' Lenten fast would begin in February. Girded by two long periods of deprivation, Christmas feasts must have been a bright interlude in hard times. Indeed, Christmas was the only time of the year when food abounded. Grain and other field crops remained from the autumn harvest, as did hoards of nuts, apples and pears. Dried fruits such as raisins, currants and figs were arriving from the Mediterranean. Most importantly, meat was plentiful. One source was the autumn slaughter of farm animals because farmers could feed only breeding or draft animals through the winter. Fresh pork and beef were thus available in large enough amounts so that even the poorest could taste them at Christmas. At other times of the year meat would have been salted or smoked, or maybe entirely unavailable, certainly to poorer people, so the freshness of the meat made it especially delicious. It's significant that the description of the sumptuous New Year's feast in Arthur's court lavishes generalised praise on its many dainties, but it picks out for special notice only the crucial detail: 'plenty of fresh meat'.

Hunting was another source of meat. Like Bertilak, most nobles pursued deer or boar. They enjoyed the sport, yet they pursued their quarry with a determination and disregard of danger that show the importance of supplementing meat from the farm with game from the wild. When Bertilak gives all this venison and boar to Gawain in exchange for the kisses, Gawain is decidedly getting the better of the bargain. Bertilak only claims he has the best of the deal when the hunt yields an inedible fox.

Hare was another prey. Rabbits, too, were popular fare. Usually they were kept in warrens or cages and fattened for the table along with poultry. Peacocks also sometimes stalked the grounds of castles and palaces, and could find themselves the prime choice for an extraordinary feast, perhaps one when royalty or a prince of the Church was present, and the host wanted to impress them by serving a peacock that had been spit-roasted, then covered over by its skin and feathers so it arrived on the table looking gorgeously alive.

Christmas Birds

Our ancestors had an astounding appetite for birds. They not only ate chickens, geese and ducks from their poultry yards, but they either raised or caught many wildfowl for Christmas. Swans were semi-domesticated and their cygnets raised for the table well into the Eighteenth Century. Baby herons and egrets were shaken from their treetop nests and kept in barns with high beams where they could perch. Holes in the roof let in rain to keep them happy. Falcons were also trained to bring down herons and other birds in flight. Smaller birds such as blackbirds, plovers, larks, and even gulls and oystercatchers were netted and then fattened up. Large birds, spit-roasted, and brought in with their legs and wings pointed upwards, were prestigious centrepieces at feasts. Smaller birds could be roasted too, but they were also baked in pies and presented as delicacies in the second or third course of a feast. Larks were still eaten in Victorian England; Charles Dickens' wife Catherine suggested them in a menu in her 1852 book *What Shall We Have for Dinner?* This fondness for birds is at the heart of the Christmas carol *The Twelve Days of Christmas*. The birds offered on each of the first seven days were all common comestibles: a partridge in a pear tree, two turtle doves, three French hens, four calling birds, five golden rings, six geese, and finally seven swans a-swimming. The calling birds were 'coaly birds', a northern name for blackbirds (which really were baked in pies just as the nursery rhyme says), or 'canary birds' as given in old versions of the song. The five golden rings may be 'gold spinks', the Scottish name for goldfinches. Interestingly, the smaller birds are listed first and the larger geese and swans later, recalling the custom of stuffing a large bird with several smaller ones, each tucked inside the other. Hannah Glasse's 1747 recipe called for a turkey stuffed with a goose, which was stuffed with a chicken, which in turn had a pigeon stuffed with a partridge inside it. Like this recipe, the first printed version of *The Twelve Days of Christmas* comes from the Eighteenth Century, but musicologists believe it dates from much earlier.

Less prestigious, but still high on the list of gourmet fare were other large birds such as swans, herons, cranes and egrets. If they were caught live in traps or raised from fledglings they were killed by slitting the roof of the mouth and letting them bleed. This prevented the flesh from darkening, and the cook had the blood to use in the chawdon sauce often served with them. These large birds were usually seasoned with ginger and mustard. This taste for a large bird as the centrepiece of the Christmas table lives on in the present popularity of goose and turkey.

Smaller birds also played their part at feasts. From pheasants and curlews down through snipe and plover and onto the smaller quail, blackbird, lark, woodcock and many more, birds were raised by gamekeepers or snared by fowlers to supply tasty morsels for the table. Often they came in pies. One Fifteenth-Century recipe for a pie of 'flesh, capons and pheasants' includes chopped beef with pork, veal or venison mixed with dried fruit and seasoned with pepper, ginger, cloves, cinnamon and saffron. It was packed in a large pie shell – called a 'coffin' in those days – and whole capons or pheasants coloured with saffron, plus whatever other wildfowl were available were nestled on it. Any gaps could be filled with egg yolks and the whole lot strewn with more spices and dried fruit before the pastry lid went on. Both game pie and mince pies descend from these ancient confections of meat and fruit.

Serving

Virtually any medieval or Renaissance recipe, except those identified as fasting recipes, can be assumed to be a potential for serving at Christmas since all early compilations of recipes were made by the cooks in wealthy households to remind them how to cook specialities for different seasons.

Food was served in courses, but the courses were not limited to one type of dish as they are today: there was no starter or a main dish, for example. Dishes of different kinds came together: soups and broths along with stews, meat dishes and sweet items. Typically the first course would be a selection of common dishes such as roasted meat and hearty stews, with pies and fritters. The second course would be a similar array of dishes, though they would include delicacies or more expensive items. Should there be a third course, it would have yet more delicacies. Sweet dishes appear in the final course or in a banquet served to the host and high-ranking guests in a private room. Among the most prestigious dishes were 'subtleties' – dishes in which one thing was made to look like another. Sugar and marzipan were prime ingredients because pastrycooks could shape them into many forms. Their skills are still used in today's Christmas cakes, chocolate Yule logs and cakes that look like snowmen or Santa Claus.

Some idea of the menu for a king's table comes from *The Forme of Cury*, a late-Fourteenth-Century collection of recipes used in the court of Richard II. Translated into modern English the first course includes venison with boiled wheat, preserved tongue, boiled meat (which could be pork, mutton or beef), boar's head, capons, roast swans, herons and pheasants, large tarts and two subtleties. This was followed by a second course of meat in a sweet and sour sauce, a pottage of chicken or capon in almond milk, roast pork, rabbits, curlews, bitterns, venison, peacock and teals, a large meat pie, almost certainly including dried fruit, fritters and one subtlety. The final course included dates cooked with spices and dried fruit, a bread pudding made and garnished with violets, roasted cranes, peacock 'endored' with egg yolk to make it look golden, roasted quails, plovers, 'grete birdes' (probably swans and herons), roasted rabbits and larks, chicken, fruit dumplings or turnovers, quince pastries, and two more subtleties.

With so many dishes present in each course, a medieval feast was both a performance and an exercise in conspicuous consumption, especially at Christmas when the rich and powerful treated the less affluent to special fare. In Arthur's court the first course includes twelve dishes for every two diners to share. The poem's Fourteenth-Century audience would have understood this as being lavish. More typically in this era (and for many centuries afterwards), the finest foods were usually only served to the high table; people lower down the social scale were seated further down the hall and served smaller, cheaper and fewer dishes. A rule of thumb was that a quarter of a chicken per person was about right for commoners, though nobles got a whole one. Sir Gawain is given double portions of the fish dishes he is served at Bertilak's castle on Christmas Eve. The poet comments that this is fitting – presumably because Gawain is a knight. With additional supplies of everything, those seated at the high table could show favour to someone lower down the hierarchy by sending a choice morsel their way, or instructing a servant to offer one of the more splendid dishes.

We do not know what King Arthur's cooks provided in the second course because the Green Knight appears just as the first course ends, and what with his head rolling about the floor and him issuing orders about the Green Chapel, nobody pays attention to the food, but typically it was only served to the highest-ranking people; others were expected to leave. For example, Constance Hieatt, an expert on medieval cookery manuscripts, notes that at the coronation feast for Richard III only the king's table got three courses; lords and ladies got two, while commoners – that is those without a title but nonetheless including dignitaries such as the Lord Mayor of London – had to leave after one course. Even the lords and ladies did not eat as well as the king: he sampled the peacock; they made do with lamb or kid.

Christmas drinking

Arthur's court followed the custom of the most prestigious knights sitting on high, but regardless of where people sat or whether everyone would have shared in the second course, everyone had 'Good beer and bright wine both'. Here's a note that rings just as cheerily today. The 'good beer' would probably have been brewed especially for the Christmas season – a custom common over northern Europe. Such brews were darker, spicier and slightly more alcoholic than the 'small beer' that was the everyday drink of virtually everyone in England until tea began to supersede it in the Eighteenth Century. In Nineteenth-Century Scotland, Yule ale was made with black treacle and sweetened with honey. The custom of brewing Christmas ales fell victim to the Nineteenth-Century temperance movements and Twentieth-Century brewery consolidations, but smaller breweries have now revived this old tradition.

Wine, too, was often served in special ways at Christmas. Though southern England had vineyards in the 1390s when *Sir Gawain and the Green Knight* was most likely composed, the north, where it was written and set, was too wet and cold for vines, so most wine would have come from Gascony in France. Typically it was a year old at most, and as there was no technology for preventing oxidation, it would have been thin. It needed sweetening with honey or sugar, and for feasts spices were added too. Since these additions cloud wine and the poet describes the wine at Arthur's Christmas feast as 'bright', then it may have been one of the more luxurious sweeter wines of Greece and Cyprus, which needed no help from honey or spice. White Rhenish wine from Germany and Alsace wines were also prized for their brilliance and clarity, so they might have been offered too.

Recipes and ingredients

While many details of wine and food have changed, it is easy to see the origins of our Christmas meals in the cooking manuscripts of the late-Fourteenth and Fifteenth Centuries. Of these *The Forme of Cury*, a title which means 'The Way to Cook', is the earliest to record recipes in English, rather than Norman-French or Latin. The headnote to the manuscript says that it was compiled by the chief Master Cooks of King Richard II's court, with advice from other masters of cooking, medicine and philosophy. Its aim was to teach cooks how to make both common foods and special dishes 'craftly and holsomely': tasty and wholesome. *The Forme of Cury* was compiled in the 1390s – the very decade in which *Sir Gawain and the Green Knight* was written. Since it describes the court of a king renowned for the luxury of his table, its recipes bring to life the food the poet imagined in King Arthur's court and Bertilak's castle.

Typically the recipes demand many expensive eastern spices, and Mediterranean dried fruits such as raisins, figs, and currants. Other imported luxuries included pomegranates, lemons, almonds and pine nuts, which were used in both sweet and savoury dishes. This history of using lots of spices, dried fruits and nuts lives on in the most traditional of our Christmas foods: in mincemeat, Christmas pudding, Christmas cake in England, and in the Dundee cake and Black Bun of Scotland.

One feature documented by cookery books of this and every other century is that Christmas is the time for sumptuous fare. *The Forme of Cury* captures the allure of such foods in the section on 'curious pottages and meats and subtleties'. It requires ingredients we now neglect: not just virtually any and all birds, but obscure bits of animals such as pigs' snouts and animal palates. More enticingly, it uses flowers such as hawthorn blossoms, primroses and

Pomegranates did not arrive in England until the Fourteenth Century. Like all foods from the Middle East they were luxurious. This image comes from the 1633 edition of John Gerard's Great Herball, or General Historie of Plantes.

violets. However, once the oddity of these ingredients and the mysteries of Fourteenth-Century spelling have been penetrated, it is possible to see the origins of some traditional dishes, and to adapt some medieval recipes for use today.

SYRIAN CHICKEN IN WHITE WINE AND ALMOND SAUCE WITH POMEGRANATE SEEDS

Under its medieval name Blanc Desorre, this is one of the dishes listed on menus for the king's table. Desorre, spelled in many ways including 'desire' means 'of Syria', and reveals it as a dish brought back from the eastern Mediterranean by the Crusaders. Such dishes can be spotted by their use of hot-climate ingredients such as the pomegranates, sugar and rice flour in this dish. The aim of all dishes that include 'blanc' in their name (including blancmange) was to make as white a dish as possible. The white theme can be maintained by serving rice with this dish, though it would have been a luxurious choice in Sir Gawain's day because like all imports from the east, it was expensive. This delicate chicken dish is a perfect foil for the spiced and often heavy food of the Christmas season, while the pretty sprinkle of pomegranate seeds, specified in the Fourteenth-Century culinary manuscript *Diversa Cibaria* that the following recipe is based on, looks Christmassy. With slightly modernised spelling the original reads 'Milk of almonds, flour of rice, flesh of capon, ginger, sugar, white wine each one of these should boil in a clean possnet and then put in the clean vessel in which it will be served and pomegranate strained above it.' Pomegranates were first mentioned in England in the early Fourteenth Century, and this recipe is the first that requires them as an ingredient. Their treasury of ruby seeds and the crown formed by the remnants of the calyx on top of the fruit made them popular with royalty including the queens, Catherine of Aragon and Anne of Austria, mother of Louis XIV. They arrived in England in late autumn so they appeared on Christmas dessert tables, sometimes cut to show the seeds, each with its own shiny Christmas-red cloak.

For the chicken:
2 chicken breasts, skinned but preferably not boned
2 chicken legs or 4 chicken thighs, skinned but not boned
1 stem parsley
1 stem thyme
1 small leafy stalk celery
1 bay leaf
salt to taste

For the sauce:
100g/3½oz ground almonds
350ml/12 fl oz chicken stock
1 tbsp rice flour
200ml/7 fl oz white wine such as Gewurztraminer or Rhine wine
2 tsp sugar
¾ tsp powdered ginger
dash of white pepper
salt to taste
3–4 tbsp fresh pomegranate seeds

Put the chicken pieces in a single layer in a large pan. Stick the parsley, thyme, celery and bay leaf among them. Season lightly with salt, then add 750ml cold water. Cover the pan, bring to simmering point and then let the liquid just gently tremble for 30–40 minutes or until the chicken is tender. Remove it and set aside. Drain the liquid and discard the herbs. Let the liquid chill in the fridge. You can do all this a day ahead of time, keeping the cooked chicken covered in the fridge until you are ready to finish the dish.

To proceed, cut the chicken from the bones, keeping it in quite small bite-size pieces. Set aside while you make the almond milk. Remove any fat from the surface of the chicken stock. Combine 350ml of it with the ground almonds in a saucepan, and simmer for 3 minutes over low heat. Let stand for 30 minutes, then strain it through a sieve. Press the dried almonds with the back of a spoon to force as much liquid through as possible.

In a medium bowl, mix the rice flour with 2–3 tablespoons of the almond milk. In a saucepan combine the rest of the almond milk with the wine, sugar and ginger. Bring to boiling point. Stir a little of it onto the rice flour mixture, gradually adding more until you have a smooth mixture. Combine this with the ingredients in the pan, stirring until it has thickened into a sauce. Season it with white pepper (not black), salt and more ginger or sugar if you think they would improve it. Add the pieces of chicken and cook for about 5 minutes, stirring occasionally until they are heated through. Pile onto a warmed serving dish. Sprinkle the pomegranate seeds on top.

SYRIAN FISH

This is another of the many medieval feasting dishes identified as 'Desorre' – from Syria – because of its use of sugar and spices. Indeed, it's another version of Blanc Desorre. The original directions for these fish balls require simply 'powder', a word that then meant a mix of spices. Probably sweet spices such as cinnamon, nutmeg and ginger were intended. You can season the fish however it pleases you. Chilli powder, though entirely anachronistic since it was not known until discovered in Mexico in the Sixteenth Century, works well.

For the fish:
450g/1lb haddock
1 bay leaf
1 stalk fennel, if available
1 stem parsley
1 stem thyme
2 eggs
salt and white pepper to taste
2 tsp ginger
freshly grated nutmeg to taste
85g/3oz flour
125ml/4 fl oz/½ cup milk
oil or fat for frying

For the almond milk:
100ml/3 ½ fl oz fish broth from cooking the fish (see below)
100ml/3 ½ fl oz sweet white wine such as a Riesling
2 tsp sugar
85g/3oz ground almonds
salt to taste

Put the fish, bay leaf, fennel, parsley and thyme in a saucepan and add 2 cups of water. Cover and bring to simmering point. Simmer for about

6–8 minutes or until the fish has cooked. Strain the mixture, reserving the liquid and the fish but discarding the herbs. Whizz the fish in a food processor with one of the eggs and a seasoning of salt and white pepper. Mix in the ginger and nutmeg to taste. Form into balls. The original recipe says they should be the size of egg yolks. Squeeze them a little to compress them. Let them rest while you make the almond milk. Combine the fish broth reserved from cooking the fish with the white wine and sugar, and bring to boiling in a small pan. Stir in the ground almonds. Return to the heat and let simmer for 2–3 minutes, then remove and let stand while you continue with other preparations. Put the flour and a pinch of salt into a bowl. Beat the remaining egg lightly and mix it with the milk. Make a well in the flour and pour in the egg and milk mixture, stirring it to form a smooth batter. Heat about 2 inches of oil in a deep fryer or a wok. When a small cube of bread dropped into it pops up to the surface in about 6–8 seconds the oil is hot enough. Drop the fish balls one at a time into the batter; retrieve them with a small slotted spoon or fork, then drop them a few

In medieval times bay wreaths were honourable adornments. They often decorated large dishes such as a boar's head or some of the huge pies of Christmas. Here a spray decorates Pheasant, Chicken and Meat pie.

at a time into the hot oil. Cook until golden all over, turning them as necessary to achieve this, and keeping those that are done first warm on a dish in the oven. When all are done, return the almond milk to the burner and bring back to simmering. By this time it will be thick. Season lightly with salt to taste. You can either pour it over the fish balls, which is what was indicated in the original recipe, or serve it in a jug at the table.

PHEASANT, CHICKEN AND MEAT PIE

The original recipe for this version of game pie comes from a Fifteenth-Century recipe reprinted in Constance Hieatt's *An Ordinance of Pottage*. Translated into modern English it reads:

> *Take good beef and boil it with pork or veal or venison cut into small bits. Add powdered ginger, cinnamon, cloves and minced dates, or if you prefer, currants, and mix with vinegar, saffron and salt, and take it [a little] in your mouth [to see] if it is well seasoned. Then lay it in pastry in a dish and put in whole capons or pheasants, or if you prefer cut them in pieces. Colour them well with saffron and put in other wild fowl, whatever you like, and put in half yolks of eggs and strew on cloves, mace, minced dates, currants and cubebs. Close it [cover with pastry] and bake for a long time and serve it in the first course.*

Clearly the writer left plenty of latitude so the cook could include whatever was available. The instruction to take a bit in the mouth also emphasises adjusting seasonings to taste, though nowadays the way to do it is to make a small patty and fry it before tasting. Likewise, you can add whatever amount of dried fruit and spices you like, but don't omit them entirely as meat pies can be surprisingly bland without assertive flavouring. We know pies of this type as game pie. The recipe specifies that this is to be served in the first course of a feast. The adapted recipe below is lengthy, but not difficult. Made in a springform tin, it can be removed and transferred to a serving plate. Of course, if you have an elegant oval game-pie mould, you could use that. Whatever you bake it in, such pies are good to have on hand for Christmas buffets, not least because they can be made ahead of time.

For the pheasant:
1 plump pheasant
salt to taste
4 whole cloves
1 tbsp oil
1 small onion, peeled and chopped
6-inch stick celery, chopped
1 small carrot, cut in two
1 bay leaf
125ml/4 fl oz white wine

For the filling:
pinch saffron
350g/12oz minced pork
350g/12oz minced beef or venison
2 rashers streaky bacon, chopped into ½-inch bites
6 juniper berries
2 tsp powdered ginger
¼ tsp freshly grated nutmeg
pinch cinnamon
salt and pepper to taste
3 chicken thighs, skinned and boned
85g/3oz mixed raisins and sultanas
about 250ml/9 fl oz jellied game or chicken stock

For the pastry:
375g/13oz plain flour
1 tsp salt
150g/5½oz lard
200ml/7 fl oz water
1 egg, beaten

To prepare the pheasant, wash, dry and season it lightly with salt. Stick a clove in each breast and each leg. Heat the oil in a pan big enough to hold the pheasant. Stir in the chopped onion, celery and carrot; add the bay leaf, then the wine. Cook for 3 minutes, then sit the pheasant on the vegetables, add water to the depth of a couple of centimetres (about an inch). Put on a very low heat and simmer as gently as possible for 30 minutes. Keep the liquid in the pan, but remove the pheasant and let it sit until cool enough to handle, then cut all the flesh from the bones, keeping the breast whole or in large pieces and cutting the rest in bite-size bits. Do not worry if it is not entirely cooked. Make sure to discard pieces of bone and stringy bits.

While the pheasant is cooking, prepare the other ingredients. Soak the saffron in 6 tablespoons of warm water. Set aside for 20 minutes. Meanwhile, mix the pork, beef and bacon thoroughly together. Crush the juniper berries and mix them into the meat mixture along with the ginger, nutmeg, cinnamon and salt and pepper to taste. Set aside for half an hour (or longer if more convenient), occasionally stirring to blend the flavours. Next, cut each chicken thigh into 4 or 5 pieces, discarding any stringy bits, but leaving on the fat. Put them in a bowl and pour the saffron and its liquid over them. Stir in the raisins and sultanas. Let stand for 10–15 minutes so the chicken imbibes the flavour of the saffron. Finally, mix the chicken pieces and raisins and any liquid with the ground meats. Make a patty of the mixture about as big as a 50p coin and fry it. Taste it. Add more seasoning to the mixture if you think it needs it.

Now, with all the meat prepared, preheat the oven to 200°C (400°F), and grease a 23mm/9-inch springform pan. Make the pastry by mixing the flour and salt in a bowl. Make a well in the centre. In a small pan, heat the lard and the water until the lard has melted and the mixture is boiling. Remove from the heat, let the bubbling die down, then pour the liquid slowly into the well in the flour, stirring as you go. Form the mixture into a ball; cover the bowl with a towel to keep it warm. Use the pastry while it is warm. Take about three quarters of it, and place in the centre of the prepared pan. With your fingers spread it over the bottom and up the sides, trying to make it as even as possible. Put the minced meat and chicken mixture in, tamping it down to make an even layer. Put the pheasant on top, distributing the pieces to cover the meat. Season the pheasant with salt and pepper. On a floured board, roll out the rest of the pastry to make a lid. Put it on top and seal the edges with your fingers. Cut off any straggly bits and make a hole about as big as a 10p coin in the centre. Re-roll any leftover bits and cut into leaf shapes. Brush the top of the pie with the beaten egg. Set the leaf shapes on top in a pattern of your choice. Brush them also with the egg. Bake in the centre of the oven for 25 minutes. Reduce the oven temperature to 160°C (325°F) and continue baking the pie for another 35 minutes. To check for doneness, stick a wooden toothpick through the central hole. When it comes out it should show no sign of pinkness. Cool on a wire rack for 20–30 minutes. Heat the jellied stock, then using a funnel or a small jug pour it about a teaspoon at a time into the hole in the pie. Let each addition of stock disappear before adding a little more. Proceed like this until the pie will absorb no more, then let it cool completely. (If you have no jellied stock, you can use ordinary stock plus powdered gelatine. Soften the powdered gelatine in the stock, using the proportions suggested by the manufacturer; typically a teaspoon to set 250ml/9 fl oz of liquid.)

CRANBERRY PEAR SAUCE

This is a modern recipe, included here because it perfectly accompanies the Pheasant, Chicken and Meat pie. Sharp fruity sauces were much appreciated with meat in medieval and Renaissance England, and are ancestors of the chutneys often served with them today. Similarly, mustard has long been a favourite English condiment with meat. A recipe for a medieval mustard follows.

280g/10oz cranberries
zest and juice of 1 large orange
115g/4oz sugar
2 medium-size firm conference pears, peeled and cored
pinch salt

Put the cranberries in a small saucepan with the orange zest and juice, the sugar, and 300ml/half a pint of water. Bring to simmering point and simmer until the cranberries have popped and the liquid is beginning to thicken. Meanwhile, cut the pears into bite-sized chunks. Stir these into the cranberries, add the pinch of salt. Cover the pan and simmer until the pears are tender but not mushy: 3–8 minutes depending on their ripeness.

HONEY MUSTARD

Mustard was served with most large birds in the Middle Ages. This recipe is easy using powdered Colman's mustard, but the original recipe called Lumbard [Lombard] Mustard in *The Forme of Cury* shows how much work had to go on in the medieval kitchen even to make the simplest of things: 'Take mustard seed and wash it, and dry it in an oven. Grind dry and pass it through a sieve. Clarify honey with wine and vinegar and stir it well together and make it thick enough. And when you use it, thin it with wine.'

55g/2oz mustard powder
55g/2oz runny honey
1 tbsp dry white wine, plus more for serving

Put the mustard in a small bowl. Make a well in the centre. Using a spoon warmed in hot water then dried, add the honey to the well and then mix to make a stiff paste. Stir in the wine. Store in a lidded jar. To serve, dilute to the consistency you like with more white wine, adding it a little at a time.

PEARS IN RED WINE AND GINGER

Medieval manuscripts include many recipes for pears, sometimes citing them as an alternative to meat in fast-day dishes. This recipe adapted from the Fourteenth-Century *Forme of Cury* is recognisable as a still popular recipe for firm winter pears stewed in spiced red wine. Translated into modern English the Fourteenth-Century recipe reads: 'Take pears and pare them clean. Take good red wine and mulberries, or sanders, and seethe [boil] the pears therein & when they are both boiled, take them up. Make a syrup of Greek wine with white powder [spice mixture] or white sugar and powdered ginger, and do [put] the pears therein. Seethe [boil] it a little, and mess [serve] it forth.' In this version blackberries replace hard-to-find mulberries. Of course, should you have mulberries, use those.

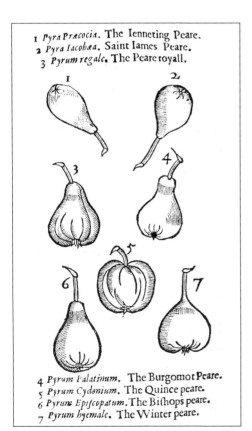

1 *Pyra Præcocia*. The Ienneting Peare.
2 *Pyra Iacobæa*. Saint Iames Peare.
3 *Pyrum regale*. The Peare royall.

4 *Pyrum Palatinum*. The Burgomot Peare.
5 *Pyrum Cydonium*. The Quince peare.
6 *Pyrum Episcopatum*. The Bishops peare.
7 *Pyrum hyemale*. The Winter peare.

Gerard's Herball *shows several varieties of English pears. They appeared in many medieval and Renaissance dishes served at winter feasts.*

1kg/2lb 4oz English conference pears, peeled
225ml/8 fl oz ruby port
115g/4oz sugar
1 tsp ginger
200g/7oz blackberries

Cut the pears in half and core them. Cut each half into 4 slices. Put the sliced pears and the port in a saucepan; cover and simmer over low heat until the pears are tender and purply. If you are using ripe pears this takes only 3–4 minutes. Hard pears take up to 8–10 minutes. Lift the pears from the liquid with a slotted spoon. Stir the sugar and ginger into the liquid, raise the heat and let it bubble for a couple of minutes or until slightly syrupy. Return the pears to the pan and simmer for another 2 minutes. Remove to a serving bowl and add the blackberries. Boil the syrup rapidly until it has reduced in volume by a third. Pour it over the pears and blackberries and let them steep in it. Serve at room temperature.

Holly

Holly probably tops the list of the most enduring and richly symbolic of all the Christmas greens. The Green Knight points out it is 'greenest when groves are bare' and it bears its scarlet fruit in winter, thus opposing the darkness of winter by asserting growth. In *As You Like It* Shakespeare uses holly as a symbol of winter, which despite its hardship is not as cruel as humans:

> *Blow, blow, thou winter wind,*
> *Thou art not so unkind*
> *As man's ingratitude;*
> *Thy tooth is not so keen*
> *Because thou art not seen,*
> *Although thy breath be rude.*
> *Heigh-ho! sing, heigh-ho! unto the green holly:*
> *Most friendship is feigning, most loving mere folly:*
> *Then, heigh-ho! the holly!*
> *This life is most jolly.*

The Green Knight uses holly as an olive branch, saying that it shows he comes in peace. Tennyson used holly to evoke the sorrow at his friend's death in *In Memoriam*:

> *With trembling fingers did we weave*
> *The holly round the Christmas hearth.*

Traditionally, holly picked on Christmas Day can cure gout, rheumatism and asthma.

CHAPTER 3

Reliving the Christmas Story

Here to record the leg of a goose
With golden chickens, pork and partridge.
A tart fit for a lord – How think you this does?
A cut calf liver with verjuice:
Good sauce to make a good appetite.
Wakefield Master, *The First Shepherds' Play*,
c. mid-Fifteenth Century

IF WE IGNORE the matter of chopping off heads, Christmas as we read about it in *Sir Gawain and the Green Knight* sounds delightful. It has games, music, dancing, plenty of good company and lots of lovely food and drink. The picture is of an ideal Christmas – and like all ideals, such Christmases were only enjoyed by a few. Those outside medieval castle walls and manor gates fared differently. Since little of their lives reached the written record, it's hard to know much about their Christmas except by catching glimpses of it here and there in old customs and old tales.

Christmas disguisers

Old customs suggest that often the best hope of eating something hot and tasty at Christmas was to sing or dance or perform at some door, hoping for a dole in return. Waits were groups of itinerant singers that went round at night, notionally guarding the streets, but also singing for their Christmas suppers and happy to take tips for either the security they theoretically provided or for their music. Carol singers carry on this

tradition. Today the gift of mince pies or donations to a charity are pleasant top-ups to a holiday already awash in good things, but in earlier times many would have gone without Christmas fare had they not earned it by providing Christmas entertainment.

Many customs involved groups of disguised men, who paraded around performing traditional dances, songs, games and even plays of various sorts. One form of fun was to dress in the clothes of the opposite sex, and to go from house to house, bringing fun in exchange for welcoming victuals. An 1832 publication called *Ancient Customs, Sports and Pastimes of the English* says that this was especially popular in the North of England. Describing 'the interchange of clothes between men and women', the author, J. Aspin writes:

> When dressed in each others' clothes they went from one neighbour's home to another to partake of Christmas cheer, dancing, and singing and suchlike merriments.

The pantomime tradition of the Principal Boy always being female and the Dame being male carries on this tradition.

Another form of dressing up involved an animal head. Once donned, its wearer and his companions went around mock-threatening householders until drinks and food were forthcoming. In parts of the south-west it was the Christmas Bull who came calling wearing a bull's head or carrying it on a pole. Sometimes he beefed up the illusion by wrapping himself in a skin; sometimes, he just swathed himself in blankets. Along with a friend acting as keeper, and an attendant group of lively lads, they knocked at doors until they were let in to perform their japes and songs, only departing when they were food and drink to the better, no doubt getting less sober as the night wore on.

Hodening was a similar custom involving a horse's head rather than a bull's. It could be an actual skull, or a wooden horse head made with a movable jaw. Someone led the horse by a rope and another rode on his back, while a third pal dressed as a woman and wielded a broom. Other companions carried musical instruments or noisemakers. As they went from house to house, the horse pretended to rear or gnash his teeth to scare people into letting them in. Once indoors, they entertained with their antics. The word 'horseplay' probably comes from hodening, and gives some idea of what might have gone on.

Wales had its own variation on this custom called the *Mari Lwyd* – Grey Mare. Led by someone wearing a horse's head, a group of men showed up and invited the householders to a competition of songs and poems. Notionally, if the householders could sing the longest, they were not obliged to open their doors, but ideally they contrived to run out of inspiration quickly, and invited in the *Mari Lwyd*.

They brought more songs and good luck, and were welcomed with food and drink. Sausages, pies, bread, and 'a stump of Caerphilly' are evoked in Vernon Watkins' *The Ballad of the Mari Lwyd*. A barrel full of unidentified good stuff comes rolling in too, plus a ham and a golden-skinned goose shining in the flames of the fire.

Mummers and mumming

'Mumming' is a general term that covers numerous local customs that involved disguised men going from house to house. The word comes from a Greek word that means 'mask', which, in the sense of 'disguise', characterised many of the amateur entertainers of Christmas.

At royal and lordly houses, the mummers would be young aristocrats who went to considerable expense and trouble to present elaborate processions and entertainments. For example, 130 men went mumming to the court of the young Richard II in 1377. In *The Court Masque* Enid Welsford quotes a manuscript account of them parading through London with 'great noise of minstrelsy, trumpets, cornets and shaums and great plenty of wax torches'. Some were dressed as squires and some as knights in a procession brought up by a mock emperor and mock pope followed by twenty-four mock cardinals, all masked and costumed. At the tail-end came '8 or 10 arrayed and with black visards [masks] like devils appearing nothing amiable'. Once at court, they proposed a game with dice loaded so that the king was sure to win the jewels they had brought as prizes. The event ended with drinks all round, followed by music from the minstrels and trumpeters and dancing.

All this was, of course, much grander than anything that could be managed at any other level of society, yet mumming was popular at every economic level, and its spirit infused many Christmas customs that involve disguises and entertainment. By the end of the Seventeenth Century mummers became best-known for their performances of plays based on tales of St. George. His mock battles always led to casualties, but those who fell in combat were miraculously raised by a doctor or another character, so apparently certain death was averted – as it was for Sir Gawain – thus providing an opportunity for celebratory drinks.

In their ragtag clothes village mummers were often scorned by lordlier people, though in *The Dunciad*, a poem excoriating clueless wannabe artists, Alexander Pope describes them sympathetically. Grafting the alliteration of their traditional medieval plays onto his heroic couplet, he writes:

Peel'd, patch'd and pye-bald, linsey-woolsey brothers,
Grave mummers! Sleeveless some and shirtless others.

Similarly, in Shakespeare's *A Midsummer Night's Dream* Theseus chooses Bottom and his friends to provide 'very tragical mirth' by playing *Pyramus and his love Thisbe* from among the many groups of players who have prepared an entertainment for his wedding. When Philostrate remonstrates that these players are 'Hard-handed men…which never labor'd in their minds til now,' – in other words, mummers – Theseus argues that many of the professional plays on offer are overly laboured. In his lordly way, he announces his preference for Bottom's play, saying:

I will hear that play;
For never any thing can be amiss
When simpleness and duty tender it.

As their presence in Shakespeare's summery tale suggests, mummers might appear at weddings and other celebrations, but the strongest and most long-lived connection of these wandering entertainers was with Christmas. In 1829 'mummers' were defined specifically as 'parties of youths who go about at Christmas fantastically dressed performing a short dramatic piece'.

Essentially mummers were amateur actors. Their masks and disguises were supposed to ensure that their neighbours did not recognise them, so their arrival was part of the magic of Christmas. Theoretically, like Halloween trick-or-treaters, they were wandering spirits who must be appeased to avert ill-luck. Startlingly, perhaps, their dramatic efforts influenced more elaborate players. Courtly mummers eventually became masquers in the court masques that reached their artistic height in the early Seventeenth Century. Mummers' skills also overlapped and infused those of the actors in the medieval mystery plays, which were put on by crafts' guilds and acted by tradesmen and workers. They were enormously popular annual events in northern and Midland towns for 200 years – from the 1370s to the 1570s – and they reveal many details about the lives of ordinary farmers and workpeople, not least, their attitudes to the Christmas story.

The mystery plays

The mystery plays are not detective stories. They get their name from the functions or crafts, known as 'mysteries', of the tradesmen's guilds that performed them. The mystery plays are cycles describing the history of Christ in a series of dramas that begin with the Creation, move through the Fall and on through the Nativity and the life of Christ to the Passion. They were given in June around the Corpus Christi holiday. Like that holiday, they celebrate the Eucharist by explicating the doctrines of the Fall and Salvation. The long days of June made outdoor performance possible, which would not have been the case had they been performed at Christmas. Nonetheless, Christmas is crucial to the plays because the Nativity plays were one of the peaks of each cycle. They cover the Annunciation to Mary, the birth of Christ, the story of the shepherds travelling to the stable, the meeting of the Three Kings with Herod, their gift-giving journey to the infant Jesus, and the Slaughter of the Innocents. Usually, the Nativity plays would have been performed in one day.

Performance

Mystery plays were presented in a unique way. The guilds built wagons fitted out as stages, sometimes including an upper section for playing scenes including angels, and a lower area that could represent the grave or hell. Called 'pageant wagons', they moved from station to station through the streets, performing at each stop. After a wagon had passed from one station, the audience there waited for the following wagon to arrive with the next play in the cycle.

The guild members were the financiers as well as players, often spending lavishly on costumes and props as well as on incidentals such as food at rehearsals. The 1551 records at Chester, for example, list the following bills:

Paid for the first rehearse	*6d*
Drink in barber's after rehearse	*18d*
For beef against the general rehearse	*6s. 8d*
Three old cheeses	*4s. 0d*

Some actors also received payments, perhaps because they were especially gifted and therefore in demand. A Chester baker claimed he was owed 2s. 6d for playing the demon in his guild's play.

When possible, guilds chose a play whose topic related to their trade. For example, the Coventry *Shearmen and Tailors' Play* includes the well-known shepherd scenes described in St. Luke's gospel. In York, the goldsmiths, who had access to precious metals, played the Three Kings. In Chester, the kings were also portrayed by the richest guilds: the vintners played their arrival at Herod's court, while the visit to the stable was taken on by the mercers – silk and cloth merchants who could be relied on for handsome costumes. As for more modest guilds, the ironmongers were responsible for the Crucifixion because they made nails, while the bakers took on the Last Supper. Guilds competed with each other to put on a good show, and when a guild did not come up to snuff, town corporations stepped in either to sort matters out, or regulate the route, and even to provide food and drink for the actors.

While many towns have records of mystery plays, complete texts survive only from York, which had forty-eight plays, Chester, which had twenty-four plays, Wakefield with thirty-two plays, and an unknown East Midlands town often called N-town that had a cycle of forty-two plays. Isolated plays survive from other towns. Coventry had one of the most popular mystery cycles, though only *The Shearmen and Tailors' Play* and *The Weavers' Play* now remain.

These plays were always works in progress. They had to accommodate the financial state of the guilds. More significantly, the Church kept one eye on the plays to make sure they were doctrinally correct – a tricky task during the Sixteenth Century, when Protestant beliefs began to take over from those of the Roman Catholics, and anything to do with religion was eyed beadily but from differing viewpoints by Tudor monarchs and their watchdogs. However, while the plays were certainly written by churchmen, they included bits of action and dialogue to appeal to local audiences. The actors, too, extemporised – often developing farcical scenes or jumping from the pageant wagons to act on the ground with the audience. An inspired performance could lead to additions to the text that became permanent. We see something of what medieval Christmas was like through the Nativity plays, especially those of the shepherds.

The shepherds' plays

The biblical account of the shepherds abiding in their fields keeping watch over their sheep by night lacks detail. The authors of the mystery plays were therefore free to imagine what the poor shepherds were like, how they lived, and how they responded to the angel's announcement of the birth of Christ. Naturally, they based their portraits on contemporary shepherds of the English countryside.

The best known of all the mystery plays is *The Second Shepherds' Play* from Wakefield in Yorkshire. It begins with shepherds on the moors grumbling about the 'spiteful' weather with 'winds full keen' and 'frost so hideous'. Even more bitterly, they complain about jumped-up henchmen of the aristocracy who oppress them. These complaints segue into moans and groans about their wives. One shepherd says his wife is 'sharp as a thistle, as rough as a briar, browed like a bristle' – a warning to bachelors in the audience that would likely have been met with roars of approval. When Mak, well-known as a light-fingered good-for-nothing arrives, he whines about having too many children. Describing his house 'full of brood' and his wife drinking by the fire he says:

> *Each year that comes to man*
> *She brings forth a child*
> *And some years two.*

However, though he claims that he is like to be 'eaten out of house and harbour' by his wife, when he steals a sheep and takes it home she becomes a helpful conspirator, quickly suggesting that they hide it in the cradle, where no-one will think to look for it. When the shepherds come searching, she and Mak pretend she has given birth yet again, and play-act so successfully that the shepherds believe them until one shepherd spots the 'baby's' woolly face. Mak's wife tries to persuade them that he was bewitched by an elf. She is saved only by the angels' chorus of 'Gloria in Excelsis', and the shepherds' decision to go to Bethlehem to worship the newborn Jesus, giving him gifts of a bob of cherries, a bird and a tennis ball.

In this version of the shepherds' story the harsh social world of Yorkshire is literally as well as spiritually one with the fallen world that Christ has come to save, and the tale of Mak and the sheep-baby is a farcical version of the Christ Child as the Lamb of God. So deftly are religious symbolism and realism woven together that the anonymous author of this play is called the Wakefield Master.

Evil Spirits on Christmas Eve

When the shepherds discover their lost sheep in the cradle at Mak's house, his wife Gyl claims that it is actually her baby, but an evil spirit has changed its shape:

> He was taken with an elf
> I saw it myself.
> When the clock struck twelve
> Was he forshapen.

Gyl is referring to the common belief that fairy folk or witches were responsible for birth defects and other misfortunes to children. In *Hamlet* Shakespeare records another belief: that on Christmas Eve evil spirits are stayed by the holiness of the night of the Saviour's birth:

> Some say that ever gainst the season comes
> Wherein our Saviour's birth is celebrated
> The bird of dawning singeth all night long;
> And then, they say, no spirit stirs abroad;
> The nights are wholesome; then no planets strike,
> Not fairy takes, nor witch hath power to charm,
> So hallow'd and so gracious is the time.

Aware of this belief in the safety of Christmas Eve, the audiences for *The Second Shepherds' Play* may have spotted the obviousness of Gyl's lie. Like today's pantomime audiences, they might have cried out a warning to the shepherds not to be fooled. Yet the belief that mischievous spirits wandered the Christmas nights was common.

The Wakefield shepherds' feast

The Wakefield Master also wrote an alternate play for the shepherds, now known as *The First Shepherds' Play*. It lacks the powerful motif of the sheep-baby, but it paints an even fuller picture of the difficult world of late-medieval England. Here again the shepherds complain of the cold and wet on the moors, and the hardness of their lives. However, instead of succumbing to Mak's wiles, this time they fall to quarrelling among themselves. One shepherd proposes papering over the cracks by eating, and produces a pork brawn – a soused pork dish that remained a Christmas favourite into the Twentieth Century. 'Set mustard with it', cries his companion, and then brings out his own stash of foods:

> *Here's the foot of a cow well sauced, I see*
> *The leg of a sow that has been spiced.*
> *Two blood puddings with a liver sausage,*
> *Eat gladly sirs*
> *Both beef and mutton.*

Another shepherd contributes both boiled and roast meat from his pack, then delves back in and draws forth:

> *Even an oxtail that should not be lost*
> *Ha, ha Good luck! I have for no cost.*
> *A good pie – this is good for the frost*
> *In the morning.*
> *And two swine snouts,*
> *And all of a hare but the loins.*

Not to be outdone the third shepherd adds:

> *Here to record the leg of a goose*
> *With gilded chickens, pork and partridge.*
> *A tart fit for a lord – How think you this does?*
> *A cut calf liver with verjuice:*
> *Good sauce to make a good appetite.*

To wash all this down there is ale from Healey, a village near Wakefield.

This scene is adapted from a similar feast in the Chester shepherds' play, though the foods the two sets of shepherds eat differ in ways that show major regional differences in food, as well as in the artistry of the authors of the two plays.

The Chester shepherds' feast

The Chester shepherds have no complaints about the weather. Instead, the first shepherd comes in with a list of diseases of sheep, all of which he seems well able to cure with the herbs in his pouch. When his companions join him they quickly agree that it's time to eat. Noting that his wife packed the best she had, one shepherd displays his food:

> *Here is bread baked today*
> *Onions, garlic and leeks,*
> *Butter that was bought in Blacon*
> *And new cheese that will grease your cheeks.*

Another shepherd responds:

> *And here is ale from Halton,*
> *And what meat I had for my pay;*
> *A pudding that no-one can despise,*
> *And a jannock from Lancashire.*
>
> *Lo here's a sheep's head soused in ale*
> *And a pig's snout to lie in the grasse.*
> *And curds too. My wife has ordained*
> *A noble supper, as is seen.*

Adding to this 'noble supper' another shepherd brings out a pig's foot. Further investigations discover hot meat, hams, a pudding, and a final offering from the first shepherd:

> *I am not ashamed to shake out*
> *My satchel to shepherds.*
> *This tongue pared round about*
> *With my teeth I will tame it.*

The shepherds eating and drinking in the 2008 performance of the Chester Mystery Plays.

The two feasts

The Chester and Wakefield 'feasts' are similar in that both groups of shepherds have lots of food, and that none of it is the penitential fish of fast days – even though Chester was then a port well-supplied with fish. Yet their differing foods help show why Christmas foods were such a highlight of the year.

Even though the Wakefield shepherds eat before Christ is born, and therefore technically are not celebrating Christmas, their food is the food of the Christmas feast. In particular, apart from the 'tart fit for a lord', which may have been filled with cheese, their meal is entirely of meat – an impossibility at any time of the medieval year but Christmas. Many of their dishes are either made from offal or the bits and bobs of meat known as 'numbles' in medieval and Renaissance England. Numbles were the internal organs such as liver and kidneys, and would have been especially plentiful during the seasonal slaughter of animals. They could certainly find their way into subsidiary dishes on grand tables, but they were highlights of poorer diets, showing up in sausages, pickled dishes and puddings, which in those days were usually meat-based.

As well as offal, the Wakefield shepherds have pieces of more highly valued meat, though usually not the prime portions. They have a hare without the loin and a goose leg but not the breast; in other words, they have the tougher bits after someone else has consumed the prime parts. Like the golden chicken painted with egg yolks, the partridge and the pork leg seasoned with spices, these meats seem clearly to be the leavings of some splendid table. Such leftovers were often given as Christmas charity. The spices in the pork leg would have been delicacies way beyond the reach of impoverished shepherds. Even meat was rare. Mak typifies most Yorkshiremen when he arrives home with the stolen sheep, and says:

> *I wish it were flayed. I long to eat.*
> *This twelvemonth I have not enjoyed one meal of sheep meat.*

The combination of poverty, the frequent fast days and the habit of slaughtering late in the year made it inevitable that the majority of medieval Britons shared Mak's position of eating meat only during the Christmas season. Yet, just as the Wakefield Master seamlessly presented the stories of a sheep-stealer and the Lamb of God in *The Second Shepherds' Play*, here he gives a realistic account of the leavings of the wealthy that reflects both their depredations on the poor and the imperfect post-lapsarian world that Christ has come to redeem. Not one single item in the shepherds' packs is whole. Nothing is perfect in the unredeemed world preceding Christ's birth.

The Chester shepherds fare quite differently. The food from their packs is specifically put up by their wives, and includes other foods as well as meat. They have vegetables, 'onions, garlic and leeks', and most significantly, dairy foods. The green cheese would have been creamy, which is why it's promised to 'grease your cheeks'. They also have curds and butter. These foods reflect the dairy economy of Cheshire rather than the sheep-rearing economy of Yorkshire, notorious for impoverishing the local population because it took food-producing arable land and turned it into wool-producing pasture. The Chester shepherds clearly relish their cheese and butter, no doubt because their richness was delicious after the salty and pickled foods of winter. They also have meat, but none of the fancier bits the Wakefield shepherds had acquired. One shepherd has unidentified but clearly leftover meat that he got as wages, plus a pudding, probably filled with meat and offal, 'a sheep's head soused in ale', a pig's snout and the remains of a tongue – all modest fare made from animal oddments. Nonetheless, along with the fresh-baked bread and an oaten Lancashire jannock, the varied foods from the Chester shepherds' packs make a good meal – though one that entirely lacks the religious symbolism that infuses the food in the plays of the Wakefield Master.

The Chester shepherds' fare is what townspeople would have expected to be eating at the time the mystery plays were performed: originally at Corpus Christi in June, though in Chester the date was later switched to Whitsun. Cheese and butter were summer foods, made to preserve the plentiful supplies of milk from animals that had newly calved and were feeding on the new season's plentiful grass. Later in the year, fresh butter would be replaced by rancid or overly salt butter from a barrel, and green cheese by hard Cheshire cheese – today a crumbly cheese, but back then so hard it was often compared to parmesan. Meat would disappear, as it did for Mak, until November prompted a new slaughter. The contrast between the good but basic foods of spring and summer and the leanness of fast meals and the elaborately dressed meat dishes of Christmas suggests what an annual delight Christmas fare would have been.

Shepherds' Gifts

The gospel account of the shepherds does not say they brought gifts to the baby Jesus, but the writers of the medieval mystery plays do. Sometimes their gifts have a symbolic significance. For example, in *The Second Shepherds' Play* the cherries brought by one shepherd suggest Christ's blood, the bird suggests the Holy Ghost or divinity, and the tennis ball symbolises kingship because tennis was a royal game. The Chester shepherds bring useful objects: a bell, a flask, and spoon for eating pottage. The boys who come with them to the stable also bring gifts, including a nut-hook. One boy explains to Jesus that he is going to find this very handy during his boyhood years:

> Nowe, child, though thou be comen [come] from God,
> And be Gode thyself in thy manhoode,
> Yet I know that in thy childhood
> Thou wilt for sweet meat look.
> To pull down apples, pears and plums
> Old Joseph shall not need to hurt his thumbs.
> Because thou hast not plenty of crumbs,
> I give thee here my nuthooke.

Reliving Christmas

The realism of the shepherds' foods is only one example of the way the mystery plays made the gospel accounts of Christ's birth comprehensible by translating them into recognisable English activities. Frequently they include stories and themes that were traditional, though not biblical. For example, Noah's wife is always presented as angrily refusing to enter the ark until after long argument from Noah and her sons. On the one hand the figure of the recalcitrant wife was a medieval stereotype, yet it is also true that people may well have questioned whether a wife would willingly embark on an apparently foolish husbandly whim to sail off with a boatload of animals.

The Nativity presents another test of credulity – one central to church doctrine. Can Mary have been a virgin, and if so, can it be supposed that Joseph would have believed that her pregnancy occurred without male

Mary and Joseph in the 2008 performance of the Chester Mystery Plays.

intervention? The plays tackle this head on. They heighten the room for suspicion by showing Joseph as an impotent old man wed to a beautiful young wife. The York play, for example, starts with him explaining his weakness and the problems of being married to a pregnant wife though he has not consummated their marriage. He admits to knowing of the prophecy of a virgin birth, but cannot believe that Mary is the chosen mother. 'And why would some young man not take her?' he asks. He interrogates Mary vigorously, asking 'Whose is the child thou art withal?' Her constant answer is 'Yours and God's,' to which he replies, 'And whose else?' The argument is lengthy, repeatedly rehearsing explanations of the virgin birth for the audience. Nevertheless they, like Joseph, would have their doubts. It is only when an angel appears to confirm the truth of it that the play ends.

A further medieval tradition of the virgin birth was that Mary experienced none of the pain promised in the Creation story: 'In sorrow and suffering shalt thou give birth.' A story in an apocryphal gospel explains that Mary gave birth alone while Joseph had gone seeking midwives. These midwives, Salome and Zelomy, appear in some mystery plays, always preceded by testimonies to their skill and experience. Quite simply, they are the best in Bethlehem. However, by the time they arrive, Jesus has already been born, so their role in the play is not to help Mary, but to confirm the miracle of the painless birth. In the N-town play Zelomy puts the issue clearly:

In birth labour she must needs have
Or else no child is born of her.

Greeting Mary, Zelomy demands:

Who was midwife of this fair child?

Women in the audience would have found this a fair enough question, familiar as they were with the harsh circumstances of medieval childbirth. Mary gives a doctrinally correct answer and offers a realistic test:

Of this fair birth that here is mine,
Pain or grieving felt I none.
I am a clean maid and pure virgin;
Test with your hand yourself alone.

Zelomy does indeed test, and immediately exclaims:

Here openly I feel and see
A fair child of a maiden is born,
And needeth no washing as others do;
Full clean and pure in truth is he,
Without spot or other pollution
His birth not hurt of virginity.

In effect, Zelomy prefigures the role of Doubting Thomas, and convinces the audience by testing the truth of the doctrine of the virgin birth in the most realistic way possible.

The end of the mystery plays

Despite their role in presenting the miracles of Christ's life in a form designed to satisfy religious doubt, ultimately, performances of the mystery plays were banned in the late-Sixteenth Century. In part, this was due to Protestant suspicion of their Catholic content. In *Ancient Sports and Pastimes of the English* published in 1832, J. Aspin says that one of the Chester manuscripts records the Pope's promise of forty days' pardon of sins to 'every person resorting in a peaceable manner, with good devotion, to hear and see the plays'. This suggests that people needed some bribe to watch reverently rather than to gossip with friends or roister round the taverns. Protestants did not approve of granting of pardons in the after-life for good behaviour in this one. Then, too, the

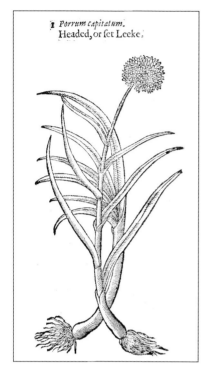

ɪ *Porrum capitatum.*
Headed, or fet Leeke,

This elegant drawing of leeks comes from the 1633 edition of Gerard's Herball. *They were a treat in the Chester shepherds' packs.*

performance was a three-day event that brought crowds into the streets at a time of year when days were longest, the weather reasonably likely to be warm and everyone ready to have a good time. Merchants clearly benefited. It is not hard to imagine that the recital of the shepherds' meals in Wakefield and Chester would have whetted appetites and sent people off to stalls selling pies and puddings and sausages. Taverns would have done a good trade too. So with crowds having a good and perhaps riotous time in the streets, the new Elizabethan church felt that religion had fallen from view, despite the plays' ostensible content. So in both Chester and York, the church called in the manuscripts for what seemed a routine round of correction, and simply never gave them back. Merchants deprived of the holiday trade and town corporations faced with what amounted to political suppression of local activities protested. However, some citizens must have sided with the church, both for religious reasons and also because public behaviour may well have been pretty out of hand during the several days of performances.

The last performance of the York cycle was in 1569, and the last performances in Chester and Coventry were in 1575 and 1580 respectively. Today the plays are revived occasionally, and at Chester the whole cycle is performed once every five years, though the days of guilds acting them on pageant wagons drawn through the streets are no more.

SLIT LEEKS BRUSCHETTA

Medieval cookbooks have relatively few vegetable recipes, most likely because the vegetable dishes were fairly simple and cooks did not need to note down how to make them as they did for the elaborate dishes served at feasts like Christmas. All vegetables would have been seasonal, and many including this dish of stewed leeks were served on pieces of toasted or fried bread called 'sops' or 'sippets' to soak up the cooking juices. With modernised spelling the *Forme of Cury* recipe reads: 'Take white of leeks and slit them, and do [put] them to seethe in wine, oil and salt. Toast bread and lay in dishes, and cast [pour] the sewe [stew] above it, and serve it forth.' In the following interpretation of this dish the leeks remain moist but not runny and are a lovely topping for bruschetta. Equally, you could add more wine or stock and serve this as a soup. No doubt the shepherds who had leeks in their packs in the Chester mystery plays simply ate them raw.

1 large garlic clove
3–4 tbsp grapeseed or other light-flavoured oil
½ tsp dried thyme
8–10 slices of French bread cut on the diagonal, about 2.5cm/1-inch thick
4 large leeks (about 900g/2lbs)
salt and white pepper to taste
white wine
2 tbsp finely chopped parsley

To make the bruschetta, slice the garlic clove into 3 or 4 slices. Put them in a small pan with 2 tablespoons of the oil over medium heat and let them cook gently without browning for 3–4 minutes. Discard them. Remove the oil from the heat and stir in the thyme. Brush the oil over the slices of bread. Toast the bread on a griddle to give it stripes or under the grill. Set aside.

To make the leeks, discard all dark green parts and use only the white and the very palest green sections. Slice the leeks lengthways then cut into 2.5cm/1-inch matchsticks. Put them in a sieve or colander and rinse under cold running water to remove any dirt. Drain and pat dry with paper towels. Heat a tablespoon of oil in a saucepan over low heat. Toss in the leeks and sprinkle lightly with salt. Put the lid on the pan and cook, shaking the pan from time to time, for 2–3 minutes. Increase the heat to medium and add the wine. Let it bubble until it has reduced by

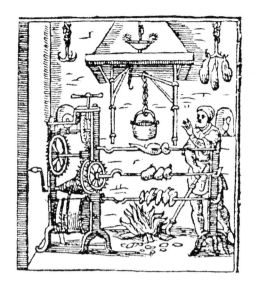

Until the Nineteenth Century poultry and meat was often roasted before a fire, sometimes in a curved dish facing the flames, sometimes as here on a spit.

half, then lower the heat and cook gently until the leeks are tender. Remove from the heat, taste and season with more salt if necessary and with the white pepper. Let cool to room temperature. Stir about half the parsley into the leeks. Top the bruschetta with the leek mixture and garnish with the rest of the parsley.

CHICKEN ENDORED

Medieval feasts were bright with colourful dishes. Cooks used spinach juice to make their food green, sanders (from sandalwood) to make it red, and either saffron or egg yolks to make it yellow. When eggs were used, the dish was described as 'endored' – a word that means gilded. Endored dishes gave the impression of splendour and were typical of feasts such as Christmas. In the Middle Ages most meat and poultry was cooked on a spit and endored afterwards. In this recipe lemon juice combines with egg to add to the taste as well as gilding to a roast chicken.

    1 roasting chicken weighing about 2.25kg/5lbs
    salt and pepper
    85g/3oz butter at room temperature
    ½ tsp dried sage
    ½ tsp dried thyme
    ½ tsp finely grated lemon zest
    juice of 2 lemons
    1 egg

Preheat the oven to 220°C (425°F). Lightly grease a roasting pan into which your chicken fits without a lot of space left over. Wash the chicken inside and out and dry it. Season the interior with salt and pepper. Mash

71

the butter with the sage, thyme, lemon zest and salt and pepper to taste. Rub about 1 tablespoon of this in the interior of the bird. Loosen the skin over the breast and put about a tablespoon of butter on each side, spreading it around by pressing the skin with your fingers. Smear the rest of the butter on the legs and the skin side of the breast. Cut one lemon in half and squeeze the juice all over the chicken. If there is not much juice, microwave the lemon halves for about half a minute to make the juice run, or use some of the juice of the second lemon. Roast the chicken in the centre of the oven for 20 minutes. Remove and baste. Return it to the oven, basting once or twice more and turning the oven to 180°C (350°F) after a further 30 minutes. Roast for another 20–25 minutes or until a skewer inserted in the thickest part of the leg elicits clear – not pink – juice. During the last few minutes of cooking, beat the egg with 1–2 tablespoons of lemon juice. When the chicken is ready brush this egg wash all over the exterior and return to the oven. Leave it for 1–2 minutes or until the wash has set into a yellow sheen. Keep watching to make sure it doesn't brown. When ready, remove from the oven, cover with a tea towel and let rest in a warm spot for 10–15 minutes. Carve at the table so everyone can see the endoring.

CALVES' LIVER WITH VERJUICE, BACON AND GRAPES

Verjuice was a vital ingredient in medieval and Renaissance kitchens. On the continent, it was the juice of unripe, unfermented grapes. English cooks who could not get grapes improvised with the juice of crab-apples or ordinary apples. Constance Hieatt, an expert on medieval cooking, suggests lemon or orange juice or even vinegar, though she notes that old manuscripts typically distinguish between verjuice and vinegar because the latter could be too sour for many uses. This recipe uses citrus juice. Combined with the grapes, it highlights the bacon and liver. If you have verjuice, use it instead.

    550g/1lb 4oz calves' liver
    salt and pepper to taste
    about 1 tbsp plain flour
    6 rashers streaky bacon
    1 small onion, peeled and chopped
    200g/7oz red or green grapes, washed
    3 tbsp freshly squeezed lemon or orange juice

Cut the liver into 4 serving pieces (or more if necessary). Season with salt and pepper, and dust very lightly with flour. In a frying pan, over moderate heat fry the bacon until it is golden but not too crispy. Set it aside. Add the onions to the pan and soften them over low heat for 3–4 minutes. Add them to the bacon. Put the liver in the pan and fry it over moderate heat. Turn it over after 2–3 minutes, depending on its thickness. Add 250ml/9 fl oz of water to the pan along with the grapes. Bring it to simmering while you break the bacon into 5cm/2-inch pieces. Put these back in the pan with the onions. Add the lemon or orange juice and cook for about 2–3 minutes more. To check for doneness, cut into the centre of a piece with a small knife. It should be smooth and faintly pink. Do not overcook it so it becomes brown and grainy-looking. Serve immediately onto warmed plates.

BRIE TART

Medieval cooking manuscripts have dozens of recipes for tarts and pies, usually filled with meat or fruit or both. One of the most surprising of these in *The Forme of Cury* is a recipe called Tart de Bry. With modernised spelling, it reads: 'Take a crust an inch deep in a trap [pie dish]. Take yolks of eggs raw and cheese ruayn [soft autumn cheese] and medle [mix] it and the yolks together. Do [add] thereto powdered ginger, sugar, saffron and salt. Do it in a trap; bake it & serve it forth.' Though medieval cheeses often differ from their modern descendants of the same name, Brie works well in this tart. Note that the sugar in the recipe was perhaps no more than a teaspoon or so to help bring the flavours together. In this form, this tart is a perfect supper or brunch dish for the Christmas season. Equally, by adding more sugar you could make it into a pudding. Either way the combination of ginger and saffron is enticing. Almonds were a favourite medieval ingredient. They are not called for in the Fourteenth-Century recipe, so are not entirely authentic, but they do add extra interest to the tart.

For the pastry:
225g/8oz plain flour
175g/6oz chilled butter, cut in 12–14 chunks
55g/2oz chilled lard, cut in 4 chunks
1–2 tablespoons chilled water

For the filling:
450g/1lb Brie
4 eggs
1 tbsp sugar
1–2 tsp powdered ginger
0.25g/pinch powdered saffron
salt to taste
1–2 tbsp flaked almonds (optional)

To make the pastry, put the flour and butter chunks into a food processor. Pulse 7 or 8 times so that the mixture looks like crumbs. Add the lard, turn on the whizz and add a tablespoon of chilled water. Stop the food processor. The mixture should be slightly lumpy and hold into a clump when you press a handful together. If necessary to achieve this, add more water a teaspoon at a time, pulsing after each addition. When the mixture is ready, take a small handful, squeeze and roll it briefly along on a lightly floured board until it makes a smooth lump. Continue this way with the rest of the mixture, piling your lumps together until you have about 10 or 12 lumps. Combine them all in a 1-inch thick disc, wrap it in clingfilm, and chill for at least 2 hours. You can leave it for up to 3 days if more convenient. To use remove it from the fridge, let stand at room temperature for half an hour, then roll it on a lightly floured board and make a tart shell in a greased 23cm/9-inch pie tin or quiche dish. Put it in the fridge, while you make the filling

Preheat the oven to 220°C (425°F). To make the filling, cut the white crust from the edge of the Brie but not from the top or bottom. Break the cheese into large lumps and briefly process them with one of the eggs in the food processor. Add the remaining eggs, the sugar, ginger and saffron, and whizz until smooth. Taste the mixture and season with salt to taste. Pour it into the prepared tart shell. If you want, scatter the flaked almonds on top. Bake for 10 minutes, then reduce the oven temperature to 190°C (375°F) and bake for another 10–15 minutes or until the filling is slightly puffy and a thin knife-blade inserted in the centre comes out clean. Let it rest for 5–10 minutes before serving, or serve at room temperature.

APPLE, PEAR AND FIG PIE

All medieval pies, whether sweet or savoury, included dried fruit and spices. This recipe is adapted from *Diversa Cibaria*. It reads, 'Take good apples and good spices and figs and raisins and pears, and when they are well mixed colour with saffron and put them in a coffin and put it forth to bake well.' That 'coffin' sounds like something for Hallowe'en, but is simply one of the usual medieval words for a pie crust. The other was 'trap'. This pie is perfect for Boxing Day or New Year's Day, and even a welcome alternative on Christmas Day for those who don't much care for Christmas pudding.

For the filling:
large pinch saffron
12 ready-to-eat dried figs
750g/1lb 10oz (about 4) cooking apples, peeled, cored and sliced
125g/4½oz sugar
½ tsp allspice
¼ tsp grated nutmeg
pinch cloves
75g/2½oz currants or dark raisins
75g/2½oz golden raisins or sultanas
3 ripe conference pears, peeled

For the pastry:
350g/12oz flour
85g/3oz lard, cut in pea-size bits
85g/3oz butter, cut in pea-size bits
2 tbsp sugar
2 tbsp or more chilled water
1 tbsp double cream

The filling should have time to cool to lukewarm (or colder) before it goes into the pie, so make it first. (You can make it up to a day ahead of time if you like.) Begin by preparing the saffron: stir it into 2 tablespoons of warm water and let it sit for at least 30 minutes. Snip the hard stalk bits off the figs, and drop the figs in a bowl of water. Leave them for 30 minutes. Put the apple slices in a saucepan with 3 tablespoons cold water, the sugar, allspice, nutmeg and cloves. Cover and cook over low heat until the apples are softening, then stir in the currants or dark raisins, the golden raisins or sultanas and the drained figs and the saffron in its liquid, which should now be a deep yellow. Stir to combine and cook for a few minutes longer until the apples are mushy and the dried fruit is plump. Slice the pears into four lengthways, take out the cores, then cut each slice into 3 chunks. Stir these into the apple mixture and let it cook just for 2–3 minutes longer. Let cool.

To make the pastry, put the flour in a large mixing bowl or the bowl of a food processor. Drop in the lard and butter, tossing them with the flour as you go. If working by hand, rub the lard and butter bits into the flour until the mixture looks like crumbs. If using the processor, pulse the mixture several times until it has the crumb appearance. Stir in a tablespoon of sugar. Now add 2 tablespoons chilled water, and bring the mixture together to form a pastry dough. You may need more water; if so, add it a teaspoon at a time. Divide the pastry into 2 portions, one a bit bigger than the other. Grease a 23cm/9-inch pie dish and turn the oven to 200°C (400°F). On a floured board roll out the larger piece of pastry until it fits the pie dish with enough to overlap the edge. Tip the filling into the dish. Roll out the smaller piece of pastry and cut into 2cm/¾-inch strips. Arrange these on top of the pie, overlapping them in basket-weave fashion to make a lattice top. Press each strip into the pastry on the side, then fold the overlap on top (discarding any excess, of course) to seal them. Brush the edge with a little cream and press with a finger or the back of a fork to decorate. Also brush the strips of your lattice, then immediately sprinkle with the remaining tablespoon of sugar. Bake at 200°C (400°F) for 20 minutes, then turn the oven to 190°C (375°F) and continue to bake until the pastry is deeply golden. Serve warm or at room temperature (not hot) with extra-thick double cream.

CHAPTER 4

The Tudor and Stuart Christmas

Provide us good cheer, for thou knowest the old guise
Old customs that good be, let no man despise.
At Christmas be merry and thank God of all,
And feast all thy neighbours, the great and the small.
                                    Thomas Tusser, *A Hundred Good*
                                        Points of Husbandrie, 1557

A T CHRISTMAS in 1509, King Henry VIII and his courtiers disguised themselves as Robin Hood and his Merry Men, and made their way into Queen Catherine of Aragon's chambers to entertain her. The king and his men in Lincoln green did not cause as much stir as that other man in green – the Green Knight who came to King Arthur's court. Their entry, like his, was unbidden but welcome as one of the festivities of the season. Like the modest revellers who cavorted or sang at houses throughout the land, Henry and his courtiers were celebrating the season in traditional mode: they came in disguise and 'after certain dances and pastime[s]' they left. At both the grandest levels of society and at the simplest, all kinds of entertainers, usually disguised, were very much a part of Christmas, welcomed and licensed to amuse and delight.

Masques

At Twelfth Night in 1512 Henry introduced a new form of dramatic entertainment. Hall's *Chronicle* records that he and nine others appeared in blue and yellow damask 'disguised after the manner of Italy, called a masque':

Apparelled in garments long and broad, wrought all with gold, with visers and caps of gold, and after the banquet [was] done, these Masquers came in, with six gentleman disguised in silk bearing staff torches, and desired the ladies to dance.

The feature new to England was not the group of costumed Christmas entertainers, but the invitation to the audience to dance. Uncertain of the propriety of this, some ladies declined. However, from this time masques at court and other aristocratic houses grew in popularity and complexity. The involvement of the masquers with their audience appealed because it allowed men and women to talk and flirt with each other. In *Henry VIII* Shakespeare shows just such an occasion when the king and a group of courtiers make a surprise visit to Cardinal Wolsey's house 'as maskers, habited like shepherds'. Pretending to speak no English, they have Wolsey's chamberlain announce their intentions:

> *They could do no less*
> *Out of the great respect they bear to beauty*
> *But to leave their flocks and under your fair conduct*
> *Crave leave to view these ladies and entreat*
> *An hour of revels with them.*

Henry chooses Anne Boleyn as his partner, and when the dancing is over he unmasks and asks her name. 'She is a dainty one' he leers, and insists that she join him when he accompanies the cardinal and other lords into the banquet in the private chamber. Here she would have been welcomed to the array of elaborate sugar and marzipan confections that followed feasts.

The other great charm of the masque was that it fostered the interest in play-acting and everything that it involved: gorgeous costumes, elaborate scenery, mechanised stage-effects and literary elegance. Popular in Queen Elizabeth I's court, they reached their zenith as a literary form in the courts of James I and VI and Charles I.

Masques were usually built around tales that flattered the person in whose honour they were performed. They were put on at weddings, ambassadorial receptions, the arrival of the king or queen in a city or house, and at holidays. Usually performed on New Year's Day or Twelfth Night, the most frolicsome days of Christmas, they became one of the highlights of the season among the wealthy.

An example from 1594 was the Twelfth Night masque given by members of Gray's Inn. It told of six knights who had apparently captured three Russians. Two goddesses, Virtue and Amity, appear to reveal that the suspects are really Envy, Malcontent and Folly. The knights take them away, and Virtue and Amity rule in their place.

Finally the knights return 'in a very stately masque, and dance a new devised measure'.

A New Year's masque for King James I in 1603 featured the elaborate machinery that became central to Seventeenth Century masques. The main character was a Chinese magician who appeared out of 'a heaven built at the end of the hall'. After he had described his eastern homeland, masquing nobles presented gifts to the king, until finally the magician released them from his supposed spells, and they danced with Queen Anne and her ladies. Courtier Dudley Carleton described another masque presented on Twelfth Night:

> *The French Ambassador was feasted publicly and at night there was a play in the Queen's presence with a masquerade of certain Scotchmen who came in with a sword dance.*

The Queen, Anne of Denmark, loved masques, and herself appeared as the chief dancer in the *Vision of Twelve Goddesses* in Hampton Court, where a Cave of Sleep and a Temple of Peace had been built as a setting. Anne and her ladies played the goddesses, entering in a torchlit parade before stepping into an elaborate dance described by Carleton:

> *Which dance being performed with great majesty and art consisting of diverse strains framed into motions circular, square, triangular, and other motions rare and full of variety, the Goddesses made a pause, casting themselves into a circle ... and prepared to take out the Lords to dance.*

Queen Anne spared little to indulge her enjoyment of masques. She hired dramatists to write them, notably Ben Jonson, and the best Italian-trained architect of the day, Inigo Jones, to design the sets. The collaboration between these two, though eventually foundering on disagreements about the relative importance of story and stage machinery, elevated the masque at its best to an art form that integrated poetry, dance, music and spectacle. (At their worst, masques could be flattering but incoherent pseudo-classical nonsense.) Queen Henrietta Maria, wife to Charles I, shared her mother-in-law's love of the masque. She and King Charles created annual masques for each other. His was performed on Twelfth Night, hers on Shrove Tuesday. *Britannia Triumphans* by William Davenant is a typical example. Performed on Twelfth Night 1638, it praises 'Britanocles, the glory of the western world' who by his good example had brought the land 'to a real knowledge of all good acts and sciences'.

Masques typically honoured such abstractions as good government or love and beauty. The value lauded and vividly presented in Ben Jonson's *Masque of Christmas* performed at court in 1616 was Christmas itself, personified as Father Christmas and his ten children: Misrule, Carol, Minced-Pie, Gambol, Post and Pair, New-Year's Gift, Mumming, Wassail, Offering and Baby-Cake, who are led on stage by Cupid. Christmas enters saying that he had trouble getting in:

> *I have seen the time you have wish'd for me, for a merry Christmas; and now you have me, they would not let me in: I must come another time! A good jest! As if I could come more than once a year: Why I am no dangerous person, and so I told my friends of the guard. I am old Gregory Christmas still, and though I come out of Pope's-head alley, as good a Protestant as any in my parish.*

Father Christmas here defends himself and Christmas festivities against the Puritan nay-sayers who claimed it was a Popish holiday with pagan roots. Father Christmas – who often appeared as emcee in mummers' plays – here notes that he has a masque of his own making. It's presented by 'a set of my sons that come out of the lanes London' – a reminder of the many entertainments put on by working people. In this case, those from Friday Street and Fish Alley are kept out of the court because 'they are not Christmas creatures: fish and fasting days, foh!' John Butter of Milk Street is let in, however, and so, after a struggle, is Venus, on the grounds that she is mother of Cupid who is present as leader of Christmas's children. Once they are all assembled, they perform a song and dance lauding each of Christmas's children, oddly to our

Ben Jonson, who wrote court masques, here crowned with the traditional bays as shown in the 1692 Folio edition of his works. Bays signified enduring fame because they stay green in winter. Their use in Christmas decorations suggested survival.

ears, focusing on both their classical links to the likes of Hercules and Venus and on their working-class roots in the alleys of London. The first is Misrule, who has a 'yellow ruff like a reveller' and carries a cheese. Carol comes in with a flute and a song-book. Minced-Pie has her pie, dish and spoons. Gambol is an acrobat. Post and Pair has playing cards. New-Year's Gift has an orange and a sprig of rosemary on his head, a collar of gingerbread round his neck, and a torch-bearer who carries marchpane and a bottle of wine. Mumming is dressed in his masquing suit. Wassail comes with a brown bowl bedecked with ribbons and rosemary. Offering wears a short cape, and in the rear comes Baby-Cake 'drest like a boy…his usher bearing a great cake, with a bean and a pease'. The point of this is to emphasise the traditional non-Puritanical Christmas. The masque also suggests that Father Christmas and his family will serve the king and that they are motivated by love – something later much needed by Charles I, who with his parents James I and Anne, was present at the first performance. Ultimately he lost his head when Puritan Parliamentarians won the Civil War, and made a clean sweep of everything they disliked – including Christmas.

Puritan nay-sayers

Only a few years after donning Robin Hood disguise and introducing the masque from Italy, Henry decided to divorce Catherine. To achieve this he separated the English Church from the Roman Catholic. He did not challenge the doctrines of the Church, but by substituting his own control for the Pope's and expropriating monastic properties he opened the door to Protestant reformers. Under his Protestant son Edward VI and daughter Elizabeth I, Protestants argued against many Roman Catholic doctrines and forbade many customs that had grown up around the numerous saints' days and holidays. Most were celebrated with games and music, with festive foods and drink – and none more so than Christmas. The combination of festivity and freedom from work fuelled the engine of Christmas. The Puritans, the most fundamental of Protestants, knew it and disapproved. Scrutinising the Bible rather than tradition for guidance, they found no authority for any celebration of the Nativity at all. The gospels were silent on the date and season of Christ's birth. Church history showed that Christmas was a latecomer to the Christian year, and clearly rooted in pagan winter festivities. Puritans got their name because they wanted to purify Christianity from what they saw as superstition and pagan excrescences. Christmas with its games and gambling, feasting and drinking, needed cleaning up in their view. They kept up a steady attack on it, and in 1647, the Puritan government that had defeated the Royalists in the Civil War forbade all Christmas celebrations, including traditional foods such as mince pies and plum porridge. Since the twelve days (and more) of Christmas were highly valued breaks in the working year, something had to replace them. The Puritans thought that a holiday on the second Tuesday of every month should do the trick. They were wrong. When Charles II returned to the throne in 1660 Christmas came back in his train. However, though it retained much that had gone before, it was far from what it had been in earlier centuries, and it was never to be the same again.

Hallowtide to Candlemas: celebrating the days of Christmas

It's impossible to understand the Puritan animosity to Christmas without taking account of the numerous Christmas customs of their day, and the ways they focused on Saturnalian feasting and license rather than the Christian implications of the Nativity. In his *Histriomastix* of 1632 William Prynne asked why couldn't his countrymen observe Christmas 'without drinking, roaring, healthing, dicing, carding, masques and staging plays which better become the sacrifices of Bacchus that the incarnation of our most blessed Saviour'. Conversely, the traditions he deplored were popular. Robert Herrick, himself a clergyman though not of the Puritan persuasion, gives the best insight into the variety of Christmas celebrations in a series of genial poems that emphasise the abundance of food and drink and the delight in sheer pleasure. The concluding lines of his *A New-yeares Gift sent to Sir Simeon Steward* sum up the physical release provided by Christmas:

Robert Herrick as shown in the frontispiece to the 1648 edition of his poems Hesperides.

And let the russet Swaines the Plough
And Harrow hang up resting now;
And to the Bag-pipe all addresse;
Til sleep take place of wearinesse.
And thus, throughout with Christmas playes
Frolick the full twelve Holy-days.

'Frolick' took many forms. Feasting was continuous, but certain days were high points. In his *Ceremonies for Christmas*, which describes the tradition of lighting the Yule log with the remains of the one from the previous year, Herrick catches the sense of anticipation of the holiday and its feasting:

Come bring with a noise,
My merrie merrie boyes,
The Christmas Log to the firing;
While my good Dame, she
Bids you all be free;
And drink to your heart's desiring.

With the last yeere's brand
Light the new block, And
For good successe in his spending,
On your Psalteries play,
That sweet luck may
Come while the Log is tending.

As the log blazed and the 'merrie boyes' enjoyed the tasty Christmas ale and ate its fine white bread rather than the usual coarse dark loaves of other seasons:

Drink now the strong Beere,
Cut the white loafe here,
The while the meat is shredding
For the rare Mince-Pie;
And the Plums stand by
To fill the Paste that's kneading.

Shredded meat was an important ingredient in the mince pies of Herrick's day, which were sometimes called shred pies on this account.

The plums that were standing by in Herrick's poem would not have been fresh plums – their season was long past – but any and all kinds of dried fruit. Thus plum porridge, plum pudding and plum cake are all dried fruit confections.

In another poem called *Christmas Eve, another Ceremonie* Herrick prays for the safety of the Christmas Pie, a substantial affair filled with spiced meat, studded with poultry and wild-fowl:

> *Come guard this night the Christmas-Pie*
> *That the thiefe, though ne'r so slie*
> *With his Flesh-hooks, don't come nie*
> *To catch it.*

After the feast of pies and meat and sweet delicacies on Christmas Day came St. Stephen's Day on 26 December. This was the day when priests opened alms boxes and distributed money to the poor, making it a bright day for them. Meanwhile, richer people might take to the countryside to

A cat stays warm as cooks go about their work in a Renaissance kitchen.

hunt, as Bertilak did in *Sir Gawain and the Green Knight.* New Year's Day was the time for exchanging gifts, with yet another feast to celebrate another year.

Twelfth Night was the most important day of the year for entertaining all-comers. On Twelfth Night 1552 Sir William Petre of Ingatestone Hall in Essex hosted over 100 guests. They ate a whole sheep, a whole sucking-pig plus two other pork joints, fifteen joints of beef, four veal joints, sixteen raised pies filled with meat and wild fowl, three geese, a brace each of partridge, teal, capons and rabbits plus a dozen larks. Dessert was on top of that. No doubt it included one of the giant Twelfth cakes that was traditional for the day. A bean was buried somewhere in its depths, and the person who got it in his piece of cake became King of the Bean. This title licensed him to rule everyone else and to be master of ceremonies. Naturally, the lucky winner took advantage of his absolute power to undermine the normal good order of the household by requiring his subjects-for-the-day to perform pranks and forfeits. There was also a pea in the cake. The lady who got that piece became Queen, who supported the King in demanding outrageous fun. Robert Herrick extols Twelfth cake and its customs in his poem *Twelfe night, or King and Queene*:

> Now, now the mirth comes
> With cake full of plums,
> Where Beane's the King of the sport here;
> Beside we must know,
> The Pea also
> Must revell, as Queene, in the Court here.

Discovering which bit of the cake had the bean and pea meant pulling it apart, but Herrick suggests that broken bits of cake may have been no bad thing because they could become 'joy-sops', presumably by dipping them in wine or beer:

> Let us make
> Joy-sops with the cake;
> And let not a man then be seen here,
> Who unurg'd will not drinke
> To the base from the brink
> A health to the King and the Queene here.

The basic drink of the season was the strong beer brewed for Christmas, but cold nights were often cheered with warm bowls of spiced drinks. One was lamb's wool: beer mulled with spices and stewed apples. As the apples broke down in the heat, pieces rose to make the woolly-looking top that gave the drink its name. It was evidently a favourite with Herrick:

> Next crowne the bowl full
> With gentle lambs-wooll;
> Add sugar, nutmeg and ginger,
> With store of ale too;
> And thus ye must doe
> To make the wassaile a swinger.

With bowls of lamb's wool and a Bean King to keep spirits high, it's no surprise that Twelfth Night was the most rambunctious night of Christmas, nor that life could not revert entirely to normal immediately afterwards. The following day was the Feast of the Epiphany celebrating the Three Kings. Then came 7 January, St. Distaff's Day, named not after a saint but after the distaff on a spinning wheel. It was so-called because women were supposed to return to their regular work, which, among other tasks, included spinning. Evidently their menfolk, many of whom were still celebrating, took the chance to make nuisances of themselves. Thus, as Herrick noted in his poem *Saint Distaff's day, or the morrow after Twelfth day*, the day was far from entirely devoted to work:

> Partly worke and partly play
> Ye must on S. Distaff's day:
> From the Plough soon free your teame;
> Then come home and fother them.
> If the Maides a spinning goe,
> Burne the flax, and fire the tow;
> Scorch their plackets, but beware
> That ye singe no maiden-haire
> Bring in pailes of water then.
> Let the Maides bewash the men.
> Give S. Distaff all the right,
> Then Bid Christmas sport good-night.
> And next morrow, every one
> To his owne vocation.

The final couplet suggests that at this point, work began to resume, yet festivities still hung on. Herrick's poems make clear that Christmas did not come to a sharp end with Twelfth Night. Many winter customs tell the same story. For example, the traditional day for the first ploughing was the first Monday after Twelfth Night. Called Plough Monday, it signalled that farm labourers should return to their tasks. However, in the spirit of Christmas, they blacked their faces, turned their jackets inside out, and dragging an old ploughshare went round the neighbourhood demanding food. If the householder obliged, all was well, but the tight-fisted paid for it by having their thresholds and paths ploughed up to guarantee a muddy mess for days to come. When all was gathered in, the men went to the local tavern, where the food they had collected was cooked and the farmers paid for the drinks. In *Lost Country Life* Dorothy Hartley reports that this custom lasted in the Midlands until tractors took over the ploughing in the 1930s.

Christmas did not entirely fade until Candlemas on 2 February, and could flicker on until Shrove Tuesday, when a day off from work with pancakes and drink was the final celebration before the long Lenten fast.

Candlemas commemorates the presentation of the infant Jesus in the Temple and the Purification of the Virgin. Candles decorated the church,

and candlelit processions were also common – hence the name of the day. Candlemas coincides with the Celtic festival Imbolc, which marked the mid-point of winter. Numerous folk customs, Celtic in origin but widely observed, clustered around the day. One that reveals the length of Christmas was the rule that Christmas greenery must be taken down and replaced by branches for the new season, as Robert Herrick explained in his poem *Ceremonies for Candlemasse Eve*:

Candles were used in churches and homes at Candlemas, which falls on 2 February.

Greenery used to decorate homes and churches included bay leaves and rosemary in earlier times.

> *Down with the Rosemary and Bayes,*
> *Down with the Mistleto;*
> *Instead of Holly, now upraise*
> *The greener Box (for show).*

In Herrick's estimation, box should be displayed until Easter, when yew took over, to be followed by birch boughs and flowers for Whitsuntide. The concluding line of his poem sums up the progress of the year:

> *New things succeed, as former things grow old.*

The spirit of bidding farewell and moving on also prevails in his poem *Ceremonies for Candlemasse Day*, when the Yule log first lit on Christmas Eve was burned for the last time, a bit being saved to bring good luck throughout the year and to light its successor next Christmas:

> *Kindle the Christmas Brand, and then*
> *Till Sunne-set, let it burne;*
> *Which quench't, then lay it up agen.*
> *Till Christmas next returne.*
> *Part must be kept wherewith to leend*
> *The Christmas Log next yeare;*
> *And where 'tis safely kept, the Fiend,*
> *Can do no mischiefe there.*

More direly, Herrick shows how the Christmas fun and plenty evoked in his poems for the season finally come to an end in his couplet *Upon Candlemasse Day*:

> *End now the White-loafe, & the Pye,*
> *And let all sports with Christmas dye.*

Bays and Rosemary

Everyone who knows the Boar's Head carol knows that the boar's head comes ceremoniously 'Bedeck'd with bays and rosemarie'. In the Seventeenth Century Robert Herrick noted that 'rosemarie and bays that are most faire were stuck about the houses and church as Christmas decorations'. His little poem *Ceremonies for Candlemasse Eve* is about taking down the Christmas greenery and begins 'Down with the Rosemary and Bayes'. In Ben Jonson's *Masque of Christmas* Father Christmas's son New-Year's Gift has 'an orange and a sprig of rosemary' and his daughter Wassail has rosemary carried in front of her. Rosemary indeed was traditional with wassail bowls. It was credited with many important qualities. Because it was a stimulant, scholars wore it to refresh their minds, hence its reputation as the herb of remembrance in Shakespeare's *Hamlet*. It also suggests remembrance in the hat of Jonson's New-Year's Gift. In his *Herball* Gerard said 'It comforteth the harte and maketh it merie' – certainly a good thing at Christmas. Gilded twigs of rosemary decorated many medieval and Renaissance Christmas foods, perhaps because of its merrymaking qualities, or perhaps because it was supposed to ward off evil spirits. As for bay, Greek myth records that the nymph Daphne was turned into a bay tree when she was trying to escape Phoebus's attentions. Bay wreaths were given to victors in ancient Greece and Rome, and awarded as honours to poets as the portrait of Ben Jonson shows on p. 80. Their use with the boar's head suggests the topsy-turvy traditions of Christmas in which dignities were transferred to the lowliest.

Customs and festivities: wassailing, misrule, Boy Bishops

The long Christmas that Sixteenth- and Seventeenth-Century Puritans' railed against not only had its myriad customs scheduled for particular days, but also festivities that continued throughout the season. Wassailing was the most frequent. It was a toast deriving from the Middle English words *'wes heil'* – Be healthy! The response was *'Drinc heil'* – Drink! Be well! Large wassail bowls were filled with sweetened and spiced beer, cider or wine, and passed from hand to hand to emphasise the community of the whole company. Toasts were drunk at every Christmas feast, but wassailers also took to the lanes and streets, taking their bowl with them and singing their good wishes and blessings at house doors. The well-known Wassailing Carol explains what they wanted:

> Our wassail bowl is made
> Of the rosemary tree,
> And so is your beer
> Of the best barley.

If this analogy didn't put the right idea in the householder's head, later verses spelled out the wassailers' expectations:

> Call up the Butler of this house,
> Put on his golden ring;
> Let him bring us a glass of beer
> And the better we shall sing.

> Bring us out a table,
> And spread it with a cloth;
> Bring us out some mouldy cheese
> And some of your Christmas loaf.

The carol ends with blessings on the master, mistress and children of the house. Misfortune for those who fail to cooperate is not explicit, but Robert Herrick's poem *The Wassaile* makes clear that blessings were a two-way exchange. The first eight verses scatter liberal good wishes on the family and its property – even on its poultry:

> Next may your Duck and teeming Hen
> Both to the Cock's tread say Amen;
> And for their two eggs render ten.

Nevertheless, after this generous shower of beneficence, comes this verse:

> Alas! We blesse, but see none here,
> That brings us either Ale or Beere;
> In a drie-house all things are neere.

The next verse suggests that the servants of such a house must be kept awake by their grumbling stomachs. Herrick concludes with a warning:

> *It is vain to sing, or stay*
> *Our free-feet here; but we'l away:*
> *Yet to the Lares this we'll say,*
>
> *The time will come, when you'l be sad*
> *And reckon this for fortune bad,*
> *T'ave lost the good ye might have had.*

Herrick doesn't imply that disappointed wassailers deliberately harmed the householders, but that the stingy would reap in kind. It could be no more than dislike or ill-will throughout the coming year. However, clearly there was a threat hanging over those who didn't cooperate.

So deeply ran the sense that wassail now implied benefits in the future that in the cider-producing counties of the south-west, it was customary to wassail the fruit trees in hopes of a good crop. Robert Herrick, who spent most of his adult life as the clergyman in a Devonshire village, makes clear the wassailing *quid pro quo* between fruit trees and their owners:

> *Wassaile the trees, that they may beare*
> *You many a Plum and many a Peare:*
> *For more or less fruits will they bring,*
> *As you doe give them Wassailing.*

A pear tree from the 1633 edition of John Gerard's Herball.

Misrule as the order of the day

With wassailers joining various sorts of mummers in entertainment for hospitality, it's easy to see that the more successful they were in their efforts, the more likely it would be that they would become exuberant then rowdy and then completely drunk. By the time they were reaching the last houses on their itinerary, they could well be in such a sorry state that their arrival would provoke groans of dismay rather than smiles of welcome. Also, some people may not have had the wherewithal to entertain multiple bands of visitors or give the Christmas boxes in the form of tips that servants expected. Jonathan Swift complained in 1710 that he would be 'undone by Christmas boxes' since he had had to follow custom and increase his tips to a crown 'besides a great many half crowns'. Nostalgia paints a picture of Medieval and Renaissance Christmases as full of generosity, good cheer and merry jests, but often generosity must have translated into 'a huge expense', 'good cheer' into 'gangs of drunken men', and 'merry jests' into 'destructive pranks'. While Puritans deplored such Saturnalian celebrations on doctrinal grounds, many sober-sided householders must also often have had good reasons for thinking that Christmas prompted disorder.

Indeed, Saturnalian misrule was literally the order of the day at the top of the social scale. Every great house from the court down appointed a Lord of Misrule as 'the master of merry disports'. These included comic masquerades, mock tourneys, and mummeries. His appointment began as early as Hallowe'en and continued until Candlemas. Anyone could be appointed, but some men had the right kind of personalities or talents. In *Cakes and Characters*, Bridget Ann Henisch reports that Richard Evelyn, an early-Seventeenth-Century Deputy-Lieutenant of Surrey chose his trumpeter Owen Flood as Lord of Misrule, because of his musical skill. In 1594 Henry Holmes of Gray's Inn was appointed because he 'was accomplished with all good parts, fit for so great a dignity … and very active in dancing and revelling'.

Once in the job, the Lord of Misrule dressed the part and was accompanied by his own court including fools, jesters and even jailers. According to Aspin, the Eighteenth-Century antiquarian, in London the various Lords of Misrule competed as to 'who should make the rarest pastime to delight the beholders'. They had free rein. Richard Evelyn gave Owen Flood the right 'to command all and every person whatsoever, as well as servants and others to be at his command wheresoever he shall sound his trumpet'. Flood had the authority to 'break up all locks, bolts, bars, doors and latches' if needed to capture those who disobeyed his orders. Once captured, the Lord of Misrule could punish his temporary subjects. Writing in the Sixteenth Century, Henry Machyn describes the Lord of Misrule's armoury of stocks and other restraining devices, writing 'The Lord of Misrule went through Cheapside with his gaolers and prisoners', some of the latter 'fastened by leg and some by the neck'. At the Inns of Court mock trials were common, with miscreants able to get off punishment by racing to the buttery and impaling a loaf with their knives.

The Lord of Misrule needed a budget to cover both the splendid clothes he had to buy and the revels he ordered. For the kings, lords, mayors and other officials who had to foot the bill, it was an expensive business. And they not only had to fork out for the Lord of Misrule; there was also the Twelfth Night King of the Bean. Though his rule lasted for only a day, a tip or other gratuity was expected for his efforts.

Large churches also gave power to those who were normally subservient by appointing Boy Bishops for the Christmas season. The boy chosen was usually an altar boy or a choir boy. In 1367 York Minster ruled that the boy who had served the longest should be chosen, provided he was good-looking. Churches kept robes, often beautifully embroidered, for their Boy Bishops. Dressed in these and accompanied by their young companions they paraded the streets asking for alms. Like a Lord of Misrule or a Bean King, the boys relished the deference of their seniors. Probably more frightening was the prospect of having to preach a sermon, but even this would be offset by the presents the miniature bishops received for their efforts.

The principle underlying the reigns of these temporary rulers was that they could invert everyday conventional behaviour by parodying real kings, lords, and bishops in licensed mockery. In an hierarchical world where rulers and masters wielded great authority and had few qualms in asserting it, the Lords of Misrule, Bean Kings and Boy Bishops gave those lower on the pecking order a brief taste of being at the top. Like Saturnalia or Kalends in ancient Rome, Christmas was therefore a time when social tensions could be released. Behaviour punishable at other times was condoned, even encouraged. Obviously since their rule was circumscribed by the holiday, they knew how far they could go without exacting retribution when the real lords and kings regained their sway. At the same time, since Christmas had pre-season events beginning in November plus its post-season carryover until Candlemas, those in authority for the rest of the year might also be guided by the thought that any stringency in their rule would be revenged when Christmas came.

The spirit of the season: Shakespeare's *Twelfth Night*

This turning-the-table spirit of the Christmas season and the obtuseness of Puritan objections to the holiday pervade Shakespeare's *Twelfth Night*. Its title has often bemused editors who question why a play called by the name of a major holiday should not feature its typical activities. Samuel Pepys, who saw it on 6 January, 1663 made the point when he called it 'a silly play and not relating at all to the name of the day'. Indeed, with its setting in distant Illyria, where the shipwrecked twins Viola and Sebastian become the love objects of the local aristocrats Orsino and Olivia, it seems as remote from Shakespeare's England as it could be. However, notably, though Viola disguises herself as a boy, Cesario, in order to enter Orsino's service, she differs from other cross-dressing heroines of Shakespeare's comedies in having no male relative to control her behaviour. This is true too of Olivia, whose ban on marrying until seven years after her brother's recent death is self-imposed, and does not stop her from instantly falling for Viola/Cesario and happily transferring her love to Sebastian, when he eventually shows up. In this respect Shakespeare's alternative title *What You Will* aptly describes their behaviour. Viola and Olivia, Orsino and Sebastian do absolutely what they like – just as people did on Twelfth Night.

Shakespeare approaches the reality of Twelfth Night, and especially the increasing controversy about its celebration, even more directly in the second plot of his play. Olivia's steward Malvolio disapproves of the jesting and boozing of her uncle Sir Toby. Chiding him and his friends, the dupe Sir Andrew and the fool Feste, for drinking and singing late at night, he says:

> *Have you no wit, manners or honesty but to gabble like tinkers at this time of night? Do you make an alehouse of my lady's house that ye squeak out your cozier's catches without any mitigation or remorse of voice? Is there no respect of place, persons, time in you?*

Sir Toby, who has no intention of taking orders from his niece's servant, responds:

> *Dost thou think because thou art virtuous there shall be no more cakes and ale?*

Malvolio clearly does think just this. Maria, Olivia's waiting-woman, has already pointed out 'Sometimes he is a kind of puritan.' Sir Andrew immediately says that if he thought Malvolio was a Puritan, he would 'beat him like a dog'. Given Sir Andrew's uselessness nobody takes this as a serious threat, yet it suggests that Puritan ideas had power to divide. Maria then makes a jibe that has long stuck with fundamentalist Protestant reformers; she implies that Malvolio is a hypocrite:

> *The devil a puritan that he is, or anything constantly, but a time pleaser, an affectioned ass that cons state without book and utters it by great swathes, the best persuaded of himself, so crammed, as he thinks, of excellencies, that it is grounds of faith that all that look on him love him.*

Taking his overdeveloped sense of self-worth as her point of attack, she comes up with a scheme to persuade him that Olivia loves him, and that if he will only dress himself with cross-gartered yellow stockings, she will know her affection is returned. Malvolio cannot resist. Nor can he resist imagining himself installed as her husband and in charge of her household. Getting rid of Sir Toby and his cronies would be one of his first acts.

This neat plot is so psychologically destructive that it elicits some sympathy for Malvolio, who is certainly no charmer, and suggests how precisely Shakespeare exposes the socio-politics of Puritan complaints. Socially Puritans were bourgeois – typically officers, merchants and businessmen rather than land-owning aristocrats. Both by faith and economic class, they wanted radical reform, which included quelling the sort of excess associated with idle minor aristocrats such as Sir Toby and Sir Andrew. Sir Toby correctly understands the desire for power that underpins Malvolio's attitudes, and pointedly defies Malvolio's request that they stop drinking:

> *Go sir! Rub your chain with crumbs. A stoup of wine, Maria!*

Frustrated by his inability to win respect from a drunkard solely because he perches higher on the social scale, Malvolio exits. He pays for his attempt to reform the behaviour of Toby by falling prey to Maria's plan, which destroys the serious persona he has created for himself. In this way, the established but scarcely responsible class represented by Sir Toby triumphs in a jape that is absolutely in the spirit of the Twelfth Night Bean Kings. Yet when all is resolved, Malvolio's final words in the play eerily predict the eventual Puritan triumph when they abolished Christmas celebrations four decades later:

> *I'll be revenged on the whole pack of you!*

No more cakes and ale

Sir Toby's complaint that Puritans wanted to strip festivities of their 'cakes and ale' was widely shared in Stuart England. Many rushed to the defence of old hospitable customs, especially of the wealthy giving money and treating the poor to the good things of the season. Writing in *The Englishman's Christmas* J.A.R. Pimlott quotes Bishop Lancelot Andrews describing Christmas in 1623 as 'a season of gathering together, of neighbourly meetings and invitations … good housekeeping and hospitality'. William Warner, writing of Christmas in the North of England explained:

> At Ewle [Yule] we wonten gambol, daunce, to carrole, and to sing, to have gud spiced sewe [sauce], and roste, and plum-pies for a king.

However, the late-Sixteenth-Century poem *Summer's Last Will and Testament*, suggests how the Malvolios of the world were having their effect. Christmas is described as 'a cut-throat churl that keeps no open house as he should do'. In 1622 James I ordered lords back to their estates 'to keep hospitality among their neighbours'. The harvest that year had been bad, and the king believed that Christmas doles of food would 'relieve and comfort' those who were 'most pinched in times of scarcity'. This suggests that the custom of giving to the poor was not always honoured. Many had simply let the tradition go.

Puritans did not directly attack Christmas charity. Their point was that the Bible makes no mention of the date of Christ's birth and there is no evidence of its celebration by early Christians. They were well aware that Christmas is rooted in the pagan Saturnalia. In a 1656 pamphlet Hezekiah Woodward called it:

> The old Heathens feasting Day, in honour to Saturn their Idol-God. The Papists Massing Day. The Prophane Man's Ranting Day, the Superstitious man's Idol Day, the Multitudes Idle Day.

In Scotland the puritan Presbyterians abolished Christmas in 1583. When the Puritans triumphed in the Civil War against the Royalists, their Scottish co-religionists and allies pressured them to follow suit. In 1644 Christmas Day fell on a Wednesday. The Puritans had declared the last Wednesday of every month as a day of penance and fasting, thus Christmas – for centuries a feast – was that year a fast. The next year the Puritans banned the religious celebration of Christmas because it lacked

In 1935, Daresbury's All Saints Church honoured the village's most famous native son, Lewis Carroll, creator of *Alice in Wonderland*, with a series of stained-glass windows designed by Geoffrey Webb. Carroll, née Charles Dodgson, was born in the Cheshire village in 1832. The windows depict the Nativity with illustrations from *Alice* on the base. This panel gives the Mad Hatter's Tea Party a Christmassy twist with lines from Lewis Carroll's poem *Christmas Greetings*. (Photograph used with permission from the Vicar and Parochial Church Council of All Saints Church, Daresbury, Cheshire).

This portrait of Dickens by Nathaniel Currier titled Boz, the pen name he used in the 1830s, shows him aged around 26, when *The Pickwick Papers*, which includes tales of Mr. Pickwick's Christmas and the Goblins and Gabriel Grub, had made him famous.

(Gift of Lenore B. and Sidney A. Alpert, supplemented with Museum Acquisition Funds, Michele and Donald D'Amour Museum of Fine Arts, Springfield, Massachusetts. Photography by David Stansbury).

In the Nineteenth Century, images of Father Christmas varied greatly. This Victorian card gives him Christmassy holly and the long beard that characterises both Father Christmas and Old Father Time.

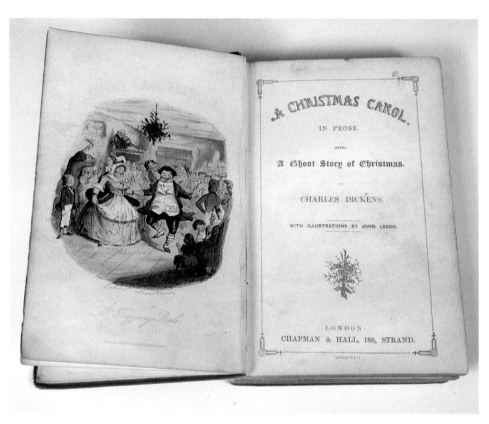

In both *The Pickwick Papers* and *A Christmas Carol*, Charles Dickens created glowing scenes of the masters and servants of yesteryear celebrating Christmas together. This frontispiece from *A Christmas Carol* shows Mr Fezziwig – Scrooge's first employer – leading the ball with Mrs Fezziwig at his home. (Photograph courtesy of Cheffins Fine Art Auctioneers, Cambridge).

In Beatrix Potter's *The Tale of Two Bad Mice,* Tom Thumb (seen here) and Hunca Munca moved into a doll's house and gave the girl who owned it a Christmas stocking to apologise for breaking items, including the toy food which they had believed to be real: their very own Christmas feast. (Figure created by Royal Albert).

Wilfred and Primrose entertained the other mice to a Midwinter Ball in Jill Barklem's seasonal *Brambly Hedge* series of children's books. (Figures created by Royal Doulton).

Mʳ GRIMALDI, as Clown.

Joseph Grimaldi (1779–1837) was one of the most popular clowns of early Christmas pantomimes. Shown here in *Harlequin and Mother Goose*, which he introduced to the Theatre Royal, Covent Garden in 1806, his costume reveals the *commedia dell 'arte* origins of pantomime, whilst the goose struggling to get out of his pocket and his bottles and glass are traditional elements of English Christmas feasts.

The child-centred Christmas with parents doing as much as possible to make festive fun for their children was a Victorian innovation. In earlier centuries, the focus was on adults eating, drinking and making merry.

Santa Claus became increasingly popular during the Nineteenth Century, but it was not until the Twentieth Century that his outfit was standardised as red with a white fur trim. Here, the Nineteenth Century German-American artist Thomas Nast portrays him as a carpenter, in the traditional carpenter's cap, making toys for Christmas.

In this version of Father Christmas, Thomas Nast evokes Bacchus, the Roman god of wine. He also includes holly, one of the most traditional emblems of an English Christmas, and adult revellers who pre-dated children as the focus of the festivities.

The German tradition that is one of the sources of the modern Santa, has him dressed in furs. Here, the dove suggests that, despite his wild appearance, he comes in peace. His holly-swagged staff recalls the holly bob carried as a symbol of peace by the Green Knight in *Sir Gawain and the Green Knight*.

The idea of green people such as the Green Knight in *Sir Gawain and the Green Knight* was common in late-medieval England. Carvings of heads with leaves growing from them are common in churches of the period. Known as the Green Man, this motif remains popular in garden ornaments today.

The Chester Mystery Plays are performed once every five years. Scenes from the 2008 performance (this page and opposite) include a shepherd and his sheep, Mary and Joseph, and the shepherds enjoying their outdoor meal.

(Photograph courtesy of David Sejrup, Chester City Council).

In England, Christmas trees were brought to Manchester by the German business community some time before 1840. Prince Albert helped popularise them when he introduced them into the Royal household in 1841. Early Christmas trees were small enough to sit on a table. Today, the rule for Christmas trees is the bigger the better. This tree at Blantyre in Lenox, Massachusetts is 103 feet tall.

Just as Medieval pastry cooks made elaborate subtleties of sugar and marzipan for Christmas feasts, so today's bakers fill their windows with cakes that mimic Christmas figures.

Fruitcakes have long been Christmas specialities in Britain. Seen here, a fruitcake topped with crystallised fruits and peel, a Dundee cake and a Christmas tin of biscuits.

The belief in the presence of supernatural creatures at Christmas has a long history, and is important in Dickens' Christmas books. This Copeland Spode plate (see below) from the 1890s shows goblins singing from a holly bough. The pattern is called The Christmas Carol. The Christmas card from the same era also shows carolling goblins.

The Nineteenth Century turned the Christmas focus onto children. When Christmas cards became popular in the second half of the century, images of children were among the most common. Christmas puddings were ball-shaped because they were boiled in a cloth submerged in water rather than in a basin.

Since the early Twentieth Century, companies have marketed their products for Christmas by packaging them in attractive containers. The Mother Hubbard biscuit barrel was made by Doulton for Huntley and Palmer in 1905.

In 1940, the Harrods' Christmas catalogue had this wartime Santa marching over its cover wearing his ARP helmet and carrying a torch to see in the blackout.
(Photograph courtesy of Company Archive, Harrods Limited).

A certificate issued to a child who joined in Harrods' efforts to spread the good things of Christmas to children in need in 1908.
(Photograph courtesy of Company Archive, Harrods Limited).

In this advertisement, Santa Claus explains that he no longer has any trouble with Christmas presents because confectioners provide him with Quality Street. At the bottom left and right are 'just a few of the many delightful boxes, caskets and fancy tins in which Mackintosh's Quality Street and other famous assortments of toffees and chocolates are specially packed for Christmas'.

Most Christmas decorations are symbolic as well as pretty. Christmas wreaths mimic the shape of the sun as a means of urging its return. Candles symbolise Christ as the light of the world.

Druids thought mistletoe had magical powers because it grows and bears fruit without having roots in the earth – characteristics that made it essential among the greenery used for decoration at Christmas. Mistletoe is a parasite that most commonly grows on apple trees.
(Mistletoe photograph courtesy of Jonathan Briggs of Mistletoe Matters in Tenbury Wells).

Many cribs show the shepherds and the Kings worshipping the Baby Jesus at the same time. In fact, St Luke's Gospel says that the shepherds went immediately to Bethlehem, whereas the Kings, also called the Magi, followed a star for 12 days before their arrival.

An initial from an illuminated manuscript showing the Adoration of the Magi, created around 1500 by Jean de Montlucon. The Magi, also called the Three Kings, were thought to have arrived 12 days after the birth of Christ. The Feast of the Epiphany on 6th January celebrates their coming and, for many centuries, Twelfth Night celebrations were the traditional end of the Christmas season.

(Photograph courtesy of Mount Holyoke College Art Museum).

James and his Snowman enjoy a cake in this Royal Doulton plate based on Raymond Briggs' classic children's book, *The Snowman*.

biblical sanction, then in 1647 they passed a law forbidding all holidays 'hithertofore superstitiously used'. This meant that Christmas could be celebrated as neither a religious nor a secular holiday. Evergreens were stripped from any church that had put them up. Shops and businesses were supposed to open as normal. In fact, many did not, and some of those that did were attacked and their goods damaged by crowds demonstrating their resistance to the Puritan ban on their favourite holiday.

The Puritans and Christmas fare

Puritans also forbade Christmas foods. Naturally, poorer people hated being deprived of the one period of the year when they could eat well. As one Puritan pamphlet of 1652 reported:

> *The poore will pawn all to the Cloaths of their back to provide Christmas pies for their bellies, and the broath of Abominable things in their Vessels.*

That 'broath of Abominable things' was probably the beloved plum porridge made from beef with prunes and other dried fruits. Along with mince pies, it was high on the list of traditional Christmas foods that the Puritans forbade as 'superstitious'. J.A.R. Pimlott quotes one doggerel tirade of 1656 that called them 'Idolatrie in a crust' because they were 'defil'd with superstition'.

On the face of it, the Puritan wrath against cakes and ale and other foods seems bizarre. Once in power under Oliver Cromwell, surely they had better reforms to see to rather than worrying about whether people had a mince pie or two at Christmas. Clearly, though, Puritans ranted against mince pies and plum porridge because they symbolised everything they hated about Christmas. Beyond this, eating long-hallowed treats at Christmas could be taken as a political marker for antipathy to Puritan rule or devotion to the Church of England, or even the Church of Rome.

Moreover, Puritans objected to the element of chance or divination in many old eating and drinking traditions. Stirring the mincemeat was supposed to bring luck. Twelfth Night cakes were a lottery for who should star as King of the Bean. Games of chance and superstitions about luck were typical Christmas pleasures, and all deeply irreligious in Puritan eyes since they flew in the face of their faith in God's Providence. Even the ancient toast *'wes heil'* – be healthy – was a secular wish rather than a religious prayer.

Thanksgiving

The Pilgrim Fathers who sailed from Plymouth to found the Massachusetts Bay Colony in 1620 were Puritans eager to establish a colony where they could practise their pure religion. Since the traditional English Christmas lacked biblical sanction, they would have none of it in Massachusetts. Governor William Bradford ordered them to work as usual on Christmas Day. Those whose conscience forbade work could observe the day indoors, but without games or feasting. Two years later he declared an autumn holiday to give thanks for their first successful farming season. Reading Edward Winslow's description of what happened, it's easy to see the similarity to the Renaissance Christmas with its games and trials of strength, its welcome to all-comers, its hunting and its feasting:

> Our harvest being gotten in, our governor sent four men on fowling, that so we might after a special manner rejoice together after we had gathered the fruits of our labor. They four in one day killed as much fowl as, with a little help beside, served the company almost a week. At which time, amongst other recreations, we exercised our arms, many of the Indians coming amongst us, and among the rest their greatest king Massasoit with some ninety men, whom for three days we entertained and feasted, and they went out and killed five deer, which we brought to the plantation and bestowed on our governor, and upon the captain and others.

Bradford confirmed this: 'And besides waterfowl there was great store of wild turkeys, of which they [the men] took many, besides venison.' Today Americans celebrate this holiday as the first Thanksgiving. Turkey reigns supreme as the centrepiece, though earlier generations also included chicken pies and joints of beef and pork. As for pudding, the mincemeat pies so reviled by English Puritans as symbolising everything they hated in Christmas became a Thanksgiving staple in America. Indeed, pies are the must-have Thanksgiving dessert: pumpkin, apple, cranberry and pecan pies are also favourites.

Perhaps, too, Puritans had a particular dislike of Christmas fare because it could be extravagantly bizarre. In his 1660 book *The Accomplish't Cook* Robert May looks back to before 'the unhappy and Cruel Disturbances of these Times', and gives elaborate instructions for a frolic for Twelfth Day. The pastrycook had to create a ship complete with cannon and gunpowder and put it on a charger surrounded with eggshells filled with scented water. Next, a stag was to be made of paste. He was filled with claret and had an arrow in his side. A castle was also necessary with battlements, portcullises and its own gunpowder supplies. The stag, which also had eggshells of perfume, was placed between the castle and the ships as were two bran-filled pies. The bran was emptied through a hole in the bottom after baking. Live frogs replaced the bran in one pie, and live birds in the other, and the pies were decorated with gilded bay leaves. Then, with everything set to go, a lady was induced to pull the arrow from the stag, so the claret poured forth 'as blood runneth out of a wound'. Next the ship and the castle fired on each other 'as in battel'. Now to 'sweeten the stink of the powder', the ladies were to take the eggshells of scented water and throw them over each other. Yet this was not the end:

> All dangers seemingly over, by this time you may suppose they may desire to see what is in the pyes; where lifting first the lid off one pye, out skip some Frogs, which make the Ladies skip and shreek; next after the other pye, whence come out the Birds, who by natural instinct flying at the light, will put out the Candles, so that what with the flying Birds, the skipping Frogs, the one above, the other beneath, will cause much delight and pleasure to the whole company: at length the Candles are lighted, and a banquet brought in … These were formerly the delights of the Nobility before good House-keeping had left England, and the Sword really acted that which was only counterfeited in such honest and laudable exercises.

This elaborate spectacle was an exaggerated form of a subtlety. During the Middle Ages and Renaissance the word indicated a deception, and when used of festive food, described something designed to look like something else. At its simplest, this could be chickens or gingerbread 'endored' with egg or saffron so that they looked gilded. More elaborately, confectioners created castles or coats of arms or whatever was appropriate to the occasion. For example, at Christmas in 1561 Queen Elizabeth I's pastrycook made her a chessboard of marzipan so she could play a favourite game – much more fun than skipping and shrieking among the birds and frogs.

The intricate Twelfth-Day subtlety May recalled so nostalgically may well have had irksome implications to Puritans. May had served in the houses of the Roman Catholic nobility – politically and socially remote from the bourgeois Puritan parliamentarians who deposed and executed Charles I. They undoubtedly saw such extravagances as typical of the thriftless court and aristocracy whose financial delinquencies had prompted the Civil War. So along with much else in Christmas of the Middle Ages and Renaissance, subtleties of this formidable nature disappeared, though their art lived on in the Twelfth cakes that continued to delight long after the Restoration. Traces of the subtlety can still be seen today in the bevy of robins and reindeer in the snow scenes atop the traditional Christmas cake, and in bakery windows where chocolate Yule logs with meringue mushrooms compete with white snowmen-shaped cakes and golden gingerbread people.

Robert May's Bill of Fare for Christmas Day

Puritans may also have felt that Robert May's Christmas menus focused attention on physical rather than spiritual delights. May's *The Accomplish't Cook* begins with suggested Bills of Fare for each month of the year. Notably, the first three are for winter holidays: All Saints' Day on 1 November, Christmas Day and New Year's Day. Each menu suggests two courses of fifteen to twenty dishes compared to the six dishes in each course during other months of the year.

The recommended first course of twenty dishes for Christmas Day is 'A collar of brawn, Stewed Broth of Mutton marrow bones, A grand Sallet [salad], a pottage of capons, a breast of veal in stoffado, a boiled partridge, a chine of beef or sirloin roast, Minced pies, a Jegote [leg] of mutton with anchove [anchovy] sauce, a made dish of sweetbread, a swan roast, a pasty of venison, a kid with a pudding in his belly, a steak pie, a hanch [haunch] of venison roasted, a turkey roast and stuck with cloves, a made dish of chickens in puff pastc, two bran [brant] geese roasted, one larded, Two large capons, one larded, A Custard.'

The second course of nineteen dishes begins with oranges and lemons, as do all the other feast-day second courses. It proceeds with an array of roasted meat and poultry quite similar to those of the first course except for the great number of small game birds: six partridge, six teal, ten plovers, six woodcock and 'a dish of larks'. Fish is included in the form of sturgeon, which was prized for its dramatic size and its veal-like flesh.

Bills of Fare.		Bills of Fare.	
1 2 A roll of beef.	1 2 A pasty of venison.	11 A Gammon of West-phalia Bacon.	11 A pasty of Venison.
1 3 Two teels roasted, one larded.	13 A kid with a pudding in his belly.	12 Ten plovers, five larded.	12 A Pig roast.
14 A cold goose pie.	14 A steak pie.	13 A quince pye, or warden pie.	13 Two geese roast.
15 A touc't mullet and bace.	15 A haunch of venison roasted.	14 Six woodcocks, 3 larded.	14 Two capons, one larded.
16 A quince pye.	16 A turkey roast and stuck with cloves.	15 A standing Tart in puffpaste, preserved fruits, Pippins, &c.	15 Custards.
17 Four curlews, 2 larded.	17 A made dish of chickens in puff paste.	16 A dish of Larks.	A second Course for the same Mess.
18 A dried neats tongue.	18 Two bran geese roasted, one larded.	17 Six dried neats tongues.	Oranges and Lemons.
19 A dish of anchoves.	19 Two large capons, one larded.	18 Sturgeon.	1 A side of Lamb.
20 A jole of Sturgeon.	20 A Custard.	19 Powdered Geese. Jellies.	2 A souc't Pig.
Jellies and Tarts Royal, and Ginger bread, and other Fruits.	The second course for the same Mess.	A Bill of Fare for new-years Day.	3 Two couple of rabbits, two larded.
	Oranges and Lemons.	Oysters.	4 A duck and mallard, one larded.
A Bill of Fare for Christmas Day, and how to set the Meat in order.	1 A young lamb or kid.	1 Brawn and Mustard.	5 Six teels, three larded.
Oysters.	2 Two couple of rabbits, two larded.	2 Two boil'd Capons in stewed Broth, or white Broth.	6 A made dish, or Batalia-Pye.
1 A collar of brawn.	3 A pig souc't with tongues.	3 Two Turkies in stoffado.	7 Six woodcocks, 3 larded.
2 Stewed Broth of Mutton marrow bones.	4 Three ducks, one larded.	4 A Hash of twelve Partridges, or a shoulder of mutton.	8 A warden pie, or a dish of quails.
3 A grand Sallet.	5 Three pheasants, 1 larded	5 Two bran Geese boil'd.	9 Dried Neats tongues.
4 A pottage of caponets. A breast of veal in stoffado.	6 A Swan Pye.	6 A farc't boil'd meat with snites or ducks.	10 Six tame Pigeons, three larded.
5	7 Three brace of partridge, three larded.	7 A marrow pudding bak't	11 A souc't Capon.
6 A boil'd partridge.	8 Made dish in puff paste.	8 A surloin of roast beef.	12 Pickled mushrooms, pickled Oysters, and Anchoves in a dish.
7 A chine of beef, or surloin roast.	9 Bolonia sausages, and anChoves, mushrooms, and Cavieate, and pickled oysters in a dish.	9 Minced pies, ten in a dish, or what number you please	13 Twelve snites, six larded
8 Minced pies.	10 Six teels, three larded.	10 A Loin of Veal.	14 Orangado Pye, or a Tart Royal of dried and wet suckets.
9 A Jegote of mutton with anchove sauce.	A 11		15 Sturgeon.
10 A made dish of sweetbread.			16 Turkey or goose pye.
11 A swan roast.			Jel-

Robert May's The Accomplish't Cook *is the most authoritative cookery book of the English Renaissance. These pages show his suggested Bill of Fare for a two-course Christmas dinner.*

The second course finishes with jellies. These now seem a fairly modest pudding, but in earlier centuries they required long hours of cooking bones, feet, trotters, and cod sounds to acquire the gelatine, which then had to be clarified. Once this was done, the jelly could be used in several ways. May has a recipe for a jelly of three colours using saffron for yellow, cochineal for red and spices for a tawny orange. He also has a recipe for 'a Crystal Jelly' made by clarifying it with egg whites and shells and flavouring it with musk, ambergris and damask rose-water. This lengthy process could only be justified for special occasions or to provide nutritious but easily swallowed food for invalids.

The Accomplish't Cook is the most interesting of the many cookery books produced before 1660. It is the most compendious – 461 pages – and the most authoritative because as May explains, he had been born into a family of cooks, trained partly in France, and worked in aristocratic households, including those of Lord Lumley, Lord Lovelace and Sir William Paston, for fifty-five years. His book also has sections on

101

Robert May had been cook in several aristocratic households, and was precise about how food should be served. This page from his book The Accomplish't Cook *shows the appropriate shapes and decorations for pies.*

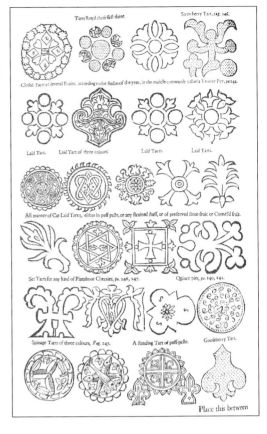

raising poultry and wildfowl so essential for Christmas and other feasts in wealthy homes. He has an elaborate list of how to carve them, each bird dignified with its own terminology for this process: 'Lift that Swan, Unbrace that Mallard, Untach that Curlew', are just a few.

He also has pages illustrating the correct shape and ornamentation for the multitude of pies so popular at Christmas and other times. As a professional chef, he is intensely concerned with appropriate presentation. He has far fewer invalid recipes than the women writers who form the majority of English cookery book authors of earlier centuries, and none of the household products such as cleaners and stain removers that they often include. Most importantly, May is a traditionalist so he gathers recipes as they had been developing since the late Fourteenth-Century *Forme of Cury*, presenting them in authoritative forms that continued to influence cooking well into the Eighteenth Century. However, while May was a traditionalist, he was not opposed to the new. His book has many recipes that show his familiarity with other countries. The first recipe in the book is a Spanish olla podrida, and he has several more Spanish recipes, as well as French, Italian, Portuguese and even a 'Turkish dish of Meat', which is beef cubes cooked in a closed pot with rice. May's directions are usually clear, so many of his recipes can be adapted for today's kitchen. Among these are his Butternut with Apples and Onions (below), a good dish to serve with the Christmas turkey or goose.

BUTTERNUT WITH APPLES AND ONIONS

This recipe derives from Robert May's directions for buttering 'gourds, pumpions, cucumbers or muskmelons' in his 1660 book *The Accomplish't Cook*. May's directions read: 'Fry them in slices … either floured or in batter, being fried serve them with beaten butter and vinegar, or beaten butter and juice of an orange.'

    1 large butternut squash
    salt and pepper to taste
    2–3 tbsp plain flour
    2 large eating apples, peeled and cored
    3 tbsp light-flavoured oil such as grapeseed oil
    1 tbsp butter
    1 medium-large onion peeled, halved and sliced
    1 tbsp finely chopped fresh parsley
    1 large navel or other orange, cut in wedges

For this recipe you do not need the bulbous end of the butternut squash. Cut off a 15cm / 6-inch section of the straight end, peel it and then slice it 8mm / $^3/_8$-inch thick. Cut into half moons. Salt and pepper them lightly, then dust with flour. Cut each apple into 8 slices. Dust them lightly with flour. Heat 2 tablespoons of the oil and the butter in a large frying pan over high heat; add the squash slices a few at a time and fry until the underside is golden and the edge tinged with brown. This takes 3–4 minutes. Turn and cook the other side. As the pieces become tender, remove them to a heated plate, and add the apple slices to the pan, letting these also fry to a light golden brown. Meanwhile, pour the remaining tablespoon of oil into a small frying pan over medium heat; add the sliced onion, and fry it gently, until it turns golden but not brown. When the apples and squash are done, pile them on a serving dish and top with the onions and parsley. Squeeze on the juice from a couple of the orange wedges, and garnish with the remainder so people can add more juice if they like. Robert May suggested serving them with butter, but for modern taste this is probably too rich.

MINCEMEAT

Many medieval meat pies included dried fruit with flavourings of spices and sugar. Mincemeat pies evolved from pies of chopped meat with a large proportion of fruit. Robert Herrick evoked the making of mincemeat appreciatively:

> *Drink now the strong Beere,*
> *Cut the white loafe here,*
> *The while the meat is shredding*
> *For the rare Mince-Pie;*
> *And the Plums stand by*
> *To fill the Paste that's kneading.*

Most mincemeat recipes lost all meat content except suet by the early Nineteenth Century. Mincemeat is easy to make. It keeps well because the dried fruits are preserved and the sugar and alcohol also have preservative power. Use butter rather than suet to make vegetarian mincemeat. A traditional mincemeat pie recipe follows and there's a recipe for Lemon Mincemeat on pp. 140–1.

115g/4oz suet or butter, frozen
1.3kg/3lb tart apples, peeled and grated
425g/15oz dark raisins
425g/15oz sultanas
350g/12oz currants
450g/1lb brown sugar
grated zest and juice of 1 orange or large lemon
1 whole nutmeg, grated (or 2 tsp powdered)
½ tsp powdered cloves
½ tsp powdered mace
1 tsp powdered cinnamon
1 tsp powdered ginger
175ml/6 fl oz rum or brandy

Grate the suet or butter on the coarse blade of a grater or in a food processor fitted with a grating blade. (Freezing makes this easier and it also prevents the suet or butter blending into the other ingredients; it should stay in small fragments.) Mix the suet with the apples, raisins, sultanas, currants and sugar. Stir in the orange or lemon zest and the

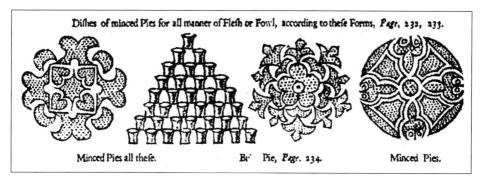

Suggested shapes for mincemeat pies from Robert May's The Accomplish't Cook.

nutmeg, cloves, mace, cinnamon and ginger. Finally, stir in the rum or brandy. Cover and stir again next day. Proceed like this for a week. Add more of any ingredient you like, making especially sure to spice the mincemeat to your taste. Pack into sterilised jars. (To sterilise jars, boil them empty in a large pan of water for 10 minutes; let them stand in the water until ready to use and then dry with paper towels.) Store in a cold spot. Makes about 6–7 pounds.

MINCEMEAT LATTICE PIE

Robert May's book *The Accomplish't Cook* has suggested patterns of cut-out pastry to decorate pies. You would need a careful hand and lots of patience to make them. A lattice-topped mincemeat pie looks equally alluring, and if you want to add a drop more rum before serving, you can just pour it into the openings in the lattice.

    200g/7oz plain flour
    pinch baking powder
    1 tbsp sugar plus extra for the top
    85g/3oz cold butter cut in bits
    50g/1¾oz lard
    about ¼ cup chilled water
    about 450g/1lb mincemeat
    1 tbsp cream

Preheat the oven to 220°C (425°F). In a mixing bowl, stir together the flour, baking powder and a tablespoon of sugar. Add the butter and lard in bits and toss them about so the flour coats them. Rub the fats into the dry ingredients with your fingers or a pastry blender. When the mixture looks like coarse crumbs, make a well in the centre and pour in about half the chilled water. With your fingers, pull the mixture together, if necessary adding more water a little at a time until you get a handleable, not sticky, pastry. Flour a cold pastry board and a rolling pin. Grease a 23cm/9-inch pie pan. Divide the dough into two portions, one about twice as big as the other. Keep the smaller one in the fridge while you roll the larger portion into a 30cm/12-inch circle and fit it into your pan. Fill it with the mincemeat. Do not trim off the edges at this point. Roll out the smaller piece of pastry into a rectangle and cut it into 2cm/¾-inch strips. Arrange these across the pie, weaving them in under-and-over style to form a lattice. (Re-roll the bits to make the shorter strips if necessary, but don't re-roll oftener than you must.) Now fold the ragged edges of the bottom layer of pastry over the ends of the lattice strips, using just enough to make a neat edge. Brush the pastry with the cream and sprinkle with a teaspoon or so of sugar. Bake for 20 minutes or until golden.

SHAKESPEAREAN WARDEN PIE

Wardens were a variety of hard pear generally used in pies rather than eaten uncooked. In *The Accomplish't Cook* Robert May includes a warden pie in the second course of his Bill of Fare for Christmas Day. His recipe calls for spicing the pears with cloves, cinnamon and ginger, and he notes that the same recipe can be used for quinces or other sorts of pears. In Shakespeare's *A Winter's Tale* Perdita plans a festive warden pie for a sheep-shearing feast and sends the Clown out shopping for ingredients:

Other Taſt of Wardens Quinces, or Pears.

Firſt bake them in a pot, then cut them in quarters, and coar them, put them in a tart made according to this form, cloſe it up, and when it is baked, ſcrape on ſugar.

Sixteenth- and Seventeenth-Century cookery books have many recipes for the hard pears called wardens. Recipes for warden pies varied. Robert May's suggested shape for a warden pear pie is shown with one of his recipes from his book The Accomplish't Cook.

Let me see, What am I to buy for our sheep-shearing feast. Three pound of sugar, five pound of currants, rice – what will this sister of mine do with rice? But my father has made her mistress of the feast, and she lays it on … I must have saffron to colour the warden pies; mace; dates – none; that's out of my note; nutmegs, seven; a race or two of ginger, but that I may beg; four pound of prunes, and as many raisins o'th'sun. (Act IV, Sc.iii)

Like Perdita's recipe, the following one has saffron for colour and flavour, and the currants and raisins from the Clown's shopping list.

Large pinch saffron threads or 1 packet powdered saffron
30g/1oz sultanas
1 tbsp currants
3 large firm conference or Bosc pears, weighing about 225g/8oz each
1 tsp powdered ginger
1 tbsp honey
1 pack frozen puff pastry
1 tbsp sugar

Put the saffron in a small bowl and add 100ml/3½ fluid ounces of warm water. Stir and let it sit for 30 minutes or longer. Put the sultanas and currants in another small bowl and cover with warm water to plump them. Peel the pears, halve them and remove the cores. Put them in a dish and dust with the ginger. Trickle the honey over them. Turn them gently so the honey and ginger spread. Slowly pour on the saffron, including the threads if you are using them. Turn the pears gently over, spooning the liquid onto them. Let them rest for 20–30 minutes to take flavour from the honey, ginger and saffron.

Grease a 23cm/9-inch pie dish with butter and preheat the oven to 220°C (425°F). Defrost the pastry. Roll out half of it and cut it into 3 strips wide enough to line the side and rim of the dish. Press it in place. Arrange the pears in the dish with their wide ends to the edge. If they don't fit evenly, cut a little of the narrow end off. Fit in these bits between the pears or in the middle. Pour the liquid from the pears on top. Discard the liquid from the sultanas and currants, and scatter them among the pears. Roll out the remaining pastry and cut it into a circle to fit the top of the pie dish. Put it in place, wetting the edges and pressing them together. Gently press the pastry down onto the pears so their shape is visible. Make cuts between the pears as air vents. Sprinkle the sugar on top of the pastry. Bake for 5 minutes, then lower the temperature to

205°C (400°F), and continue baking for another 15–20 minutes or until the pie is golden. Serve warm or at room temperature, cutting between the pears to make 6 servings, each with its own pear half. To serve 8, use 4 pears, each weighing about 175 grams / 6 ounces.

ROBERT HERRICK'S LAMB'S WOOL

Lamb's wool was a favourite version of mulled ale in Elizabethan England and still popular in the Nineteenth Century. It got its name from the roasted or stewed apples that float on top in a woolly-looking mass. Robert Herrick lists the ingredients in his poem *Twelfe Night; or King and Queene*:

> *Next crowne the bowl full*
> *With gentle lambs-wooll;*
> *Add sugar, nutmeg and ginger,*
> *With store of ale too;*
> *And thus ye must doe*
> *To make the wassaile a swinger.*

The following recipe can be multiplied as needed to serve a crowd. The amount of spice and sugar can also be adjusted to taste. It's important to use an apple such as Bramley's Seedling that quickly collapses into a fluffy mass in cooking to get the froth of soft apples on top.

3–4 apples (about 500g/1lb 2oz), preferably Bramleys or McIntoshes
200g/7oz soft brown sugar, or to taste
1½ tsp ground ginger
½ tsp freshly grated nutmeg, plus more for serving
2 bottles (350ml/12 fl oz each) winter ale

Peel, core and slice the apples. Put the slices in a saucepan with 100ml/3 fl oz water. Cover and cook over low heat for 4–5 minutes until they are softening. Stir in the sugar, ginger and nutmeg. Cook until the apples have fallen into a soft mass, about another 7–8 minutes. Pour in the ale and continue cooking until the mixture is very hot. Ladle into mugs and quickly grate a little more nutmeg onto each one. Makes 4 drinks.

Turkey

A native of North and South America, the turkey was unknown in Europe until Spanish conquistadores brought them to Spain in the early Sixteenth Century. They were an instant hit because they were meatier, tenderer and easier to handle than swans and herons. Having been domesticated in England during the reign of Henry VIII, the Puritan Pilgrim Fathers took them from England to Massachusetts, so when they saw wild turkeys wandering from the woods they knew exactly what they were. Visitors to New England today might not spot that these flocks of narrow bronze-black birds are related to the chunky big-breasted turkeys that star on many Christmas tables. Centuries of hybridisation produced the change, in the interest of having lots of white meat. As for the name, when turkeys first arrived in Europe no-one knew their provenance. The English decided they must have come from the East, so they were named after Turkey, a source of much of the dried fruit so popular at Christmas. The Spanish stuck with *péru*, also denoting the supposed country of origin, while the French opted for India as the most likely source and identified them as the bird *d'Inde*, now changed to *dinde*.

CHAPTER 5

Between the Old and the New, 1660–1840

This is quite the season indeed for friendly meetings. At Christmas everybody invites their friends about them, and people think little of even the worst weather.

Jane Austen, *Emma*, 1815

WITH THEIR total ban on all Christmas celebrations, the Puritans made the sharpest possible break with Christmas as it had been developing in Britain for hundreds of years. Their changes did not please many people. The diarist John Evelyn, an Anglican, bemoaned the lack of Christmas Day services in the 1650s, and when he went to one in London in 1657, Puritan soldiers burst in during Communion and imprisoned both the clergyman and the congregation. Poor people deprived of the beer, bread and meat provided by the wealthy protested their loss, sometimes by rioting. *The Arraignment, Conviction and Imprisonment of Christmas*, a satirical pamphlet of 1645 anonymously printed by Simon Minc'd Pye for Cissely Plum Porridge to avoid persecution, described the response to the ban:

The poor are sorry for it, for they go to every door a-begging, as they were wont to do (Good Mrs., somewhat against this good Time); but Time was transformed (Away, begone, here is nought for you); and so instead of going to an Ale-house to be drunke, were fain to work at the Holidayes. The Schollers came into the Hall, where they hungry stomacks had thought to have found good Brawn and Christmas pies, Roast-beef and Plum-porridge; but no such matter ... Alas, poor tallow-faced Chandlers, I met them mourning through the streets, and complaining that they could get no vent for their Mustard for the want of Brawn.

The insensitivity to deeply-rooted Christmas traditions notwithstanding, the Puritans could not have succeeded, either in winning the Civil War or in their reforms, had they not tapped into shared feelings. It was possible to disagree with Puritan religious beliefs, yet to agree that uninhibited Christmas celebrations had little to do with the Nativity or with good public order. The metaphysical poet Henry Vaughan acted on the Royalist side in the Civil War, yet his poem *The True Christmas* argues that sticking up 'Ivie and the Bays' is a step toward 'Heathen ways'. Arguing against the customary revels, he writes:

> *The brightness of this day we owe*
> *Not unto Music, Masque or Show*
> *Nor gallant furniture, nor plate;*
> *But to the Manger's mean estate.*
> *His life while here as well as birth,*
> *Was but a check to pomp and mirth;*
> *And all man's greatness you may see*
> *Condemned by His humility.*
> *Then leave your open house and noise,*
> *And welcome him with holy Joys.*

At the same time, Sixteenth-Century pamphleteers had been complaining that Christmas was no longer being kept with the old open-handed hospitality. The Tudor kings Henry VII and VIII and Edward VI were the last to have a Lord of Misrule to orchestrate their Christmas festivities. Though the masques so popular with Queen Elizabeth I and the Stuarts thrived until the eve of the Civil War, aesthetically they had fallen from the heights achieved when Ben Jonson was writing them. The fact that James I had to order his lords back to their country duty of dispensing Christmas alms suggests that this tradition was declining. Thus, it's fair to see the Puritan attack on Christmas as both a pious devotion to the Bible, and at the same time to note that traditional celebrations were weakening even before the Puritans scythed them down.

When Charles II returned to the throne in 1660, some old ways came in his train. His advisor the Marquis of Newcastle encouraged him to support the customs that punctuated the year, including 'carols and wassail at Christmas, with goodly plum porridge and pies, which are now forbidden as profane ungodly things'. Once more, shops and businesses closed to keep Christmas Day as a holiday, and churches and households were decorated with greenery. Charles revived the custom of courtiers bringing the monarch New Year's gifts – usually cash or plate. Charles also followed the custom shared by rich and poor alike: he gambled furiously at Christmas, often losing heavily.

More significantly, while dissenters from the Anglican Church continued to treat 25 December as an ordinary day of business well into the Nineteenth Century, for the majority the return of the king signalled that they could celebrate as they liked without fear of reprisals. Some old customs such as eating mince pies revived intact and still remain as popular as ever. Other traditions such as parades of Boy Bishops and Lords of Misrule were things of the past. Between these two extremes, many customs suffered a sea change and emerged in new forms. Mummers and masquers were less common, but the love of disguises and Christmas entertainment found fresh channels in music and pantomime. Male-dominated Christmas revelry was quelled as festivities took to the indoors, where families gathered to eat and to play games around the fire. Christmas after the Restoration became a patchwork cut from both old and new cloth.

Twelfth Night and its cakes

One of the oldest customs was the celebration of Twelfth Night with the biggest feasts of the whole Christmas season. Twelfth cakes were the highlight of the evening. Like Christmas cakes, Twelfth cakes were dense with dried fruits and sturdy enough to withstand an enthusiastic confectioner working on their surface. Made of the omnipresent dried fruits of British celebrations, Twelfth cakes contained a bean. Whoever got it became the King of the Bean and reigned for the evening, demanding obedience to outrageous rules and powering up the revels of the most uninhibited day of the Christmas season. This custom goes back to Saturnalia, when the one who got the bean in his pottage had license to command whatever he wanted. Also Saturnalian were the drink-fuelled pranks and fun. Robert Herrick gives some idea of the enthusiasm for drinking in his poem *Twelfe Night, or King and Queene*:

And let not a man then be seen here,
Who unurg'd will not drinke
From the base from the brink
A health to the King and the Queene here.

A pea was commonly added to the cake to determine the Queen. At Samuel Pepys' celebrations in 1661 there were two Queens because the pea was sliced in two as the cake was cut. The bean was never found, so the party improvised:

After a good supper we have an excellent cake, where the mark for the Queene was cut; and so there was two queenes, my wife and Mrs. Ward; and the King being lost, they chose the Doctor to be King, so we made him send for some wine.

Trinkets in the cake signified supporting roles for those who got them. Some roles had little status. In her history of Twelfth Night *Cakes and Characters*, Bridget Ann Henisch quotes a description of a ship-board Twelfth Night celebration at which the bean for the king and pea for the queen were accompanied by a clove for the knave, a forked stick for the cuckold, and a rag for the slut. The lieutenant who got the forked stick was the laughing stock of the evening. To avoid such a fate, battles could ensue to get the pieces with the best parts. Samuel Pepys must have been only one of many who regretted seeing an expensive cake wrecked as guests seized the bits they wanted, perhaps dipping them in the wassail bowl before chomping them down. His account of his 1669 Twelfth cake describes a new fashion, which tamed disorder by writing the names of the king, queen and other characters on slips of paper, which guests then drew at random:

In the evening I did bring out my cake – a noble cake, and there cut it in pieces, with wine and good drink; and after a new fashion, to prevent spoiling the cake, did put so many titles into a hat, and so drew cuts; and I was the Queene; and Theophilia Turner, King – Creed, Sir Martin Marrall; and Betty, Mrs. Millicent, and so we were mighty merry till it was night.

By the early Nineteenth Century stationers were printing sheets of coloured satirical characters that could be cut out as needed. Sometimes, confectioners supplied such characters free with the cake. In 1838, William Hone explained how to organise a Twelfth Night party:

First buy your cake. Then before your visitors arrive, buy your characters. Next look at your invitation list, and count the number of ladies you expect; and afterwards the number of gentlemen. Then take as many female characters as you have invited ladies; fold them up, exactly of the same size, and number each on the back taking care to make the king No.1 and the queen No.2. Then prepare and number the gentlemen's characters. Cause tea and coffee to be handed to your visitors as they drop in. When all are assembled and tea over, put as many ladies' characters in a reticule as there are ladies present; next put the gentlemen's characters in a hat. Then call a gentleman to carry the reticule to the ladies, as they sit, from which each lady is to draw one ticket, and to preserve it unopened. Select a lady to bear the hat to the gentlemen for the same purpose ... Next arrange your visitors according to their numbers; the king No.1, the queen No.2 and so on. The king is to recite the verse on his ticket: then the queen the verse on hers, and so the characters are to proceed in numerical order. This done let the cake and the refreshments go round and hey! for merriment!

Hone complained that characters sold by stationers were 'commonplace or gross' with humorous characters often being 'vulgar' – by which he meant risqué. Their names revealed the role the person who drew them was to play. Typical examples from a 1794 character set include Miss Tender and Draggle-tail Doll. An 1840 set featured Mr. Lovemoney, Old Gouty Roger, Mrs. Flash-Along, Lady Tulip and Miss Gillyflower. Some cards suggested how the character should be acted. A 1798 set included Miss Frolic, shown blindfolded in a game of Blind Man's Buff, with the note:

> *Miss Frolic spreads for hearts a snare,*
> *She'll catch you if you don't take care.*

The same set had John Bull, waistcoat buttons bursting open and the tag:

> *With Pipe and Pot and Belly full*
> *Well pleased is honest John Bull.*

Any of these could have appeared alongside such characters as Tattle and Fondlewife in Congreve's *Love for Love*, or Mrs. Malaprop and Lady Teazle in Sheridan's *School for Scandal*. This is one place where it's easy to see the English love of acting at work. The link between the characters and the theatre and fiction is especially clear in William Makepeace

Thackeray's *The Rose and the Ring*. In his introduction to this fantastical story, he explains that it originated in an effort to create Twelfth Night entertainment for his daughters when they were all in Italy in 1854:

> *In that city, if you wanted to give a child's party, you could not even get a magic lantern or buy Twelfth-Night characters – those funny painted pictures of the King, the Queen, the Lover, the Lady, the Dandy, the Captain, and so on – with which our young ones are wont to recreate themselves at this time. My friend Miss Bunch … begged me to draw a set of Twelfth-Night characters for the amusement of our young people. She is a lady of great fancy and droll imagination, and having looked at the characters, she and I composed a history about them, which was recited to the little folks at night, and served as our fireside pantomime.*

Thackeray's illustrations do indeed resemble the more elaborate sets of characters, while his story is modelled on fairy tales, and can easily be imagined as a pantomime. It tells of the court of Valoroso XXIV, King of Paflagonia, and Giglio, the nephew he has usurped, and his daughter Angelica, with the Fairy Blackstick taking a hand as she sees fit. It has

HERE BEHOLD THE MONARCH SIT,

parts for young and old people, and lends itself to the amateur theatricals typical of Twelfth Night parties. British Christmas entertainments have always let people play roles different from those that shape their everyday lives. This delight in role-playing was no doubt felt especially keenly in centuries when class and gender strait-jacketed everyday behaviour. When Henry VIII transformed himself into Robin Hood to surprise Catherine of Aragon, he was fantasising about another way of life just as much as the lowly subject who got the lucky bean and played at being king, or the respectable middle-class wife who had her chance as Lady Racket or Miss Playful. The

William Makepeace Thackeray drew this caricature king in the style of the Twelfth Night characters used to play games when Twelfth cakes were cut. It appears in his fantastical tale The Rose and the Ring.

The Queen from Thackeray's The Rose and the Ring.

WITH HER MAJESTY OPPOSITE.

luck of the draw freed everyone who shared in the Twelfth cake to shed inhibition. Writing in the 1820s Leigh Hunt captured their feelings:

Christmas goes out in fine style, – with Twelfth Night. It is a finish worthy of the time. Christmas Day was the morning of the season; New Year's Day the middle of it, or noon; Twelfth Night is the night brilliant with innumerable planets of Twelfth-cakes … All the world are kings and queens. Everybody is somebody else … Cakes, characters, forfeits, lights, theatres, merry rooms, little holiday dances, and last not least, the painted sugar on the cakes, so bad to eat but so fine to look at.

Looking was as near as many people got to a Twelfth cake. They were big, heavy and expensive. Charles Dickens' admirer Angela Burdett-Coutts sent him one weighing ninety pounds. She mailed it to Genoa, where he was then living. It survived the journey – a testament to its solidity – requiring no more than some cosmetic touch-ups from a local confectioner, who was so amazed by its size and decoration that he displayed it in his window.

Gazing at window displays of Twelfth cakes was one of the Christmas pleasures of London. Bakers put their biggest creations in the centre of their displays with smaller cakes, including Twelfth buns, round about. The buns were cheap samples for those who could afford no more. Noting that 'a great deal of jollity goes on in England at the eating of the Twelfth cake all sugared over', the Scotsman James Boswell, a newcomer to London in 1763 and not yet the biographer of Dr. Johnson, decided to get his share of the fun by walking from St. Paul's to the Exchange, treating himself to a Twelfth bun at every bakery he passed.

At the other end of the scale, Queen Victoria's cake for 1849 was 30 inches across; presenting an iced plateau for an *al fresco* party of

Thackeray's portrait of Lady Gruffanuff, the governess in The Rose and the Ring.

Eighteenth-Century aristocrats waited on by servants and entertained by a violinist and harpist. Describing it the *Illustrated London News* wrote: 'As a specimen of fancy workman-ship, the ornaments to the cake do credit to the skill of Mr. Mawditt, the Royal confiseur.' The City Twelfth cake for 1846 was even more elaborate. Weighing in at nearly a hundredweight, it was shaped as a fountain. Water made of sugarwork poured down from a confectionery pineapple and into a basin filled with more candy water. Two sponge cake birds sat on the rim dipping their beaks into the bowl, while blancmange dolphins spouted barley sugar.

Yet while these amazing creations were thrilling observers in the 1840s and 50s, Twelfth cakes, which had been made for centuries, were soon to disappear – or rather to be deconstructed. Before the end of the century the cake itself had become the more modest Christmas cake, still iced in sugar and highly decorated but now just as likely to be home-made as the work of an expert cook. One explanation of this change may be that the invention of domestic kitchen stoves with reliable ovens meant that cakes could be made relatively inexpensively at home, whereas Twelfth cakes were way out of the financial reach of all but the wealthiest.

Christmas cakes retain the fruit-cake recipe and the decoration typical of Twelfth cakes, but the bean and trinkets changed into a silver coin which came to rest in the Christmas pudding. The characters found another home. Their ghosts appear at the Christmas table when the crackers are snapped and everyone dons the paper crown that is the proper wear for Christmas dinner. Even the paper slips that once designated a character are still with us in the jokes and riddles tucked inside the crackers. Notably, corny cracker jokes keep the farcical pranks of the King of the Bean just flickering. They help set the convivial mood of the meal by raising the universal groans that bring everyone together.

Witty jokes would be no good at all; anybody who didn't get them would feel excluded from the festivities. In any case, wit ups the tone; a little Saturnalian foolery is what's needed at Christmas.

Christmas at home

Christmas parties of families and friends gathered round a cake and a wassail bowl, or modestly enjoying whatever special fare the season offered, must have occurred during earlier centuries, but literary and other historical records spotlight royal occasions and the hospitality of great aristocrats who kept open house at Christmas. What happened in houses of medieval and Renaissance craftsmen, merchants and farmers is more obscure. Did the men who cavorted as guisers and mummers share their rewards with their wives at home? In the Eighteenth and Nineteenth Centuries poor women sometimes received Christmas gifts of clothing or money from charities. The Eighteenth-Century Parson Woodforde recorded in his diary regularly sending a shilling to some of his poor parishioners' wives. How did they spend it? What was Christmas like for children? Little is known. The happenstance of literary survival partly accounts for this, but it is clear that medieval and Renaissance Christmas celebrations were public rather than domestic: at court there were feasts and entertainments; in city streets there were processions and music; in villages and towns, wassailers and mummers made their rounds of farms and houses. However, by the late Seventeenth Century literary records show that Christmas was disappearing from the streets and settling down at home.

Ironically, the Puritan laws against Christmas may have spurred its domestication. They could control public festivities such as processions and mumming; they could go into churches and tear down mistletoe and holly. It was harder to supervise what went on behind closed doors. Opponents claimed that Puritans 'plunder[ed] pottage pots' and 'ransack[ed] ovens' to make sure no-one was cooking forbidden fare. In 1659 a minister at Elgin, Scotland inspected his parishioners' houses to see if anyone was hiding a goose for an illegal Christmas feast. As late as 1819 one Scotswoman, embarrassed by the unexpected arrival of the minister, hid her Christmas dinner under the bed. However, such pantry investigations were not common, and could never have been entirely effective. Many a secret mince pie must have been eaten on the quiet and nowhere more safely than by the fireside of home.

A more significant long-term change underlying the new domestic Christmas was the economic growth that began in the Renaissance and transformed Britain in the following centuries. The country became more mercantile and more industrial and more of a colonial power. People got richer. The middle class spent their money on houses. They had more space. Men who worked in offices took pleasure in the homes, furniture, gardens, and families that their wealth supported. By the early Eighteenth Century Daniel Defoe was characterising Christmas as 'days of entertaining among friends and relations'. The changes that brought this about did not occur all at the same time. They extended into the Nineteenth Century and beyond, gradually involving more and more of the people in the family Christmas that is now the norm.

Christmas in Jane Austen's novels

Jane Austen's novels give several glimpses of Christmas at home in the era between Pepys and Dickens. *Sense and Sensibility* opens with a discussion of how John Dashwood is to interpret his father's dying request that he help support his stepmother and half-sisters. Beginning with a generous impulse to give the girls £1,000 apiece, he is quickly persuaded by his penny-pinching wife that 'sending them presents of fish and game in season' is quite enough. Such gifts actually relegate his half-sisters to the general class of neighbours, all of whom could expect gifts of produce or meat, especially at Christmas. Mrs. Dashwood's miserliness about any other help her husband could have provided suggests that the sending of food was a seasonal obligation too powerful to ignore. In contrast, in *Emma* it is sign of Mr. Woodhouse's and Mr. Knightley's proper feelings that they send gifts of apples in autumn and meat at slaughter time to Mrs. Bates.

More specifically, Jane Austen shows Christmas as full of the pleasures (and sometimes the irritations) of families reunited for the holiday. In *Persuasion* Mr. and Mrs. Musgrove return from Lyme, where their daughter is recovering from an injury, so they can be home when their younger children get back for their school holiday. Anne Elliott finds them all gathered together:

On one side was a table occupied by some chattering girls, cutting up silk and gold paper; and on the other were tressels and trays, bending under the weight of brawn and cold pies, where riotous boys were holding high revel;

the whole completed by a roaring Christmas fire, which determined to be heard in spite of all the noise of the others.

To Mrs. Musgrove all this activity is a restorative. 'A little quiet cheerfulness at home' is just what she needs to recover from worrying about her daughter, but Anne reflects that it is too boisterous a scene to suit the elderly Lady Russell, though she could enjoy the equal din of the Bath season.

Similarly, in *Emma* opinions differ about what's fun and what's not. Emma's sister Isabella and Mr. Knightley's brother John arrive from London with their five children to spend Christmas in the village where they grew up. With John and Mr. Knightley enjoying brotherly chats while Isabella and the children visit friends, everything runs merrily until dinner at the Westons' house on Christmas Eve. 'It was a very great event that Mr. Woodhouse should dine out on the 24th of December', but he sallies forth without his usual anxieties about the weather. On the other hand, John Knightley complains about being separated from his children:

To spend five dull hours in another man's house…four horses and four servants taken out for nothing but to convey five idle, shivering creatures into colder rooms and worse company than they might have had at home.

He is aghast at Mr. Elton's nonchalant attitude to the snow and its possible effects:

'Christmas weather,' observed Mr. Elton. 'Quite seasonable and extremely fortunate we may think ourselves that it did not begin yesterday, and prevent this day's party, which it may very possibly have done, for Mr. Woodhouse would hardly have ventured had there been much snow on the ground; but now it is of no consequence. This is quite the season indeed for friendly meetings. At Christmas everybody invites their friends about them, and people think little of even the worst weather. I was snowed up once at a friend's house for a week. Nothing could be pleasanter.'

John Knightley's grumping about Christmas Eve visiting is vindicated when snow breaks up the party early.

Christmas foods

Jane Austen's Christmases are much more familiar to us than the processions, feasts, masques and misrule that we read of in earlier centuries, though processions and parades are fast returning. The effort to gather together as a family with distant members travelling home for Christmas, the resulting bustle of activity, the excited children, is the same in millions of homes today. Christmas presents are missing from these scenes. Children in Jane Austen's time might have received a game or a book, but those mountains at the end of the bed or under the Christmas tree were still decades away. It is the neighbourly gifts of game or meat and Mrs. Musgrove's trays of brawn and pies that indicate where the heart of Christmas still lay: on the table.

Every country has special foods for Christmas, often as long-enduring as our own mince pies, but commentators on England in the Seventeenth, Eighteenth and early Nineteenth Centuries noted the special English enthusiasm for the foods and the feasts of Christmas. In the late Seventeenth Century Henri Misson, a French visitor to England, wrote about Christmas Pie:

Every family against Christmas makes a famous Pye: It is a great Nostrum the composition of this Pasty; it is a most learned Mixture of Neats' [calves'] tongues, Chicken, Eggs, Sugar, Raisins, Lemon and Orange Peel, various kinds of Spicery.

In 1754 the *London Magazine* described the season as 'sacred to good eating and drinking', and in 1823 Victoire de Soligny wrote:

Probably there is not a single table spread on Christmas Day throughout the land – from the King's to the lowest artizan's that can scrape together enough to buy him a dinner at all – that is not furnished with roast beef and plum pudding.

Numerous descriptions of Christmas record the pleasure in the meal, and the hospitality still sometimes offered by the wealthiest in the land. In 1684 one of Charles II's courtiers, Sir John Reresby of Thrybergh in Yorkshire, entertained over eighty guests throughout the Christmas season, and on New Year's Day he hosted 300 people. In 1712 Lord Fermanagh wrote that by 28 December he had already 'killed two oxen this week and four sheep and of poultry we keep no account'. Guests came constantly to his Buckinghamshire estate. 'My servants say there were 400 people,' he wrote, 'and I do believe there were rather more than that last Tuesday…Besides the vast expense, it has been very tiresome.'

Such huge numbers were by no means usual. More typical was the meal for thirteen guests given by Timothy Burrell of Ockenden House in Sussex on New Year's Day, 1707. It included plum pottage, a calf's head and bacon, two geese, a pig, a sirloin of roast beef, a loin of veal, boiled beef, baked puddings, three mince pies, two capons, two pullets and two dishes of tarts. These dishes would have been served in the courses familiar since the Middle Ages: several dishes of many sorts presented as the first course, followed by a second course, also composed of different kinds of dishes, though usually with boiled meats coming first and roast meat and more luxurious dishes arriving later in the meal, with the dessert of fruit, nuts and sweetmeats coming after.

Numerous other accounts reveal the pleasure in Christmas meals, the range of foods that might be served at them, and often also, the impulse to share them, not only with family and friends but also with the poor.

The diary kept by Parson James Woodforde of Norfolk from 1759 until 1802 shows what he ate for his Christmas dinners. As a 19-year-old student at Oxford in 1759 rabbits were served, one between three students. They also downed eight bottles of port accompanied by Cheshire cheese. In December 1772 the first course of another Oxford Christmas included cod with soles and oyster sauce, sirloin of beef, pea soup, and orange pudding, followed by a second course of wild ducks, forequarter of lamb, salad and mince pies with plum cake to follow.

Once established in his Norfolk parish of Weston Longueville Parson Woodforde's income was around £400 a year. He was comfortable, but not wealthy. It's reasonable to assume that he ate in a manner typical of the provincial gentry, who lived well but not ostentatiously. His Christmas dinners always included plum pudding and mince pies, and beef was the usual *pièce de resistance* along with other meat and poultry dishes. In 1793, for example, he had boiled rabbit and onion sauce alongside a roast sirloin of beef, followed by plum pudding and mince pies. In 1795 boiled fowl and bacon partnered the beef. On Boxing Day 1794, when he had not been well the previous day, he was able to sample calf's fry and rabbit. 'I drank plentifully of Port Wine after dinner,' he writes. 'Instead of one Glass, drank 7 or 8 and it seemed to do me much good.'

Parson Woodforde also regularly recorded the Christmas meals of beef, plum pudding and beer he gave for six or seven poor men of his parish. Invariably they went home with a shilling and sometimes also cast-off clothes or food for sick family members.

Many undoubtedly shared Parson Woodforde's choice of beef for Christmas dinner, but it was not a must-have; all kinds of meat and poultry were welcome on the Christmas table. In 1660 Samuel Pepys had 'a good shoulder of mutton and a chicken', and in 1662, when his wife was ill, he dined by her bedside on a 'brave plum porridge and a roasted Pullet', then sent out for a mince pie because she had been

Candles

Many Christmas symbols and customs emphasise light in the darkest days of winter, in this way asserting faith in the eventual return of the sun. Lighting candles was one of the most important. Brand's *Antiquities* published in 1777 records the tradition: 'Our Fore-Fathers, when night was come on, were wont to light candles of uncommon size, which were called Christmas candles…these were to illuminate the house and turn the Night into Day, which custom in some measure is still kept up in Northern Parts.' It was kept in eastern parts, too. Parson Woodforde of Norfolk wrote in his diary on Christmas Day 1790: 'I lighted my large wax candle being Christmas Day during Tea-time this Afternoon for about an Hour.' Evidently, he did not share the belief held in some parts of the country that the Christmas candle should be large enough to burn from when it was lit until the end of the day or some mischance would happen to the family.

unable to make one. In *Emma* the Westons served their guests a saddle of mutton on Christmas Eve. In *The London Art of Cookery* published in 1783, John Farley included Bills of Fare for December. Inevitably, all food was seasonal, but little or nothing was specific to Christmas. In the first course was a leg of lamb, pork cutlets, a fricandeau of meat (probably veal), a haricot of mutton, a rump of beef, a large fish dish, and oyster loaves. The second course had fowls, oyster patties, crawfish, partridges, a ragout of lambs' tails, sweetbreads, roast hare, golden pippins and macaroons. All this was a veritable feast, fit for Christmas indeed, but equally fit for any other winter meal in a wealthy home.

Mince pies and other pies of the season

As well as dishes cooked for the major meals of the festive season – dinner on Christmas Day, New Year's Day and Twelfth Night – cooks provided many dishes that could be served throughout the season. Work on preserving fruit into sweetmeats began as early as summer, while closer to Christmas the slaughter of the animals produced meat for dishes such as the brawn that Mrs. Musgrove kept ready for those who wanted a snack. Brawn, originally the name for the meat of a wild boar, evolved in the Seventeenth and Eighteenth Centuries into a rolled pork joint that was soused after baking. Eventually brawn became a terrine-like preparation made from a brined pig's head, boiled until it was tender in a wine or vinegar-sharpened broth. The gelatinous meat was removed and packed into a container, and weighted down so it set firmly. Garnished with rosemary and bay leaves to suggest its family relationship to the boar's head of medieval feasts, it was always eaten with mustard, whether served as a first course dish for Christmas and New Year's Day as Robert May suggested in 1660, or set on a sideboard with pies and other cold foods as Mrs. Musgrove did in Jane Austen's *Persuasion*, published in 1816.

The pies that accompanied the brawn were, if anything, even more essential for Christmas. Meat is now no longer included in mince pies but it was basic in early recipes. Indeed, given the frequency with which meat was cooked with spices and dried fruit in the Middle Ages, it was but a tiny step to create a pie filling such as the following from an anonymous book of 1545, *A Proper new Booke of Cokerye declarying what maner of meates be best in season for all times of the yere*. With modernised spelling the recipe reads:

Pies of mutton or beef must be fine minced and seasoned with pepper and salt, and a little saffron to colour it, suet or marrow a good quantity, a little vinegar, prunes, great raisins and dates, take the fattest of the broathe of powdered beef, and with it you will have royal pastry, take butter and egg yolks and so temper the flour to make the pastry.

A recipe of 1588 in Edward Allde's *Good Hous-Wiues Treasurie* calls for veal or mutton with three pounds of suet for every four pounds of meat. In addition to the meat and dried fruit, it also says 'If ye have any Oranges or Lemmans, you must take two of them'. Apples and wardens – as mentioned, a kind of hard pear – were also recommended additions. Here we can see the mixture of fresh and dried fruits common today. Suet remains an ingredient, but meat has now entirely gone. It was disappearing by the Eighteenth Century, possibly because the availability of cheap sugar from Caribbean plantations encouraged a lavish use that edged out meat. By the Nineteenth Century Britain had few meaty mincemeat recipes, though they survive in North America, where deer-hunting remains a popular rural tradition, and many hunters' families still make mincemeat with venison.

Mince pies were not the only pies of the season. Meat pies of many kinds were a must. For example, on the twelfth day of Christmas 1660 Samuel Pepys breakfasted on a cold turkey pie and a goose, and then

Pies of many kinds always appeared at Christmas.

went to his cousin Thomas Pepys for dinner, 'which was very good; only the venison pasty was palpable beef, which was not handsome' (recipe pp. 136–7). Venison was game largely restricted to aristocratic tables, so it had more cachet than beef. Game pies made with combinations of venison, pork, poultry and wildfowl were also prestigious dishes for winter feasts. (For a medieval pie with pork, chicken and pheasant see the recipe on pp. 47–50). Ingredients for these pies were not fixed; the filling depended on the luck of the chase or the success of a fowler with his nets.

At social levels where acquiring game was difficult, pork pies were made from the pigs kept by many families, urban and rural alike, to provide fresh meat for Christmas and bacon and ham for the winter. Like other pies of the season, pork pies were a way of making use of every scrap of meat. Even trotters could be used – indeed they were vital – to make the jelly that filled up the pie case. This left the handsome legs to be roasted as joints or cured as hams.

One advantage of meat pies is that unlike the roasted and boiled meats of the Christmas meal they can be made ahead of time, and sit comfortably in the pantry or on a sideboard to be cut as wanted. A corollary disadvantage is that they were vulnerable to raiders. One of Robert Herrick's Christmas lyrics *Christmas Eve, another Ceremonie* prays for its safety:

> *Come guard this night the Christmas-Pie*
> *That the thiefe, though ne'r so slie*
> *With his Flesh-hooks, don't come nie*
> *To catch it.*

When Pip has to take food to the escaped convict at the beginning of Charles Dickens' *Great Expectations* the pork pie resting in the cool of the larder seems a good choice since he knows Mrs. Joe won't miss it immediately (recipe pp. 175–7).

Mrs. Joe's pie was clearly a handsome thing but intended only to serve a small group: just herself and Joe with Mr. Pumblechook and Mr. Wopsle and perhaps a morsel for Pip. However, in earlier days pies presented not just a chance to make good use of whatever bits of meat and poultry were available, but also an opportunity to create a dish that impressed with its size. The large pies of an earlier era lived on into the Eighteenth and Nineteenth Centuries as Christmas pies or Yorkshire pies, which were made in immense sizes to be served at public dinners.

Decorating a pie with pastry scraps is a long tradition.

In *The Art of Cookery made Plain and Simple* published in 1747, Hannah Glasse gave a recipe that included a turkey, a goose, a fowl, partridge and a pigeon as well as numerous other creatures. She explained how to arrange them:

> *Open the fowls all down the back and bone them; first the pigeon, then the partridge, cover them, then the fowl, then the goose, and then the turkey, which must be large. Season them all well first, and lay them down in the crust, so as it will look only like a whole turkey; then have a hare ready cased, and wiped with a clean cloth. Cut it to pieces … and lay it as close as you can on one side; on the other side woodcocks, moor game and what sort of wild fowl you can get. Season them well and lay them close; put at least four pounds of butter into the pye then lay on your lid, which must be a very thick one.*

Mrs. Glasse insisted on thick pastry made with a bushel of flour because 'These pies are often sent to London in a box as presents, therefore the walls must be well built.' One such pie was reported in *The Newcastle Chronicle* on 6 January 1770:

> *Monday last was brought from Howick to Berwick, to be shipped to London, for Sir Henry Greg Bart., a pie the contents whereof are as follows, viz: 2 bushels of flour, 20 pounds butter, 4 geese, 2 turkeys, 2 rabbits, 4 wild*

ducks, 2 woodcocks, 6 snipes, and 4 partridges, 2 neats' tongues, 4 curlews, 7 blackbirds and 6 pigeons; it is supposed a very great curiosity; was made by Mrs. Dorothy Patterson, housekeeper at Howick. It was near nine feet in circumference at bottom; weighs about twelve stone; will take two men to present it at table; it is neatly fitted with a case, and four small wheels, to facilitate its use to every guest that inclines to partake of its contents at table.

Virtually all pies of the period were filled with melted butter or other fat after they were baked. This filled in the gaps left as the meat shrank in cooking, helping to preserve it and adding much-needed succulence to pies of lean game and wildfowl. They continued to be shipped from the North to London well into the Nineteenth Century. Similarly, Edinburgh bakers dispatched enormous Black Buns to all parts of Britain. Weighing up to sixteen pounds, these treacle-dark fruit cakes baked in a pastry shell were the old Twelfth cakes of Scotland.

The sturdy pastry walls of many pies were treated as simply a container. In the Sixteenth and Seventeenth Centuries stoffados were a dish in which large birds or pieces of meat or even fish were covered with a plain flour and water pastry, sometimes called a huff paste. It was discarded after fulfilling its role of preventing the dish from drying out. Christmas pies were similarly made of an inedible pastry to keep the filling moist. Little Jack Horner was clearly only interested in the filling:

Little Jack Horner sat in a corner
Eating a Christmas pie.
He put in his thumb
And pulled out a plum
And said 'What a good boy am I.'

Plum porridge, plum pottage and plum pudding

To Jack Horner the word 'plum' signified all dried fruits – prunes, raisins, currants and so on. Their popularity in British Christmas fare lies behind old names like plum pudding and plum cake. Recipes for plum pudding, now usually called Christmas pudding, have been appearing in cookery books since the Seventeenth Century, though they were not identified as specifically Christmas fare until much later. Culinary historians trace its origin to plum porridge (also called plum pottage and sometimes plum broth), which had been a festive staple since the

Middle Ages. Unlike the dense pudding at the end of the meal, plum porridge was served as a thick soup in the first course. It was made from meat broth, dried fruit, spices, and a thickening of breadcrumbs or grain such as wheat or oatmeal. It was a substantial dish. An odd one too. In 1728 César de Saussure, writing in *A Foreign View of England in the Reigns of George I and George II*, said:

> *Everyone from the King to the artisan eats soup and Christmas pies. The soup is called Christmas porridge and is a dish few foreigners find to their taste.*

In a 1774 play called *Christmas Tale* David Garrick also asserted that no foreigner could digest this thick spiced mass of meat and 'plums'.

What could have turned plum porridge into plum pudding – our Christmas pudding – was increasing the breadcrumbs and decreasing the liquid and then turning the whole mass into a floured pudding cloth, and boiling it for several hours. Alternatively, the suet pudding, already well known, could have been fortified with more spices and lots of dried fruit. Or perhaps these two transformations occurred together: plum porridge marrying with suet pudding to become plum pudding. Cooks generally produced several at a time, boiling them on the fire or in the

kitchen copper used for laundry. They would then serve one at Christmas, keep one for New Year's Day and another for Easter. By the early Nineteenth Century plum porridge had virtually disappeared. Plum pudding had taken its place, and Charles Lamb was explaining 'I always spell plumb-pudding with a b, p-l-u-m-b. I think it reads fattier and more suetty.'

Anyone making a Christmas plum pudding today can buy suet ready-grated, or grate it quite easily in a food processor. Until well into the Twentieth Century, it had to be done by hand, and was one of the greasiest kitchen jobs of the year. Indeed, confecting plum puddings,

Christmas cakes, and mincemeat involved much more work in earlier times. Taking hours away from everyday occupations to spend on making the time-consuming dishes of the season was a way of marking the holiday as special. In *Jane Eyre* Jane and the servant Hannah embark on a thorough top-to-bottom cleaning of the house followed by 'such a beating of eggs, sorting of currants, grating of spices, compounding of Christmas cakes, chopping up of materials for mince-pies'. The dried fruits of their day were dirty; they needed not just washing and sorting but stoning too. Sugar as well as spices often had to be grated and fruit and peel chopped by hand. Jane does her work delightedly because she is happy to welcome back her new-found relatives. Yet food-writer Elizabeth David, who was prevailed upon to make a Christmas pudding for the residents of the Greek island of Syros in the early 1940s, wrote that though she had wonderful local products to work with, making the pudding took days. She had to stone gooey raisins; cut up sticky citron peel with a blunt knife; grate breadcrumbs, tend a charcoal fire for three

Dried Fruit

Dried fruits arrived in Britain with Crusaders returning from their exploits in the eastern Mediterranean. Raisins, currants, prunes, figs and dates were such a hit that cooks added them to dishes where we would find them odd: to fish stews and meat dishes, for example. The word 'mincemeat' recalls its origin as a meat dish. The medieval raisins of Corinth were so-named from the Greek port which was their source. Pronounced the Greek way 'Korintos', it became 'currants' in English. Raisins of the sun or great raisins are our black raisins. Sultanas were from Turkey and took the name of the sultan's wife, because their pale colour reflected a prestigiously fair complexion. Prunes, figs and dates were also popular. Since they were imported from far away, dried fruits were relatively expensive so they were used for special occasions – hence their presence in British festive dishes. As well as Christmas pudding, Christmas cake and mincemeat, they appear at Christmas and New Year in the Scottish Black Bun and Dundee cake, again at Easter in simnel cake, and in special occasion breads such as the Welsh *bara brith* and in many regional harvest breads.

or four hours, make sure the water didn't go off the boil and finally construct a hay box, where the pudding could finish cooking. She describes the process vividly in *Spices, Salts and Aromatics in the English Kitchen* (1970), but looking back on it thirty-three years later in *Elizabeth David's Christmas* (2003) she confessed that she disliked Christmas pudding and had never made one since that epic Greek effort.

Holidays

Until the Twentieth Century literally millions of Britons had little more in the way of kitchen equipment than the Greek islanders for whom Elizabeth David made the pudding. Though they could produce a Christmas meal by having a joint or poultry cooked in the local baker's and boiling plum porridge or a Christmas pudding over a fire, their Christmas differed from that of the affluent.

One of its main pleasures was that most workers had time off, usually about three days, though the amount depended on their job. Historian J.A.R. Pimlott noted that at the end of the Eighteenth Century workers in the cutlery factories of Sheffield had four to eight days; lace-makers in Devon and Somerset had a week, while some northern miners had a fortnight. As ever, farm workers had little work in December and early January simply because the agricultural year was not under way. In earlier centuries, most workers laboured on farms, and winter conditions could have limited work for many who did not (unless they were household servants, whose work was interminable). However, by the Eighteenth Century lots of people worked in offices and factories. Many laboured every day of the year except Christmas Day and Good Friday. It's a sign of Scrooge's miserliness in *A Christmas Carol* that he begrudges his clerk Bob Cratchit the day off at Christmas. It was not until the Bank Holiday Act of 1871 that Boxing Day was formally acknowledged as a usual holiday for bank personnel. Later acts extended this to other workers and factories often followed suit, but while Boxing Day became a holiday, workers were not necessarily paid for it. Indeed, the lengthy Christmas holidays traditional in some industries were not always popular with workers because they received no pay, and sometimes could ill afford to do without it.

Christmas boxes

One important source of extra cash was the Christmas boxes that gave Boxing Day its name. These were annual tips to anyone who gave a service, and were so called because servants kept sealed earthenware boxes with slots for tips. Traditionally, they broke them open on the day after Christmas, when they had a day off and could enjoy it with their savings and any additional money given by their employer at Christmas. These gifts were called 'Christmas boxes' because of the box associated with the day. Alms from church poor boxes were also distributed on Boxing Day.

As well as servants and the poor, a myriad of others who ministered to the affluent qualified for Christmas boxes. In 1786 Parson Woodforde records that he gave the bell-ringers their annual gift of 2 shillings and sixpence; his maltster's assistant got a shilling and the blacksmith's son sixpence. For some the number of Christmas boxes could be onerous – or at least seem so. The Eighteenth-Century Bow Street magistrate Sir John Fielding complained:

> If you should send for a carpenter to drive a nail or two, or an upholder to take down a bed, a blacksmith to mend your poker, or a brick-layer to mend a hole in a wall, you will certainly see all their apprentices at Christmas, and add to these your baker, butcher, brewer, grocer, poulterer, fish-monger, tallow-chandler, glazier, corn-chandler, dustman, chimney-sweeper, watchman, beadles, lamp-lighters, not to forget the person who sells brick dust to your footman to clean his knives, and you will have some idea of the Christmas boxes of a private family.

Sir John was not the only one to protest. Lady Eleanor Butler, one of the famed Ladies of Llangollen, was accosted by her neighbour's bailiff for a Christmas box in 1791, but demanding 'What for?' she sent him off. Such behaviour was risky: failure to give could be avenged by poor service in the year ahead.

Christmas boxes gave large numbers of people cash in hand at Christmas. A verse of John Gay's suggests the pleasure of opening it:

> When Christmas comes about again,
> O then I shall have some money;
> I'll hoard it up, and box and all
> I'll give it to my honey.

Christmas boxes were spent on some of the luxuries of the season: drink definitely, but also nuts, oranges, gingerbread, hot chestnuts and other food sold in the city streets.

Pantomimes and other entertainments

Servants and other working people also spent their Christmas plenty on traditional Christmas entertainments. Gambling had always been a Christmas activity. Henry VIII had a special draft on the Treasury to pay his gambling debts, and James I is reported to have insisted that everyone who came to court bring at least £300 to cover the gambling expenses of the Christmas holiday. The stakes were not so high at other social levels (though losses could be as high proportionately). Parson Woodforde kept careful tally of his Christmas wins and losses playing cards with the niece who lived with him. Packs of cards were often given along with meat and other doles to poor tenants in the country so they could enjoy a Christmas game. Bear-baiting, cock-fighting and other animal sports were also seasonal events that appealed to those who loved a bet.

Beyond gambling, cities, especially London, offered many entertainments. In 1754 the *London Magazine* described 'hops' attended by kitchen servants and plays that attracted an audience of 'beaux, wits and critics from Cheapside and Whitechapel'. By the early Eighteenth Century, these playgoers may well have seen a pantomime.

The first pantomimes were simply acts inserted into the intervals of operas. Pantomimes began their ascent into the highly stylised farce they are today in 1717 when John Rich, the manager of Lincoln's Inn Fields Theatre created a pantomime featuring Harlequin and Columbine – two characters from the Italian *commedia dell'arte*. Rich was a skilled acrobat. Portraits show him dancing on the stage as Lun – short for lunatic and the equivalent of the Italian stock-type the *zanni* or zany. Traditionally, Harlequin was in love with Columbine, his shrewd female counterpart. Since neither of them spoke in the earliest pantomimes, the audience needed to know the story – or the story had to be nugatory with burlesque, acrobatics, dancing and music being the centre of attention. Though dialogue is now a major feature of pantomimes, it remains true that their stories are so well-known that maintaining a logical narrative line is of little importance. Similarly, appearances and disappearances enacted by Fairy Godmothers and others of that ilk trace back to the Eighteenth Century, when part of the charm of the pantomime was the ingenuity of its stage machinery. Even the inevitable men in animal costume and the frequent breaks for song have always been part of pantomime.

Early pantomime stuck close to the *commedia dell'arte*, adding characters such as the Clown and Pantaloon to the basic Harlequin and

Columbine, and charming audiences with its mixture of burlesque and spectacle. Thackeray described going to a pantomime called *Harlequin Hamlet* in which Hamlet's umbrella was whirled away in the storm, Hamlet and the watch on the battlements of Elsinore kept treading on each other's toes as they tried to keep warm in the storm, and the ghost manifested as 'an awful figure throwing his eyes about' to elaborate sound and stage effects. Thackeray notes that the old Italian figures still survived, even in a Shakespearean adaptation:

> *After the usual business, that Ophelia should be turned into Columbine was to be expected; but I confess I was a little shocked when Hamlet's mother became Pantaloon, and was instantly knocked down by Clown Claudius.*

Thackeray's account comes from *Round About the Christmas Tree*, one of a long series of articles he wrote in the 1860s, by which time pantomimes had become Christmas entertainments, traditionally starting on Boxing Day. Augustus Harris, manager of the Drury Lane Theatre where panto had long been popular, is credited with establishing it in its modern form with fairy tale characters ousting the *commedia dell'arte* figures in the 1870s. Tales such as Cinderella – ever the most popular pantomime theme, and Aladdin, which runs Cinderella a close second – appealed to children, but since they had to be taken to the pantomime by their parents, the entertainment had to appeal to them too. In this way *doubles entendres* and political jokes became part of the panto's stock-in-trade. Other vital conventions that developed in the Nineteenth Century are the Principal Boy being played by a pretty young woman, and the Dame being a man. Just as in Shakespeare's comedies, this cross-dressing raises many opportunities for sexual innuendo. Also dating back to a much earlier era of theatre-going is the involvement of the audience, either singing as requested by the actors, or yelling out 'boos' and 'Look behind you!' as required by the plot.

Together these conventions break every rule that shapes other kinds of drama. The jokes creak; the audience intrudes; the plot can scarcely limp along; the characters lack verisimilitude; the action never strays beyond slapstick and farce; and famous stars play absurd parts. To put it briefly, pantomime presents a topsy-turvy world in which anything ridiculous can happen. It is the world of Saturnalia and of Twelfth Night under the Bean King's rule. The audience can jeer and cheer; they laugh at things funny and unfunny. The pantomime releases them from the straitjacket of good taste and good order – just as the Lords of Misrule did centuries ago.

BRAISED RABBIT WITH CARROTS AND CABBAGE

Rabbit often appeared on Eighteenth-Century Christmas tables. It's a good choice for the holiday season because it is flavourful without being rich. Indeed, if you want to keep down the calories over Christmas choose rabbit for supper for one cold night, perhaps Christmas Eve. This dish can be made ahead and reheated. Slow cooking brings out the flavour of the rabbit and vegetables.

2 rabbits, preferably wild
salt and white pepper to taste
3 tbsp plain flour
2 tbsp olive oil
30g/1oz butter
6 large cloves garlic
350ml/12 fl oz rabbit or chicken stock or vegetable broth
175ml/6 fl oz white wine
4 juniper berries, lightly crushed
2 bay leaves
6 stems thyme
6 carrots, cut into thick 3-inch sticks
small Savoy cabbage, weighing about 700g/1½lb
about 10 rashers thin-cut streaky bacon

Have each rabbit cut into 6 pieces (2 front legs, 2 back legs, and 2 pieces of the saddle). Use the ribcage for making stock or some other purpose as it is too bony for this dish. Season the rabbit with salt and white pepper, then dust with flour. In a large shallow braising dish, heat the olive oil and butter over medium heat. Put in the rabbit pieces a few at a time so the pan is not overcrowded and cook until golden on both sides, which takes about 6–7 minutes per side. Remove the pieces when they are done. Put in the garlic cloves and cook until they are slightly golden and a little soft. Add them to the rabbit pieces. Pour the stock and wine in the pan, add the juniper berries and let it bubble until it has reduced by a quarter. Season to taste with salt and pepper. Now replace the rabbit and garlic in the pan. Tuck the bay leaves, thyme and carrot pieces in between the rabbit. Pull the large outer leaves from the cabbage and reserve. Cut the cabbage into 6–8 wedges and add these to the pan. Arrange the bacon on top, overlapping the slices a little and using as many as you need to cover the rabbit and the vegetables; the exact number therefore depending on the size and shape of your pan. Arrange the outer leaves of the cabbage on top, again covering the surface. These leaves and the bacon help keep the dish moist and flavourful. Put the lid on the pan, and simmer as slowly as possible over very low heat for 2 hours. Or start the pan on top of the stove, and transfer it to a 150°C (300°F) oven once it has started simmering. It's important to have a good seal to the pan so if the lid doesn't fit tightly cover the pan with a sheet of foil before putting the lid on. For serving, discard the outer leaves of the cabbage. Remove the rabbit and bacon to a serving dish and surround with the carrots and cabbage. Boil up the liquid in the pan and strain it over the rabbit and vegetables. Serves 6.

VENISON PASTY

'We have a hot venison pasty for dinner,' Page promises Falstaff in Shakespeare's *Merry Wives of Windsor*, making clear it's a luxury to assuage previous 'unkindness'. Venison pasty is not finger-food like a Cornish pasty. It is a pie filled with a wine-enriched venison stew. Pepys was cross that the venison pasty served at his cousin's on the Twelfth Day of Christmas was 'palpable beef', but indeed, beef can be substituted for venison. 'This is a dish in which ornament is not only allowable but is actually expected,' wrote F. Marian McNeill in *The Scots Kitchen, Its Lore and Recipes*. Pastry trimmings are the raw material for decorations. Personal fancy determines what shapes to cut them in, but leaves are common.

675g/1½lb venison steaks or stewing venison
¼ tsp ground mace or nutmeg
½ tsp allspice
2 tbsp cooking oil
25g/1oz butter
salt and pepper
1 medium onion, peeled and chopped
150ml/¼ pint red wine from Bordeaux or Rioja
2 tbsp Scotch or rum
300ml/½ pint game, beef or chicken stock
2½ tbsp plain flour
250g/9oz frozen puff pastry
1 egg, beaten

To make the filling, cut the venison into small chunks about 1 or 2 centimetres square. Cut off any skin or membranes but keep the fat. Put the meat in a shallow dish and sprinkle it with mace or nutmeg and allspice. Stir the pieces to coat all sides, then trickle on the oil and stir again. Leave for 2–4 hours, stirring occasionally. Melt the butter in a large pan over medium heat, season the venison with salt and pepper then sauté it in batches to avoid crowding the pan and brown. As it browns remove from the pan. When it is all done, add the chopped onions and cook for 3–4 minutes or until softened. If there is not enough oil to fry the onions, add a little more. Now increase the heat, and pour in the wine and the Scotch or rum. Let it bubble for a minute then add the stock and return the meat to the pan. Simmer over a very low heat for an hour or until the meat is tender. To thicken, mix the flour with 2 tablespoons of cold water. Stir in some of the hot liquid from the pan, then add the flour mixture to the ingredients in the pan. Stir over medium heat until the liquid in the pan thickens into gravy. Set aside to cool to room temperature.

Defrost the pastry in the refrigerator or according to the maker's directions. Flour a pastry board lightly and grease a 23cm / 9-inch dish with butter. Pour the venison in the dish. Turn the oven to 220°C (450°F). Roll out the pastry on the floured board so it fits the dish. Place it over the top letting it drape slightly over the side so you get a good seal between the pastry and the dish. Save all scraps of pastry and pile them on top of one another. (Don't form them into a ball as this destroys the puffiness of the pastry.) Re-roll the scraps and cut into leaf or any other shapes. Brush the pastry surface with the egg, then place the pastry shapes on top. Brush these with egg also. Make 3 to 4 cuts or holes in the centre of the pie to act as vents. Bake for 15 minutes at 220°C (450°F) to brown the pastry, then lower the heat to 200°C (400°F) and bake for a further 15 minutes. If the gravy begins bubbling through the vents before this time is up remove the pie. Let cool for 10–15 minutes before serving. Serves 4–6.

Potted ham and chicken looks festive with its cream and pink stripes. (Recipe overleaf.)

POTTED HAM WITH CHICKEN

Elizabeth Raffald's recipe for how to pot ham with chicken explains a popular Eighteenth-Century way of turning leftovers to delicious use: 'Take as much lean of a boiled ham as you please and half the quantity of fat. Cut it as thin as possible, beat it very fine in a mortar with a little oiled butter, beaten mace, pepper and salt, put part of it in an earthen pot. Then beat the white part of a fowl with very little seasoning, it is to qualify [contrast with] the ham. Put a layer of chicken, then one of ham, then chicken at the top, press hard down and when it is cold pour clarified butter over it.' This comes from *The Experienced English Housekeeper*, and is the basis of the following recipe. The striped effect of the layers is best shown by cutting out a wedge before serving so they are visible. Alternately, serve it in slices on toast or crackers to reveal the layered effect. Turkey can replace chicken, and of course, whizzing in a food processor replaces pounding in a mortar, making this dish an easy and tasty way of preparing meat left from a Christmas meal. The method works for many kinds of meat: Mrs. Raffald has recipes for potting ox cheek, venison, veal, tongue, hare, woodcocks, moor game and 'all kinds of small Birds'. With meals in her day being composed of many dishes, ways of preserving the remains were essential.

    115g/4oz baked ham, including some fat
    115g/4oz very soft butter
    ¼ tsp powdered mace
    ½ tsp soft brown sugar
    tiny pinch cloves (optional)
    salt and white pepper to taste
    115g/4oz cooked chicken or turkey
    ¼ tsp dried thyme
    1–2 bay leaves (optional)
    extra butter (optional)

Cut the ham into small chunks and put them in the bowl of a food processor. (Use the small bowl if you have one.) Pulse several times to chop the ham, then add half the butter, the mace, brown sugar, the tiniest pinch of cloves and a light seasoning of pepper. Pulse to mix, then run the processor until everything is a uniformly smooth mass, occasionally stirring with a spatula if necessary. Taste to check the seasoning, and adjust with mace, sugar, pepper and salt as you see fit.

Put half the mixture into an even layer in a large buttered ramekin and reserve the other half. Rinse out the processor. Cut the chicken or turkey into small chunks and put them in the processor with the rest of the butter, a pinch of the thyme and a seasoning of salt and pepper. Pulse to chop and then run the processor until the mixture is smooth. Taste for seasoning and add extra thyme and more salt and pepper if you like. Take half this chicken or turkey and pat it in an even layer on top of the ham. Now repeat these two layers with the remaining mixtures finishing with a layer of chicken. Tap the base of the dish sharply on the counter a few times as you put in the layers to knock out any air spaces. If you plan to use this potted meat within 2–3 days, simply press a bay leaf or two on the surface then cover with clingfilm, pressing it down right onto the top layer of chicken to preclude any air getting in. If you want to keep it for 4 days or more, melt 85g/3 ounces of butter very slowly. Let it rest then pour off the clear part on top of the chicken so that it entirely covers it. Let it chill in the fridge then cover with clingfilm. Do not keep it more than a week. Makes 10–12 hors d'oeuvres servings.

A RAGOO OF ENDIVES

In the Eighteenth Century gardeners understood how to grow and store vegetables and fruit so they would have supplies throughout the year. *Adam's Luxury and Eve's Cookery* is an anonymous book of 1744, written for 'all who would live Cheap, and preserve their Health to old Age'. The first part of the book explains how to grow fruits and vegetables, while the second provides recipes. Then, as now, endive was a winter vegetable that would be available for Christmas and New Year meals. This recipe reads: 'Get the best white Endive; pick it, and blanch in boiling water, then squeeze it and mince it a little … fry it with Butter, and then moisten it with Broth … When it is relishing, thicken it with the Yolks of Eggs and Cream.'

    4 medium endives
    salt to taste
    40g/1½oz butter
    2 egg yolks
    100ml/3½ fl oz single cream

Cut the endives widthways into 2cm/¾-inch sections. Drop them in a pan of boiling lightly salted water and let them simmer for a minute. Drain well, reserving the liquid. Melt the butter in a frying pan. Add the endive and fry it for a minute, then add about 125ml/4 fluid ounces of the liquid it was boiled in. Let it bubble for a minute or two until it feels tender when you stick a fork in it. In a small bowl, stir the egg yolks and cream together. Off the heat stir this into the endives, then return to a low heat and stir until the mixture thickens. You can add more of the endive liquid if you want to thin it. Check the seasoning and serve.

THE AUSTENS' LEMON MINCEMEAT

After the death of their father, Jane Austen and her sister Cassandra lived with their mother and an old friend Martha Lloyd. Jane took charge of tea, coffee and wine; Cassandra kept bees, and Martha Lloyd oversaw the cooking. She kept a notebook of her recipes, which still survives. One of them is for Lemon Mincemeat. This Eighteenth-Century mincemeat differs from modern mincemeat recipes in using boiled and pureed lemons as the base, with candied orange and lemon peel and orangeflower water to heighten its distinctly citrus flavour. Martha Lloyd's recipe has no apples, though someone later added them to the manuscript, rightly noting they are 'a great improvement'. The following recipe is adapted from Martha Lloyd's.

    2 large lemons
    425g/15oz currants or raisins
    250g/9oz sultanas
    6 apples, peeled and grated
    225g/8oz candied lemon or orange peel
    550g/1lb 4oz white sugar
    280g/10oz shredded suet or frozen butter
    ¾ tsp grated nutmeg
    ½ tsp cinnamon
    ½ tsp powdered mace
    2 tbsp orangeflower water
    125ml/4 fl oz Malaga, brandy or rum

Squeeze the juice from one of the lemons and set it aside. Cut the other lemon into half a dozen pieces, and put them in a saucepan with enough water to cover. Put on the lid and simmer for about 25 minutes or until the pieces are very tender. Whizz them into a puree in a blender or pass them through a coarse sieve. In a large bowl, mix the lemon puree, currants, sultanas, apples, candied peel and sugar. Stir in the suet. (If you want this to be a vegetarian mincemeat, omit the suet and instead grate an equal amount of frozen butter into the mixture using the large holes of a cheese grater.) Stir in the nutmeg, cinnamon and mace. Then strain the lemon juice and stir it in along with the orangeflower water and Malaga, brandy or rum. Grate the zest from the remaining lemon, and add it to the mixture. Cover the bowl and leave for 2–3 days, stirring from time to time. Taste to check the flavour. You may want to add more sugar or spices or more liquid in the form of lemon juice.

ORANGE PUDDING

The famous diarist Parson Woodforde ate an orange pudding at a Christmas dinner at his Oxford college in 1772. Oranges were a winter favourite in puddings, sweetmeats and preserves such as marmalade. In Elizabeth Raffald's *The Experienced English Housekeeper*, published in 1769, the recipe reads: 'Boil the rind of a Seville orange very soft, beat it in a marble mortar with the juice. Put to it two Naples biscuits grated very fine, half a pound of butter, a quarter of a pound of sugar, and the yolks of six eggs. Mix them well together. Lay a puff paste round the edge of your china dish, bake in a gentle oven half an hour. You may make a lemon pudding the same way by putting in a lemon instead of an orange.' The amount of butter has been reduced in the following recipe, and instead of all that pounding in a marble mortar, a blender or food processor cuts down the work time.

1 large Seville or navel orange
6 egg yolks
30g/1oz (about 3–4) Lady Fingers or similar biscuits, grated finely
115g/4oz sugar
175g/6oz butter, melted
100g/3½oz puff pastry

Peel the zest off the orange with a vegetable peeler, leaving behind all the white pith. Cover the strips of zest with water and simmer for about 25 minutes or until soft. Meanwhile preheat the oven to 180°C (350°F), and grease a glass or earthenware pie dish with butter. Put the softened peel in a blender or food processor with the juice of the orange and the egg yolks and whizz until the peel has disintegrated into minute fragments. Mix the grated Lady Fingers with the sugar, and then stir in the butter. Roll out the pastry and cut it into strips about 5cm/2 inches

141

wide and fit them round the side and edge of the dish. You don't need a base for this tart. Pour the orange filling in the dish and bake for 25 minutes or until it is golden on top and a knife blade slipped into the centre comes out clean.

APPLE SNOW

A mass of apples whisked with egg whites was one of the simpler subtleties of Renaissance cooking. Stuck with a twig of rosemary, it looked like a snowy mountain. This pretty dish survived into the Eighteenth Century, when it appeared in Elizabeth Raffald's *The Experienced English Housekeeper* as a 'Dish of Snow'. To get the desired mountainous effect, Mrs. Raffald directed 'Heap it as high as you can, and set green knots of paste in imitation of Chinese rails. Stick a sprig of myrtle in the middle of the dish and serve it up.' This dish uses egg whites left over from Raffald's Orange Pudding above. Use apples that fall into a soft mass such as Bramleys.

  6 Bramley apples, peeled, cored and sliced
  115g/4oz sugar or more to taste
  4 egg whites

Put the sliced apples into a saucepan with a couple of tablespoons of water, and 2 tablespoons of the sugar. Bring them to simmering point over low heat and cook until they are completely soft. Mash them into a smooth mass and let cool. Whisk the egg whites stiffly. Scatter the remaining sugar on them and whisk until they look glossy. Fold the egg whites into the apples. Pile into a peaked mountain on a shallow dish. Stick a festive twig in the centre. Rosemary was the choice in Elizabethan England, and it could be dabbed with a little of the egg white to imitate snow. Fir or holly would be festive for Christmas, and if you love the miniature robins, snowmen, reindeer and other pretty little things that congregate on top of Christmas cakes, you could add these too.

Fires

Christmas is the season of good cheer and nothing is more cheering in the depth of winter than a good fire. In Jane Austen's *Emma* Mr. Elton is glad to go to dinner with the Westons because they are sure to have good fires. In *Persuasion* Jane Austen suggests the homely comforts of the Musgroves' house by describing the chattering children and their parents around 'a roaring Christmas fire, which determined to be heard in spite of all the noise of the others'. In Charlotte Brontë's *Jane Eyre*, Jane getting ready for her new-found cousins' return threatens: 'I shall go near to ruin you in coals and peat to keep up good fires in every room.' The importance and pleasure of keeping warm in winter needs no belabouring. It's a powerful sign of Scrooge's meanness in Charles Dickens' *A Christmas Carol* that he begrudges coal for Bob Cratchit's fire so much that Cratchit can scarcely keep it alight. Further back in time, the tradition of the Yule log emphasises the need for fuel. The huge log was brought in lit from a small piece of last year's log saved for the purpose. Keeping a bit of the log supposedly preserved the household from evil spirits; psychologically it was a reminder of the vital importance of fuel for winter.

CHAPTER 6

The Pre-Victorian and the New Victorian Christmas

Go, seek, when Christmas snows discomfort bring,
The counter Spirit found in some gay church
Green with fresh holly, every pew a perch
In which the linnet or the thrush might sing.
William Wordsworth, *Ecclesiastical*
Sketches, XXXIII Regrets, 1822

O N CHRISTMAS EVE 1798, Jane Austen sat down to write a letter to her sister Cassandra to tell her about the promotion of their brother Frank, a naval officer. On Christmas Day a letter arrived from Cassandra, so Jane completed her unfinished Christmas Eve letter by replying to her news:

I am full of joy at much of your information: that you should have been to a ball, and have danced at it, and supped with the Prince, and that you should meditate the purchase of a new muslin gown, are delightful circumstances. I am determined to buy a handsome one whenever I can.

After more clothes' talk, she concludes a long paragraph of chit-chat with 'I wish you a merry Christmas'. Just that. Nothing about Christmas Day festivities; nothing about Christmas dinner, or about presents except her 'charities to the poor': gifts to village women of stockings and shawls 'amounting in all to about half a guinea'. Ten years later on 27 December, 1808 Jane was again writing to Cassandra. On 22 December she and her mother had hosted an evening party:

The tray had admirable success. The widgeon and the preserved ginger were as delicious as one could wish. But as to our black butter, do not decoy anybody to Southampton by such a lure, for it is all gone.

Maybe this little party with the widgeon, the ginger and black butter – a preserve of apples and dark berries – was a Christmas celebration, but if so she doesn't identify it as such, and again she is silent about Christmas dinner, Christmas presents and any other traditional Christmas festivity.

The impression of Christmases at the Austen home is much as we see it in Jane Austen's novels, where we glimpse the Musgrove family around the fire with Christmas brawn and pies, or the Woodhouses and Knightleys dining with the Westons on Christmas Eve. Christmas celebrations were low-key compared to either the revelry of the Middle Ages or the ebullient parties and cornucopia of presents typical today. If the history of Christmas in Britain were represented as a line on a graph, it would peak in the early Sixteenth Century, before the Reformation tamed its Saturnalian and medieval frolics; descend inexorably into the slough of 1647, when Christmas celebrations were banned; trace gently up to the post-Restoration plateau where it rested until the early Nineteenth Century, and then soar unwaveringly to today's heady peaks.

The Seventeenth-Century dip is easily explained by the Puritan vendetta against Christmas. Then, too, the country had become less feudal, and therefore depended less on old customs. Similarly, the social changes of the late Eighteenth and the Nineteenth Century nourished a new *Zeitgeist* that reawakened dormant Christmas feelings. Christmas began to flourish in new ways, mixing old traditions with newly-minted pleasures and appealing customs imported from other countries. This potent mixture spoke to Nineteenth-Century concerns and needs. For religious and political reasons the affluent were more worried by the poverty around them, and could be soothed by a holiday whose traditional principle was community. Significantly, the 1840s, renowned as the 'hungry forties' because of widespread unemployment and poor harvests, were also a decade of Christmas innovations. Christmas trees, Christmas crackers and Christmas cards are all 1840s' phenomena. They caught on quickly because large numbers of people were literate. Magazines and newspapers flourished. They filled their December pages with Christmas articles and advertisements. Novelists, too, wove tales around Christmas, so while there is no single event like the Puritan ban on Christmas that accounts for the Nineteenth-Century changes in its celebration, a wealth of literature records the emotions and feelings that prompted new ways of celebrating it.

Washington Irving

The tales of the American writer Washington Irving kick-started the Christmas revival. Irving was an established writer in his native New York when he came to England in 1815. His most famous story *Rip van Winkle* was written at his sister's Birmingham home. In 1822 he published *Bracebridge Hall, or The Humorists, A Medley*, which includes several stories celebrating Christmas at Bracebridge Hall, a fictional Yorkshire manor house, loosely based on Aston Hall near Birmingham. Among these *Christmas* recalls the customs of bygone years with friends and family gathered by the fireside. *The Stage Coach* portrays Geoffrey Crayon travelling through Yorkshire to experience England's surviving rural customs. He meets an old friend Frank Bracebridge, who invites him to share Christmas at Bracebridge Hall. *Christmas Eve* describes the music, dancing and old games such as Steal the White Loaf, Blind Man's Buff and Snap Dragon, while the waits arrive to sing carols. *Christmas Day* describes the Christmas church services and Squire Bracebridge's open house, at which tenants and villagers feast on beef and ale. *The Christmas Dinner* records an old-fashioned meal with the boar's head presented medieval-style 'bedecked with bays and rosemary', and the pheasants served, like the peacocks of the past, in all the glory of their tail feathers. The day ends with the wassail bowl going cheerily around, the children performing a masque, and the parson telling ghost stories.

Irving's influence

All the customs Irving mentions certainly existed at some point in the past, but whether they all occurred in one place at one time outside his imagination is hard to tell. Paradoxically, he is now little read in Britain, but his powerful effect on Christmas is still felt through his pioneering evocation of Christmases of yore, and most particularly through his influence on his admirer Charles Dickens, who became a close friend.

Irving had grown up among the ethnically Dutch residents of upstate New York. They went to church on Christmas Day; their jolliest celebration was a round of New Year's visits to share Christmas cookies. English customs therefore charmed him with their novelty. His picture of an English Christmas is not a report but a pastoral tale based on literature and perhaps also on the memories of his Scottish father and his English mother.

Yet why, it may be asked, should these traditions capture the imagination of Irving and the multitude that followed him in celebrating

Christmas as they imagined it in earlier centuries? Significantly, Irving was writing shortly after the tumultuous years following the American War of Independence, the French Revolution and the War of 1812, in which British guns bombarded the newly-built White House. Such seismic shifts seemingly opened crevasses between life as it had been and life as it had become. Even when the effects were welcomed, as Irving certainly welcomed his country's independence, they prompted anxiety. With the harsher aspects of the past veiled by time, nostalgic pictures of earlier days comforted because they suggested continuity even as times changed.

Wordsworth

Less floridly, Wordsworth also longed for the return of old customs. His poem *The Minstrels*, one of his *Duddon Sonnets* of 1820, gently evokes the visit of rural musicians one frosty night:

> *Through hill and valley every breeze*
> *Had sunk to rest with folded wings:*
> *Keen was the air, but could not freeze*
> *Nor check, the music of the strings.*

The cold notwithstanding, the musicians play on until they have greeted everyone personally:

> *And who but listened? – til was paid*
> *Respect to every inmate's claim,*
> *The greeting given, the music played*
> *In honour of each household name,*
> *Duly pronounced with lusty call,*
> *And 'Merry Christmas' wished to all.*

Again, in *Rural Ceremony*, number XXXII of the *Ecclesiastical Sketches* 1822, Wordsworth described Lakeland children carrying garlands to the church as their ancestors had done in 'Papal time'. He continued his meditation on the function of ceremony in the next sonnet, *Regrets*. He wishes England had kept more old 'graceful rites' because they give 'to Memory help when she would weave A crown for Hope'. Yearning for whole-hearted Christmas celebrations, he exhorts:

Go, seek, when Christmas snows discomfort bring,
The counter Spirit found in some gay church
Green with fresh holly, every pew a perch
In which the linnet or the thrush might sing,
Merry and loud and safe from prying search,
Strains offered only to the genial Spring.

Dickens and Christmas: *Pickwick Papers*

Like Irving, who was born in 1783 during the early years of American independence and named after its iconic figure George Washington, and Wordsworth, who had been in France during the French Revolution, Charles Dickens also grew up in the long shadow of revolution. The Napoleonic Wars still raged when he was born in 1812. In their aftermath, he and most of his compatriots feared a repeat performance of France's radical revolutionary solution to social divisions in England. The thematic engine of Dickens' novels is therefore the search for a non-revolutionary way to change society for the better. Christmas as envisoned by Washington Irving became his model for what society should be, and no-one admired Irving's ideas more than he or propagandised more thoroughly for a renewed sense of Christmas as a time of goodwill and sharing.

Dickens painted his first significant Christmas picture in *Pickwick Papers*, published in parts in 1836 and 1837. This is an adult-centred

Christmas with lots of drinks and bonhomie. The only child is a servant called 'the fat boy'. Dickens himself, then only twenty-five years old, writes from the perspective of an old man looking back on his youth:

We write these words now, many miles distant from the spot at which, year after year, we met on that day [Christmas], a merry and joyous circle. Many of the hearts that throbbed so gaily then have ceased to beat; many of the looks that shone so brightly then, have ceased to glow; the hands we grasped, have grown cold; the eyes we sought have hid their lustre in the grave; and yet the old house, the room, the merry voices and smiling faces, the jest, the laugh, the most minute and trivial circumstances connected with those happy meetings crowd upon our mind at each recurrence of the season, as if the assemblage had been but yesterday! Happy, happy Christmas, that can win us back to the delusions of our childhood days; that can recall to the old man the pleasures of his youth; that can transport the sailor and the traveller, thousands of miles away, back to his own fire-side and his quiet home!

Fortified with brandy, the Pickwickians drive through the frosty countryside into Dingley Dell, where they go to celebrate the wedding of Mr. Wardle's daughter. There they throw themselves into an evening of seasonal festivity with cards and conviviality:

Long after the ladies had retired, did the hot elder wine, well qualified with brandy and spice, go round and round, and round again.

After the marriage the Pickwickians embark on a 25-mile walk to disperse the effects of the wedding breakfast and prepare for the evening's dinner and ball. Next day is Christmas Eve, and Mr. Wardle – like Squire Bracebridge – observes it as his forefathers had 'from time immemorial'. Family and servants gather in the kitchen, where 'a huge branch of mistletoe' provokes 'a scene of general and most delightful struggling and confusion' as all are kissed and 'the fat boy took the opportunity of appropriating for his own use and summarily devouring a particularly fine mince pie'. Games follow including Blind Man's Buff:

The poor relations caught the people they thought would like it, and when the game flagged, got caught themselves. When they were all tired of blind-man's buff, there was a great game of snap-dragon, and when fingers enough were burned with that, and all the raisins were gone, they sat down

149

by the huge fire of blazing logs to a substantial supper, and a mighty bowl of wassail, something smaller than an ordinary wash-house copper, in which the hot apples were hissing and bubbling with a rich look and a jolly sound that were perfectly irrestistible.

'This,' said Mr. Pickwick, looking around him, 'this is, indeed, comfort.'
'Our invariable custom,' replied Mr. Wardle. 'Everyone sits down with us on Christmas Eve, as you see them now – servants and all; and here we wait, until the clock strikes twelve, to usher Christmas in, and beguile the time with forfeits and old stories.'

Encouraging his guests to 'fill up' from a wassail bowl so deep that it will take two hours to empty it, Wardle sings an old song significantly called *A Christmas Carol*. It's a poem by Dickens extolling Christmas as 'the King of Seasons All'. Its title exemplifies the contemporary interest in looking back to old customs such as singing carols. Many had been forgotten, but in this era folklorists were collecting old carols and clergymen were writing new ones. Dickens' use of the form is one of the many instances of the Nineteenth-Century interest in dusting off traditions and shaping them up to fit the new Victorian era. Wardle's story, which follows, similarly picks up on the tradition of telling wonderful tales – a tradition King Arthur loved in *Sir Gawain and the Green Knight*. Dickens was to use both the concept of carols and of ghost stories again in his *A Christmas Carol* a few years later.

Wardle's ghost story prefigures Scrooge in a mean-spirited local sexton Gabriel Grub, who was carried off by goblins one Christmas Day a few years earlier. He is digging a grave when a goblin appears atop a

The goblin perching on the gravestone in the story of Gabriel Grub recounted in Dickens' Pickwick Papers.

nearby gravestone. The goblin chides him with his gratuitous ill-will. Soon a horde of supporting goblins fills the churchyard, playing leap-frog, vaulting over the gravestones, buffeting Gabriel and reminding him of his churlishness. Eventually he repents, but when he wakes on Christmas Day he cannot face the neighbours he has injured, so he leaves the village. Thus the tale that the goblins had spirited him away takes hold.

Death hangs around this graveyard story, and death is on the scene again on Christmas Day. It peeps in at breakfast, when two student surgeons chat about the corpses they need for dissection. After a walk to church, the 'substantial lunch, with the agreeable items of strong-beer and cherry-brandy' and skating party on a pond capture everyone's attention. However, death suddenly appears again. The ice breaks, plunging Mr. Pickwick into the water. His rescuers send him to bed to recover with bowls of hot punch:

When Mr. Pickwick woke next morning, there was not a symptom of rheumatism about him; which proves, as Mr. Bob Sawyer very justly observed, that there is nothing like hot punch in such cases: and if ever hot punch failed to act as a preventive, it was merely because the patient fell into the vulgar error of not taking enough of it.

This comment, though softened with irony, suggests that only alcohol-fuelled cheer and Wardle's brimming punch bowls can keep death at bay. Dickens has played the ringmaster, bringing forth one Christmas spectacle after the other, but never letting the audience lose sight of death perched like a lion on a drum behind him. He drives the point home, as Pickwick, saved by the punch bowl, prepares to leave:

Mr. Pickwick slides

Mr. Pickwick's adventures on the frozen pond in Dickens' Pickwick Papers.

The jovial party broke up next morning. Breakings up are capital things in our school days, but in after life they are painful enough. Death, self-interest and fortune's changes, are everyday making up many a happy group, and scattering them far and wide; and boys and girls never come back again.

This *obiter dicta* scarcely fits the stereotype of Dickensian Christmas themes, but it underpins virtually all his Christmas tales. Indeed, arguably Dickens' enormous influence on the Victorian Christmas comes from his sense that death is ever-present at the feast, ready to take centre stage unless pre-empted by food, drink and determined jollity. More than any other writer except the anonymous poet of *Sir Gawain and the Green Knight*, Dickens taps into the fear of death in the season that most imperils life.

Dickens and Christmas: outfacing death with *A Christmas Carol*

Death also dominates *A Christmas Carol*. Its first words are 'Marley was dead'. The first page emphasises his death, and the second identifies Scrooge with him:

Scrooge never painted out Marley's name. There it stood, years afterward, above the warehouse door: Scrooge and Marley. Sometimes people new to the business called Scrooge Scrooge, and sometimes Marley, but he answered to both names. It was all the same to him.

Days were all the same too, all equally devoted to making money:

Oh! But he was a tight-fisted hand at the grindstone. Scrooge! A squeezing, wrenching, grasping, scraping, clutching, covetous old sinner! Hard and sharp as flint from which no steel had ever struck one generous fire: secret and self-contained and solitary as an oyster. The cold within him froze his old features, nipped his pointed nose, shrivelled his cheek, stiffened his gait, made his eyes red, his thin lips blue, and spoke out shrewdly in his grating voice. A frosty rime was on his head, and on his eyebrows, and his wiry chin. He carried his own low temperature with him; he iced his office in the dog-days, and didn't thaw it out one degree at Christmas.

Asked to help buy food and drink for the poor, Scrooge demands, 'Are there no prisons?…And the Union workhouses?…Are they still in operation?' Marley's ghost spells out the message that with such attitudes, Scrooge is forging a chain for himself. Pointing to his own heavy chains, he bemoans his lost opportunities in life. 'You were always a good man of business,' Scrooge says consolingly:

> *'Business!' cried the Ghost, wringing its hands again. 'Mankind was my business. The common welfare was my business; charity, mercy, forbearance, and benevolence, were all my business. The dealings of my trade were but a drop of water in the comprehensive ocean of my business!'*

Marley's ghost promises Scrooge visits from three spirits, who will show him the error of his life. For the historian of Christmas the spirits illustrate the fears and yearnings of the early Nineteenth Century, and how they shaped a new way of celebrating Christmas. The first spirit, the Ghost of Christmas Past, returns Scrooge to his childhood, when his benevolent employer Mr. Fezziwig celebrated with feasting and dancing, servants and master all enjoying themselves together:

> *There were more dances, and there were forfeits, and more dances, and there was cake, and there was negus, and there was a great piece of Cold Roast, and there was a great piece of Cold Boiled, and there were mince pies and plenty of beer.*

The young Scrooge enjoyed himself and even had a fiancée, but he declines into a workaholic skinflint. Here it is easy to see the conflicted feelings of the Nineteenth-Century bourgeoisie: proud of Britain's wealth and power, yet aware that the effort to make money – whether as a businessman or a working-class drudge – had an emotional and social price, including the separation of business owners and their workers into opposed classes.

Now the Ghost of Christmas Present appears; green-robed, bare-chested, holly-wreathed and sitting on a throne of Christmas plenty:

> *Turkeys, geese, game, poultry, brawn, great joints of meat, sucking pigs, long wreaths of sausages, mince-pies, plum puddings, barrels of oysters, red-hot chestnuts, cherry-cheeked apples, juicy oranges, luscious pears, immense twelfth-cakes and seething bowls of punch.*

Bob Cratchit, Scrooge's browbeaten clerk, earns too little to afford all these good things, but Scrooge watches him enjoy himself with his

The Spirit of Christmas Present in Dickens' A Christmas Carol *is sometimes taken as a version of the traditional Father Christmas, who was associated with feasting and abundance rather than with presents.*

family at a Christmas dinner of goose with apple sauce and mashed potatoes, followed by a Chrismas pudding 'like a speckled cannon-ball…blazing in half a quartern of ignited brandy, and bedight with Christmas holly stuck in the top'. Later they roast chestnuts in the fire and drink 'hot stuff from the jug'. Scrooge, his sympathy now awakened, asks whether crippled Tiny Tim will live, and learns of the empty chair at future Christmas tables. The ghost reminds him that he had said the surplus population should hurry up and die. When two scrawny children called Ignorance and Want creep forth, the ghost recalls Scrooge's rhetorical demand about whether there were not prisons and workhouses for such as they. In effect, he throws back at Scrooge the *laissez-faire* arguments typically trotted out against the social reformers of the 1830s and 1840s. The extraordinary popularity of *A Christmas Carol* and Dickens' subsequent Christmas tales suggests that his audience was not entirely at ease with the cruel economics of those who opposed legislation to improve the conditions of the poor.

Finally, the Spirit of Christmas Yet To Come shows Scrooge a death-bed. Men debate how much money the dead man left, while the charwoman and others run off with the dead man's shirt and teaspoons, even his bed-curtains to sell to a Fagin-like fence. Next, Scrooge sees Bob Cratchit's home again, where the family are mourning Tiny Tim. Finally, he arrives at a dank graveyard, and the ghost points to a gravestone with 'Ebenezer Scrooge' engraved on it. 'Am *I* the man who lay upon the bed?' he exclaims. He insists he will change:

I will honour Christmas in my heart, and try to keep it all the year. I will live in the Past, the Present, and the Future. The spirits of all three will strive within me. I will not shut out the lessons that they teach. O! tell me I may sponge away the writing on this stone!

As the ghost fades away, Scrooge awakens. It's Christmas Day, and he grasps at life. He buys a huge prize turkey for the Cratchits. He makes an impressive gift to charity. He goes to church. He watches merrymakers. He raises Bob Cratchit's salary, and shares a bowl of punch with him. He goes to dinner with the nephew who had said:

I have always thought of Christmas time…as a good time; a kind, forgiving, charitable, pleasant time; the only time I know of, in the long calendar of the year, when men and women by one consent seem to open their shut-up hearts freely, and to think of other people below them as if they really were fellow passengers to the grave, and not another race of creatures bound on other journeys.

This is an heroic assertion of community in the face of mortality. Dickens' solution to social misery is to spread the Christmas spirit of sharing and goodwill throughout the year. This conjuration of Christmas goodwill as a social balm suggests that the will to act is sufficient to effect a desired result. Given the real intransigence of the evils of industrial England, such magical thinking had – and still has – immense appeal because it is less demanding than political action. However, the piecemeal volunteerism of charity cannot succeed against the inevitability of death, and the increasing power of Dickens' presentation of social evils in his novels of the next two decades suggests that he knew this.

The reformed Scrooge shares a bowl of punch with his poor clerk Bob Cratchit at the end of Dickens' A Christmas Carol.

155

His assertion of the power of the Christmas spirit was an inspired attempt to visualise it as an answer to social evils, but the point about death is that it always comes, and the point about Christmas is that it comes but once a year.

The success of *A Christmas Carol* was immediate. It sold 6,000 copies during the first five days of publication, and has never been out of favour. Only a year after its publication in 1843, there were already three dramatic versions on the London stage, and Dickens, a skilled amateur actor, began annual readings that were enormously popular and financially rewarding. Since then, theatrical, film, cartoon and television versions have proliferated. No other Christmas story is better known.

Everything old becomes new again

Dickens was not alone in seeing Christmas as the model of proper human relations and a pointer to solutions to England's problems. A year after the publication of *A Christmas Carol* Benjamin Disraeli, then a Member of Parliament and later Queen Victoria's favourite Prime Minister, published *Coningsby*, a political novel expounding the aims of the Conservative group Young England. Disraeli led it, though its members were mostly young aristocrats, such as Lord John Manners, heir to the Duke of Rutland, and George Smythe, later Lord Lamington. They believed that paternalistic government with an ethic of *noblesse oblige* could solve Britain's social ills. Rather than reforming legislation directed at particular problems, which had been the response of governments of the previous decade, Disraeli's novel shows an alternative way to achieve harmony in the description of Christmas at an aristocratic house:

> *The Buttery Hatch was open for a whole week from noon to sunset; all comers might take their fill, and all carry away as much bold beef, white bread, and jolly ale as a strong man could bear in a basket with one hand. For every woman a red cloak, and a coat of broadcloth for every man. All day long, carts laden with fuel and warm raiment were traversing the various districts, distributing comfort and dispensing cheer.*

Inside, 'all classes are mingled in the joyous equality that becomes the season'. There are carols on Christmas Eve, mummers on Christmas Day and a Lord of Misrule entrusted with the task of reviving old customs. Among these, a boar's head is paraded ceremoniously into the hall preceded by a real live Duchess working as an herb-woman scattering rosemary. Other guests don the old armour displayed around the hall or ride the hobby horse or carry cups of sweetened wine or lighted candles. This medievalised Christmas was justified by Young England theory:

> *A mere mechanical mitigation of the material necessities of the humbler classes, a mitigation which must inevitably be limited, can never alone avail sufficiently to ameliorate their condition … their condition is not merely a 'knife and fork question', to use the coarse and shallow phrase of the Utilitarian school … You must cultivate the heart as well as content the belly; and that the surest means to elevate the character of the people is to appeal to their affections.*

The longing for an earlier era, perceived as kinder and gentler, shines out from this description. So does the fear of a society in which the working class had enough money and power to determine their own fates. In effect, like Dickens, Disraeli believed the spirit of the past could keep the future at bay. Like *A Christmas Carol*, *Coningsby* was a great success. Its first edition sold out within a fortnight, an edition of 50,000 copies appeared in America, and numerous further editions appeared during the Nineteenth Century.

As much as these novels helped spread nostalgia for the past and resistance to radical change, they were themselves shaped by emotions that were already widely shared: a concern for the state of the vast impoverished class of England and bewilderment about how it might be helped. The most popular Christmas poem of its day, Alfred Lord Tennyson's *Ring Out Wild Bells*! shows the longing for a reformed dispensation without any significant action to bring it about:

> *Ring out the feud of rich and poor,*
> *Ring in redress to all mankind . . .*
>
> *Ring out a slowly dying cause,*
> *And ancient forms of party strife;*
> *Ring in the nobler modes of life,*
> *With sweeter manners, purer laws.*
>
> *Ring out the want, the care, the sin,*
> *The faithless coldness of the times …*
>
> *Ring in the valiant man and free,*
> *The larger heart, the kindlier hand.*

The spirits of Christmas

While Tennyson, and even Disraeli, imply that it is quite possible to adopt new Christmassy attitudes to achieve desirable change, Dickens shows less confidence in unaided human will. He generally relies on supernatural beings to convert the stony-hearted: the goblins in the story of Gabriel Grub, and the ghosts in *A Christmas Carol*. More fantastical beings appear in his later Christmas tales. In *The Chimes*, published in 1844, the Goblin of the Great Bell of the church reinvigorates the semi-starved Trotty Veck, brought close to despair by the ignorant assertion that the poor have only themselves to blame for their condition.

In *The Cricket on the Hearth* of 1845, a fairy who has been masquerading as a cricket brings happiness back to the Peerybingle home by proving that John's doubts of his much younger wife are unfounded. In the 1848 story *The Haunted Man* a phantom promises John Redlaw relief from the sad memories that bedevil his Christmas by erasing all recall of past injustices. This seems like a blessing, but Redlaw has the spell reversed when he realises that at Christmas personal sorrow recalls the sorrows of Christ, and thus teaches redemption and forgiveness.

Dickens' association of the supernatural with Christmas was not by his own invention. Ghost stories were a Christmas tradition that shaped *A Christmas Carol*, as its subtitle *A Ghost Story for Christmas* makes clear. Nor were ghosts the only spirits of Christmas. Northern European folklore is peopled with them. For example, in Scandinavia gnomes called Jultomten supposedly emerge from their hiding places and either reward the family with gifts or punish them with tricks. To appease them, food is left out at night. In Seventh-Century England the Venerable Bede noted that at Christmas people left food on their tables overnight for spirits, reflecting an old belief that the dead revisit their families at Christmas.

Goblins appeared at Christmas in Dickens' Pickwick Papers *and again in* The Chimes, *from which this illustration is taken.*

One notable Shakespearean example is the ghost of Hamlet's father, who appears around Christmas. Debating whether it is a good or evil spirit, Marcellus notes:

> *Some say that ever gainst the season comes*
> *Wherein our Saviour's birth is celebrated,*
> *This bird of dawning singeth all night long,*
> *And then they say no spirit dare stir abroad,*
> *The nights are wholesome, no planets strike,*
> *No fairy takes, nor witch hath power to charm,*
> *So hallowed, and so gracious, is that time.*

This suggests the ghost is benign, so Hamlet is encouraged to speak to him. He learns that his father was murdered by his brother, Claudius, who then usurped the throne and married Hamlet's mother. The ghost's revelations seem the more horrific because we know that at the very moment he is speaking, Claudius is celebrating in traditional Christmas style:

> *The King doth wake tonight and takes his rouse,*
> *Keeps wassail, and the swagg'ring up-spring reels;*
> *And as he drains his draughts of Rhenish down*
> *The kettle-drum and trumpet thus bray out.*

The outcome of Hamlet's encounter with the ghost is a string of events that leads to numerous deaths, including his own. Reviewing Marcellus' speech, it seems that the 'some' who 'say' that supernatural spirits are harmless at Christmas are mistaken – especially given widespread northern European belief in less-than-benign gnomes, elves and other spirits of the season. Notionally the groups who went from house to house singing or performing for drinks disguised themselves because they were supposed to be sprites who could injure the householders unless appeased – just like the trick-or-treaters of Hallowe'en.

Father Christmas

The most powerful supernatural spirit of Christmas in England was Christmas itself, personified as Father Christmas. He fuelled the mirth and abundance of the season, inspiring the Bean Kings, Lords of Misrule and all those who drank up and made merry. In Ben Jonson's 1616 court entertainment *The Masque of Christmas* he calls himself 'Old Christmas, Christmas of London…Captain Christmas', and 'Gregory Christmas'. He protests that the guards had tried to keep him out, saying he must come another time. 'A good jest,' he responds, 'as if I could come more than once a year!' His aim is to put in a good word for the preservation of Christmas and the masque ends with Father Christmas advising King James to keep Christmas sport at least once every year.

Father Christmas meets Santa Claus

Jonson's portrayal of Christmas exemplifies the way that Christmas is both always tied to the past but constantly changing to become contemporary. The Father Christmas of 1616 with his focus on revelry and food is utterly different from today's Father Christmas, who, apart from being fat, has no link with food. His sole task is to bring presents to children, not delivering them any old how but magically freighting them on an airborne sleigh and clambering down chimneys to load them into waiting Christmas stockings or pillowcases. (He can also hand them over in person in a department store or at a Christmas party, but most children lose faith in this manifestation of the great man; they much prefer his nocturnal gift-giving.)

This change in Father Christmas emerged quite suddenly in the Nineteenth Century, when the old English Father Christmas began to merge with Santa Claus, a hybrid character traceable to America's immigrants. The Germans and Swiss who settled in Pennsylvania had several magical Christmas gift-givers. One was *Christkindl* – the Christ Child sometimes represented as a blonde angel. Among English speakers *Christkindl* became 'Kriss Kringle', a name Americans still sometimes use for Santa Claus. Other German Christmas figures were more judgemental. Knecht Ruprecht [Rupert] had a sack of good things for good children, and also a whip for punishing bad children. Belsnickel scattered nuts and fruit for children brave enough to risk a blow of his whip as they gathered them up.

Both Belsnickel and Knecht Ruprecht were roughly dressed. Belsnickel often wore animal skins and furs, which may be the source of the furs trimming Santa's suit. Its colour comes from a Fourth-Century saint, St. Nicholas, historically portrayed wearing his red bishop's robe. A widely venerated medieval saint, he was the patron of sailors because he quelled a storm when seamen called on him. He was also patron saint of thieves because he compelled a group of them to return their pelf.

Most importantly though, he was noted for his charities. Once he tossed purses of gold through a window as dowries for three girls, who were about to be sold into slavery. For this he became patron saint of virgins. The purses were represented as golden balls in painting. When the Medici bankers of Renaissance Florence included them in its coat of arms, St. Nicholas became patron saint of lenders, and later of pawnbrokers. His miraculous resuscitation of three murdered boys made him a patron saint of children. All these miracles are celebrated on his saint's day on 6 December. Since it falls within the old Christmas season it is celebrated in many countries, but nowhere was it more popular than the Netherlands, where the arrival of *Sinterklaas* initiates the Christmas holiday.

Washington Irving wrote about Santa Claus flying across the skies in a gift-bearing wagon in his 1809 book *A History of New York*. Like his English tale of Bracebridge Hall, this story had a powerful effect because it encouraged the descendants of New York's Dutch immigrants to think of St. Nicholas as a symbol of Dutch identity.

Irving's book had progeny. Its most powerful descendant was Clement Moore's poem *A Visit from St Nicholas*. Moore apparently wrote it in 1822 to amuse his children, though it has been suggested that it was written by Henry Livingston and introduced into Moore's family by a governess. Whatever the case, the poem appeared in the Troy, New York newspaper every year starting in 1823, and not only became enormously popular, but helped shape St. Nicholas into Santa Claus – the anglicised form of the Dutch *Sinterklaas*.

In the poem eight tiny reindeer pull a miniature sleigh. Called Dasher, Dancer, Prancer and Vixen, Comet, Cupid, Donner and Blitzen, they stop on each rooftop, so St. Nicholas can nip down the chimney and stuff toys into the waiting stockings. In most ways, he looks like our Santa Claus:

> *His eyes how they twinkled! His dimples how merry!*
> *His cheeks were like roses, his nose like a cherry!*
> *His droll little mouth was drawn up like a bow*
> *And the beard of his chin was as white as the snow…*
> *He had a broad face and a little round belly,*
> *That shook when he laughed like a bowlful of jelly.*

Unlike our present burly Santa, but like his reindeer and sleigh, he is tiny: 'a right jolly old elf' – clearly one of the supernatural spirits who roamed northern Europe at Christmas. He's also a smoker:

161

The stump of a pipe he held tight in his teeth,
And the smoke it encircled his head like a wreath.

The Santa Claus outfit with hood and white fur trim is a late arrival on the Christmas scene. The traditional English Father Christmas looked quite different. The stage directions in Jonson's *Masque of Christmas* detail his garments. He wears 'long stockings, a close doublet, a high crown'd hat, with a brooch, a long thin beard, a truncheon, little ruffs, white shoes, his scarfs and garters tied cross'. A woodcut of the era shows him with a straggly beard, a long cloak and high hat a bit like that of a traditional Welsh lady. In the Eighteenth Century poet John Bampfylde charmingly described him 'in furry pall y-clad, his brows enwreathed with holly never sere'. Dickens' Ghost of Christmas Present, often interpreted as a form of Father Christmas, is similarly holly-wreathed and wears a fur-trimmed gown. It's green though, not red, and worn open to the navel. As late as the early Twentieth Century, Santa Claus was sometimes dressed in blue, but Thomas Nast, a German-American illustrator, regularly portrayed him in the red garments of the traditional St. Nicholas, with a wide belt, and the fur trimmings typical of German Christmas figures such as Belsnickel. In some of Nast's early pictures Santa wears a brimmed hat, but gradually this became a hood. In England, the holly wreath continued to appear, sometimes on top of the hood, in the Nineteenth Century. Failing this, artists gave him a staff with holly on its top.

Santa Claus is more closely related to the gift-giving St. Nicholas than to Father Christmas, who brought only good cheer. Eating, drinking and revelling – not gift-giving – remained at the heart of British Christmas celebrations throughout the Nineteenth Century. Notably, the reformed Scrooge joins his nephew in Christmas dinner, buys a turkey for the Cratchits, and shares a bowl of punch with Bob. However, he doesn't bring presents. Traditionally in England gifts were exchanged among friends and family on New Year's Day – a custom that traces back to the Roman Kalends. Christmas boxes of money or necessities such as warm clothes were given to dependants on Boxing Day. Middle-class children might also receive Christmas boxes of money or books, but the piles of toys now typical of Christmas did not begin to show up until the idea of Santa Claus as their magical donor took hold. That was too late for Charles Dickens' ten children. His eldest daughter Mamey recalled that when they were little in the 1840s and 50s they were taken on a Christmas Eve visit to a Holborn toy shop, where they could choose a gift. Neither Father Christmas nor Santa Claus brought them. The first Father Christmases in department stores appeared in Liverpool's Bon Marché in the 1870s and in Fortnum and Mason's in 1898.

The Christmas Tree

As Santa Claus was beginning to arrive in Britain from America, other new customs were arriving too. One of the most important – the Christmas tree – had its roots in Germany. Quite when the first Christmas trees appeared is not known. The tradition of decorating with evergreens at midwinter festivals existed all over Europe. An early reference to decorated trees describes fir trees ornamented with paper roses in the town squares of Riga in Latvia and in Reval, Estonia in the Sixteenth Century. After people had danced round the trees they set them alight. Later records from Alsace describe small fir trees set up on tables, and in 1605 Strasbourg had Christmas trees decorated with paper roses (symbolising the Virgin), wafers (symbolising the Eucharist), apples, sweets and pretzels – the latter suggesting arms crossed in prayer. After this time the Christmas tree or a Christmas pyramid made from fir branches tied in a triangle spread all over northern Europe. In England Christmas trees were first mentioned in the early Nineteenth Century, when German governesses introduced them to their employers' homes. In 1840 William Howitt wrote about the established Christmas-tree custom in Manchester, which had a significant German business community: 'Pine tops are brought to market for the purpose, which are generally illuminated with a paper for every day in the year.'

   Despite these early examples of English Christmas trees, Queen Victoria's German husband Prince Albert is generally regarded as their pioneer. When their first child was born in 1841, he suggested putting up a Christmas tree in Windsor Castle, and as other children were born, each of them got a personal tree. The Royal Family's Christmas trees were widely reported in the press, and in 1848 a photograph was published. Nevertheless, while the Royal example undoubtedly encouraged the quick adoption of the new custom, Charles Dickens does not mention Christmas trees in his Christmas books of the 1840s. However, in 1850 he wrote about them as 'a pretty German toy' in his new magazine *Household Words*, describing them fulsomely, yet as though his readers would already know of the custom:

There were rosy-cheeked dolls hiding behind green leaves; and there were real watches (with movable hands at least and an endless capacity for being wound up) dangling from their innumerable twigs … there were jolly broad-faced little men, much more agreeable in appearance than many real men – and no wonder for their heads took off, and showed them to be full of sugar plums; there were fiddles and drums; there were tambourines, books, work-boxes, paint-boxes, sweetmeat-boxes, peep-show boxes, and all kinds of boxes; there were trinkets for the older girls; there were baskets and pincushions … real fruit made artificially dazzling with gold leaf; imitation apples, pears, and walnuts, crammed with surprises; in short, as a pretty child before me, delightedly whispered to another pretty child, her bosom friend, 'There was everything and more.'

This description goes on for over a page, and shows a major change from the adult-centred Christmas he had described in Dingley Dell less than fifteen years before. Now the tree with its toys is clearly designed to charm the little girls and other children, and it is very much an indoor decoration set up on a table for the enjoyment of a private household. Though sweets and fruit are among the good things on display, there is no substantial food – no giant pies or birds or cakes or puddings. Christmas as shown here is no longer the time when people eat their fill of food that might be scarce at other times, no longer the season for adult revels, but a holiday when children are primary, and abundance takes the form of a myriad of sweets and toys to charm them. A few years later, writing his essay *Round About the Christmas Tree*, Thackeray also describes it as decorated with sweets, crackers and 'giftlings' for children and young people.

The table-top Christmas tree with toys hanging from its branches remained the standard in Britain until well after the Second World War, and is still the tree that appears on Spode Christmas plates, first produced in 1938. However, it was many years before every family could afford its own tree. Public Christmas trees were set up so children could be taken to visit them. A giant tree appeared at the Crystal Palace in 1854. Welwyn Garden City had an outdoor tree in 1938, and from 1946 onwards Trafalgar Square has had an enormous tree donated by the people of Norway.

Christmas cards

The 1840s were probably the most innovative decade for Christmas in British history. It not only saw the publication of Dickens' Christmas

Christmasing

London street-sellers called laurel, ivy, holly and mistletoe 'Christmasing'. Writing about the trade in *London Labour and the London Poor* in 1849 Dickens' friend Henry Mayhew estimated how much was sold and at what cost. He believed that 375,000 evergreen branches were sold in the streets; smaller inns would spend from 2 to 10 shillings on it, while larger inns and clubs would spend £1. He and one of his 'informants' estimated that Londoners ate 100,000 Christmas puddings. 'Flinging in any mince pies that may be decorated with evergreens ... every plum pudding will have a sprig of holly in him. If it's bought just for the occasion it may cost 1d to be really prime and nicely berried. If it's part of a lot, why won't it cost a halfpenny? What does that come to? Just above £200. Think of that, then, just for sprigging puddings!' Holly was half the price of mistletoe, so sometimes replaced the kissing bough. It was easier to find in the gardens and countryside round London, where young men would go gathering it. A 17-year-old explained 'It's hard work, Christmasing.' Scavenging for holly around Mortlake, in ten days he gathered only enough to make 6 shillings plus half a pork pie and a pint of beer, which he paid for in holly. Mistletoe typically grows in orchards, which were harder to invade without the risk of being caught in a trap. This explains its higher price.

books, and the introduction of Christmas trees, but it also produced the first Christmas crackers and Christmas cards. Unlike Santa Claus, who emigrated from America and the Christmas trees that came from Germany, Christmas cards and crackers were English inventions.

The question must arise, why did people take it into their heads to start sending cards to each other? The answers suggest something of the mood of the era.

One source of Christmas cards was the custom of leaving calling cards on neighbours and acquaintances. In the Nineteenth Century stationers began producing coloured scraps – little motifs of pretty children, birds, flowers or anything of charm. Some women compiled scrapbooks as a hobby, and it was but a short step to sticking Christmassy scraps on the calling cards left in December. Clearly this took them a step closer to the Christmas card as we know it.

Valentine cards were already familiar, and in the early days of Christmas cards, stationers simply recycled Valentine images with Christmas messages. The link with St. Valentine's Day suggests the emphasis on love and goodwill at Christmas. This theme dominates the first purpose-made Christmas card drawn by John Calcott Horsley and sold by Henry Cole in 1843. It has three panels: narrow side panels showing the poor being fed and clothed, and a central panel with a family sitting down to a hearty Christmas dinner, the paterfamilias extending a welcoming gesture to allcomers. The 1840s are called 'the hungry forties' because so many people were living on the edge of starvation. Dickens emphasised hunger in his Christmas books, especially in *The Chimes*. The new magazine *Punch*, founded in 1840, regularly carried Christmas pieces urging charity by satirising the greedy. In 1841, for example, they ran an article called *How Mr Chokepear keeps a Merry Christmas*. He has everything fine, with plenty of food and fun, but no thought for others. 'Christmas of the belly' *Punch* described it, urging 'Keep you the Christmas of the heart. Give – give.' Again in 1843 *Punch* demanded 'What have you done for the happiness of those about you? Nothing! Do you dare with those sirloin cheeks and that port-wine nose to answer – Nothing?' This emphasis on sharing remained strong in early Christmas cards, either expressed in verses or shown graphically in Christmas puddings and other foods.

One source of the Victorian focus on alleviating poverty was the invigoration of the Church of England by the evangelical movement, whose ministers actively proselytised among the poor and whose parishioners ran soup kitchens and distributed food and clothes for the winter. Yet while the renewed sense of religion infused new energy into the Christmas tradition of community, religious images were never a staple of Christmas cards. Children were a prime focus, often presented as cute little people dressed in their best and gazing moonily at robins or Christmas puddings, or more mischievously, simply having fun in the snow. It's worth noting that putting the spotlight on children is typical of the 1840s, when two of the first English novels to be written from a child's point of view became best-sellers: Charlotte Brontë's *Jane Eyre* (1847) and Charles Dickens' *David Copperfield* (1850).

The link between Christmas cards and Valentine cards meant that pretty motifs of all kinds were valued. These included many Christmas card pictures that no longer seem Christmassy: springtime flowers, for

Children were a favourite motif on Victorian Christmas cards. They became the focus of Christmas celebrations during the Nineteenth Century.

example, and butterflies, birds of many kinds, seascapes, even seductive nymphs and classical goddesses could appear along with the goblins that were still remembered as Christmas sprites. Among more seasonal themes, holly, mistletoe, plum pudding, Father Christmas, bells and robins dominated.

At a shilling apiece the first Christmas card was so expensive that it was not possible for any but the most affluent to send them. However, in the 1860s new printing technology brought the price down, and by 1887 Christmas cards were being sold for as little as 8d a dozen. At this price, they could take off. Getting cards prompted people to send out their own. Five million Christmas cards were already being sent in the 1880s. By 1938 it was 470 million and in 1949 it had risen to 590 million. Today the Royal Mail delivers 2 billion cards and letters in the four weeks preceding Christmas. Normally it handles about 80 million items a day, but on the peak Christmas posting day, 15 December, the figure is around 125 million. Among this tsunami of mail are an estimated 750,000 letters to Santa and 750 million Christmas cards.

Christmas cards today

Today, animals have replaced the children of Victorian Christmas. Their popularity began in the 1960s at the same time that fluffy animals began to exert a major appeal in toy shops. Like toy animals, they must be cute: puppies, kittens, penguins and deer all qualify. Snakes, lizards, armadillos and hyenas wouldn't do at all. Other favourite motifs are winter scenes, birds, evergreens, candles and bells. Interior scenes with a Christmas tree or Christmas stockings and a window or door revealing the wintry outside are another favourite image. Old-fashioned Christmas scenes of horse-drawn coaches or snow-bound villages are common too, but religious cards are not. In December 2008 the *Daily Mail* reported that only one in a hundred cards showed a religious scene. Though various public officials huffed and puffed their regret at this, religious cards have never been popular in Britain. Indeed, while images have changed since the Nineteenth Century, Britain has always had a greater fondness for cute scenes and jokey cards than either Americans or continental Europeans. One card which combined the cute with the comic was identified by the *Daily Mail* as among the oddest of 2008. It showed a chorus line of paper-hatted meerkats, one of them looking decidedly tiddly. The greeting asked which one looked as if he had robbed an off-licence.

Christmas card motifs reveal much about the Christmas ideas with which their senders identify. Nineteenth-Century cards with their children, flowers and birds suggest a longing for beauty and purity that may have been prompted by the physical murk of smoky slum-ridden cities. Many cards of the day were created by talented artists including Walter Crane, Marcus Ward and Kate Greenaway. People often kept them in albums or cut out the prettiest bits and stuck them in scrapbooks. Today the fondness for wintry motifs such as snowflakes and fir trees evokes Christmas as a winter festival. The prettiness of some of the images suggests that now that the survival of life in the dark and cold is a bit more assured, the charms of winter can be appreciated. Animals also emphasise life, especially the cuddly baby animals that dominate the Christmas cards. As for the jokey cards like those squiffy meerkats, though they may look bizarrely modern, they emphasise the revelry that has always been central to the English Christmas, and indeed is rooted in Saturnalia and other ancient winter celebrations. A card showing a pan of Brussels sprouts also appeared in the *Daily Mail*'s list of bizarre images. Though they were not widely known until the Nineteenth Century, many people would now find Christmas dinner without them unthinkable. They typify the domesticity that has moved steadily to the centre stage of Christmas.

New Year's Day

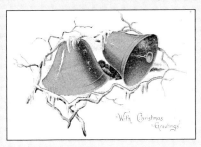

With Christmas Greetings

When Christmas was a twelve-day season, New Year's Day was the day for gift-giving. In *Sir Gawain and the Green Knight* King Arthur's knights give their gifts on New Year's Day before going into the hall for the New Year's feast. This practice survived in the Tudor and Stuart courts. New Year's Eve and New Year's Day remained, even as Christmas shrank down from twelve days. Dickens' daughter Mamey recalled their house as 'overflowing' on New Year's Eve. She remembered her father standing, watch in hand, waiting for the first chime of the New Year: 'A few minutes of breathless silence and all eyes fixed on him as he stood by the open door – whatever the weather might be – then a beautiful voice saying "A Happy New Year. God bless us all."'

In Scotland the Presbyterians banned Christmas celebrations in the Sixteenth Century, so New Year, called Hogmanay, became the most important holiday of the winter. This brought its own celebratory dishes including haggis, shortbread, Black Bun, and visits from first-footers: groups of men who go from house to house to let the new year in. Dark men bring luck; women and fair-haired men are unlucky, so householders must watch that they don't step over the door sill first. First-footers come armed with bottles of whisky and sherry, and are greeted with drinks and food. First-footing is common also in the North of England, if less elaborate. If necessary, a dark man of the household is sent out of doors before midnight and must wander about in the cold until the New Year has arrived, when he can knock on his own door and be welcomed back in with kisses and drinks. Failing this, care must be taken next day that a man, preferably dark, is the first person to enter the house. First-footers bring gifts of salt for health, bread for prosperity, and coal for warmth and shelter in the coming year.

Nineteenth-Century Christmas foods

Since the Nineteenth Century sought Christmas inspiration in the past, it is not surprising that mince pies, pork pies, and a big bird or beef joint all retained their Christmas dinner appeal, as did drinks such as mulled wine and punch. Nonetheless Christmas eating changed in the Nineteenth Century as these dishes and a few others became codified as seasonal essentials, while others disappeared.

By the end of the Nineteenth Century meats such as rabbit, veal and mutton had lost favour at Christmas. Meat pies and hams played supporting roles, while beef or poultry starred as centrepieces. In 1843 Dickens described Bob Cratchit's family having goose, and eating it all except one bone. Scrooge buys them a turkey, evidence that meaty-breasted turkeys were more desirable than slimline geese. By 1862, when Anthony Trollope published *Orley Farm*, Felix Graham complains about the overwhelming combination of 'a turkey twice as big as it ought to be' and 'the mountain of beef', but most people welcomed the turkey as the *pièce de resistance*. Trollope shows Moulder ceremoniously carving a 24-pound specimen, which had been left to hang for two weeks and wiped down with vinegar every day to make sure it was flavourful – indeed, high – but still eatable:

> For the next three or four minutes Moulder did not speak a word. The turkey was on his mind with the stuffing, the gravy, the liver, the breast, the wings, and the legs. He did not help first one person and then another …but cut up artistically as much as might probably be consumed, and located the fragments in small heaps or shares in the hot gravy; and then having made partition of the spoils, he served it out with unerring impartiality.

The prestige of a massive turkey was great, but so was its price. Until 1955 more people ate chicken than turkey on Christmas Day. Before the days of battery-raised hens they were delicious and too expensive for everyday consumption, so they were perfect for Christmas. Brussels sprouts appeared in Eliza Acton's *Modern Cookery for Private Families* in 1845, and gradually won their role as the essential vegetable of Christmas when home gardeners began to grow them later in the century.

Nineteenth-Century cookery books gave plain everyday versions of some recipes with richer versions for Christmas. Plum pudding with a few raisins was a common pudding and not very expensive; a dark pudding rich with fruit and redolent of spice and spirits was for Christmas Day. The plain pudding is a measure of Mrs. Mason's parsimony in *Orley Farm*:

> *The pudding was also small, nor was it black and rich, and laden with good things as a Christmas pudding should be laden.*

The pattern of jazzing-up basic recipes for Christmas was common. In George Eliot's *Silas Marner* Dolly Winthrop makes lard cakes for Christmas by enriching ordinary bread dough with lard and dried fruit. She encourages Silas to take a dish of meat to be baked in the baker's oven, a common practice among poor people who had no ovens of their own, saying:

> *But now upo' Christmas Day, this blessed Christmas as is ever coming, if you were to take your dinner to the bakehus, and go to church, and see the holly and the yew, and hear the anthim, and then take the sacramen', you'd be a great deal the better.*

The Lammeters live at a higher level, with Priscilla making a large batch of the pork pies that were traditional for the season. The 'savoury pork pie' in Dickens' *Great Expectations* is never tasted because Pip has given it to the escaped convict, but it had a starring role at the end of a Christmas dinner of fowls and pork. Pip gets only 'the scaly tips of drumsticks ... and those obscure corners of pork of which the pig, when living, had had least reason to be vain'. Joe compensates him with half a pint of the plentiful gravy Mrs. Joe had made. Uncle Pumblechook brings her a bottle of sherry and a bottle of port, and she offers him both brandy and gin.

After the meal, there are oranges, apples and nuts to be eaten in state in the parlour. The Eighteenth-Century author Martha Bradley thought this dessert too simple for her wealthy readers. She had suggested sweetmeats instead, and gave recipes for an orange-flower candy and chocolate almonds made by forming chocolate in almond-shaped moulds. However, for Pip and the majority of his countrymen, the apples and pears of the English harvest and the year-end oranges and nuts from Spain were essential Christmas fare.

In the London streets, about 15 million oranges were sold every year, mostly by women and girls, many of them Irish. They could expect the best prices at Christmas because oranges were used in punch, and

Oranges were in season around Christmas and were often the only treat in a poor child's Christmas. As shown in this illustration from Henry Mayhew's 1849 account London Labour and the London Poor, *they were sold in the street, typically by women and children.*

tucked into the toes of Christmas stockings. Even so, Henry Mayhew writing in *London Labour and the London Poor* estimated they yielded little profit. One woman he spoke to made only ninepence a day. Nut-sellers fared even worse. They sold hazelnuts, coconuts and Brazil nuts – an 1824 newcomer to England. By 1849 when Mayhew was writing, they sold at twelve or sixteen for a penny.

Factory-made biscuits packed in bright tins were also Nineteenth-Century newcomers to the Christmas feast. They were yet another innovation of the 1840s: the brainchild of Jonathan Carr, a Carlisle baker, who mechanised the process of stamping them out. Companies such as Huntley and Palmer and Peek Frean's followed. Until the end of the century their biscuits were relatively expensive: sixpence a pound for ginger biscuits was a quarter of the day's wage for the people who made them, so a packet or tin of biscuits was only possible as a Christmas luxury for many people.

Chocolates fell into the luxury category, too. Though chocolate had been known since the Seventeenth Century, it was used for drinks or occasional creams and other puddings because its high cocoa butter content made it unpalatable to consume straight from its packet. A series of Nineteenth-Century commercial developments in Holland and Switzerland solved the problem by separating the cocoa butter from the cocoa solids, so manufacturers could recombine them in the proportions necessary for chocolate sweets. Like all sweet luxuries, a box of chocolates and later selection boxes of chocolate bars for children became essential for Christmas.

Abandoned Christmas foods

As new foods came in, some older Christmas specialities were abandoned or lost their Christmas roles. In 1835 Charles Dickens ordered a Christmas meal in an inn: roast beef, roast duck, plum pudding, mince pies and cod with oyster sauce. The last dish sounds unseasonal now, but in 1772 when the diarist Parson Woodforde ordered Christmas dinner at New College, Oxford, he too had cod, specifying 'two fine Codds boiled with fryed Soals round them and oyster sauce, a fine Sirloin of Beef roasted, some peas soup, and an orange pudding in the first course'. Cod was considered a winter fish, and only disappeared later in the Nineteenth Century as courses of several main dishes gave way to the single turkey, chicken or beef in the starring role. Saddles of mutton like those Mr. Weston served in *Emma* and other meat dishes such as rabbit, veal and the succulent preparations of offal and innards also became unChristmassy. Of these, boar's head is the best remembered because of Oxford's Boar's Head Carol sung as it came into the hall 'bedeck'd with bays and rosemary'. Once a regular part of Christmas in either this form or turned into brawn, it is now rare. Similarly, plum porridge, a thick soup of bread, spices and dried fruit, which had been popular since the Middle Ages, disappeared in the early Nineteenth Century.

Crackers

No Christmas meal would be complete today without the crackers to initiate the feast. Like Christmas trees and Christmas cards they were an 1840s' invention. Their creator was Tom Smith, whose company is still a major producer of Christmas crackers. Originally he was a confectioner, apparently inspired to wrap his sweets prettily when he saw attractively packaged bonbons in Paris. After coming up with the traditional tripartite form, he realised he could add the paper hats and riddles or jokes and a tiny toy. Thackeray describes them strung on Christmas trees, where they helped flirtations along:

The kindly Christmas tree, from which I trust every gentle reader has pulled a bonbon or two, is yet aflame and sparkles with the sweet fruits of its season. You young ladies, may you have plucked pretty giftlings from it; and out of the cracker sugarplums which you have split with the captain or sweet young curate; you may have read one of those delicious conundrums which the confectioners introduce into the sweetmeats, and which apply to the cunning passion of love. Those riddles are to be read at your age. As for Dolly, Merry, and Bell, who are standing at the tree, they don't care about the love-riddle part, but understand the sweet almond portion very well. They are four, five, six years old. Patience little people! A dozen merry Christmases more, and you will be reading those wonderful love-conundrums too.

This traditional version of the creation of the cracker omits some intriguing bits of history. The paper hats, usually nowadays crowns, seem to be descendants of the masquing costumes beloved in earlier days, and the jokes and toys revert to the japes of the Middle Ages and Renaissance. Crackers were an innovation of the Nineteenth Century, but were Janus-faced in looking back as well as forward. Indeed, the Nineteenth-Century Christmas now often evoked nostalgically, weaves the old with the new so masterfully that the Christmas which emerged looked like it had always been that way.

PORK PIE

The most famous pork pie in English literature is the one that Pip gives to the convict in Dickens' *Great Expectations*. However, they had been popular for many centuries because they were a way to use small pieces of meat from the pigs that were slaughtered in late autumn. There are many regional variations: Melton Mowbray pork pies are made from unbrined meat seasoned with pepper; an Eighteenth-Century recipe for Cheshire pork pies includes apples. Few people now make their own pork pies, though Mrs. Joe evidently did, and in George Eliot's *Silas Marner* Priscilla Lammeter is famous for her pork pies. Making a pork pie is not hard, at least not now that we have food processors to do the chopping, but they are rather a production: a wonderful thing to make on a cold day when you don't want to leave the house. Or, make the jellied stock a day ahead of time if you like, or even go for the shortcut of making it with gelatine as explained below. The taste of a home-made pork pie suggests the flavours of the food of Eighteenth and Nineteenth-Century country mansions. The hot-water pastry used for pork pies is the easiest pastry to make, though you need to work with it while it is still warm.

For the jellied stock:
about 450g/1lb pig's trotters (2)
2 carrots, peeled and halved
2 celery sticks, peeled and halved
1 medium onion stuck with 4 cloves
1 bay leaf
1 sage leaf or sprig of thyme
½ tsp black peppercorns
about 1 litre/1¾ pt chicken or vegetable stock
125ml/4 fl oz Madeira or sherry

For the pork filling:
225g/8oz gammon
350g/12oz minced pork
450g/1lb belly pork
salt and pepper to taste
about 1 tsp dried sage
about ½ tsp dried thyme
about ½ tsp mace or nutmeg

For the pastry:
500g/1lb 2oz plain flour
55g/2oz icing sugar
1 tsp salt
200g/7oz lard
200ml/7 fl oz water
1 egg, beaten

To make the jellied stock, preheat the oven to 180°C (350°F). Put the trotters in a pan that can go from the stove to the oven. Cover them with water, bring to the boil, simmer for 5 minutes, then drain the water away and rinse the trotters to get rid of the scum. Return the trotters to the pan along with the carrots, celery, onion, bay leaf, sage or thyme, peppercorns, stock and sherry. The liquid should cover the solid ingredients. Add more stock or water if it doesn't. Bring to the boil on the stove, then transfer to the oven and let it simmer for 3 hours, turning the heat down to 150°C (300°F) after 30 minutes. Strain the liquid. You can do all this the night before making the pie. Alternatively, you can make jellied stock with powdered gelatine and chicken or beef stock, see p. 50.

To make the filling, cut about a third of the gammon into small dice no bigger than 1cm/½-inch. Mix with the minced pork. Chop the belly pork and the remaining gammon into chunks and process them a few at a time in a food processor or pass them through a meat grinder until coarsely chopped. Mix them with the minced pork. Season them well with salt, pepper, sage, thyme and mace, and mix thoroughly. Take a portion about the size of a 50p coin and fry it for a minute on each side, then taste it to see if it is seasoned to your liking. Add more of any flavouring that seems necessary. Mix in the chopped pork and the gammon, distributing the pieces throughout.

To make the pastry, mix the flour, icing sugar and salt in a large bowl. Make a well in the centre. Put the lard and water in a saucepan, bring to the boil and when the lard has melted slowly pour it into the well in the flour mixture and stir it in. Use your hands to quickly mix a smooth dough. Put a cloth over the bowl and let it rest, while you turn the oven to 180°C (350°F) and grease with lard a tin for the pie. You can use either a game pie mould, or a 7-inch springform tin or a removable-base 5cm/2-inch deep cake tin. Alternatively, make a number of smaller pies in individual-size ovenproof dishes. While the pastry is still quite hot take about three quarters of it, put it in the centre of your tin then spread it evenly all over the base and up the sides of the tin. Let it dangle over the edge or stand higher than the tin. Put the pork and ham mixture in. Now roll out the rest of the pastry. (Don't worry about tears, as these are easy to repair with this sort of pastry.) Cover the top of the pie. Make a hole as big as a 5p coin in the centre. Press the edges together and trim off the excess. Make some leaf or petal or other shapes with the scraps of pastry. Brush the surface with egg. Place your decorations on top, and then brush with egg again. Put the tin on a baking sheet and slide it into the oven. Bake for 30 minutes, then reduce the heat to 160°C (325°F) and bake for another 30 minutes. Depending on the dimensions of the tin you are using you may need to bake it a little longer. To check, remove it from the oven and wiggle a skewer or knife blade in the hole in the middle and look for any pink moisture in the meat. If you spot some, return it to the oven, if necessary laying a sheet of aluminium foil over the top to stop the pastry browning too much.

When the pie is done remove it to a cooling rack and leave it for 45 minutes. Reheat 300ml/half a pint of the jellied stock to lukewarm, then using a funnel or a small jug with a good pouring spout, dribble a little at a time into the pie. It will fill up spaces left as the meat shrank in cooking. Cool the pie completely so the stock turns back to jelly again. Serve cold with chutney and salads. You can reheat portions of the pie if you like. The pastry will soften, but will still taste good.

COD WITH OYSTER SAUCE

In her book of bills of fare *What Shall We Have for Dinner?* Dickens' wife Catherine, writing as Lady Maria Clutterbuck, listed Cod (or codling) with Oyster Sauce no less than fifteen times. Oyster sauce was a traditional accompaniment with cod from at least the Eighteenth Century. Dickens mentions cod with oyster sauce at a pre-Christmas supper in 1835, and Agatha Christie mentions oyster soup at the start of Christmas dinner in the early Twentieth Century. Cooks also used oysters in poultry stuffing, and even inserted them into large joints of mutton or beef as seasoning. The popularity of oysters at Christmas only declined as they became rarer and more expensive later in the century.

700g/1lb 9oz cod fillet, cut in 4 pieces
salt and pepper to taste
55g/2oz butter
1 tbsp plain flour
8 oysters opened, their juice saved
1 tbsp white wine
about 150ml/5 fl oz milk or single cream
tiny pinch mace or nutmeg
Worcestershire sauce to taste

Preheat the oven to 180°C (350°F). Grease a baking dish large enough to hold the pieces of fish without them touching each other. Season the fish with salt and pepper. Using about half the butter, divide it into little bits and put one on top of each piece of fish. Cover the dish with aluminium foil, and bake the fish for 8 minutes or until it is opaque all through.

While the fish is cooking, make a paste of the remaining butter with the flour. Combine the drained oyster juice with the wine, then add enough milk or single cream to make it up to 300ml/half a pint. Bring it to simmering point. Remove from the heat and add the oysters. Return to a very low heat and cook without boiling for about 30 seconds to 1 minute or until the oysters look plumped up. Remove them to a warm plate with a slotted spoon, and take off their beards – the blackish edges. Now return the liquid to the heat, still low, and stir in about a third of the flour/butter mixture. When it has blended in, stir in another third, and then the final third, stirring all the time. You should now have a thick sauce. Taste it and season with salt (which may not be necessary as

This illustration from The Strand *shows how plum pudding assumed greater importance at Christmas during the Nineteenth Century. Previously, plum porridge would have been an essential dish, but pudding replaced it.*

178

the oysters can be salty), mace or nutmeg, pepper and Worcester sauce. Return it to simmering point, remove from the heat, return the oysters to it, then serve the cod with the oyster sauce over it. This serves 4 as a main dish. To make it as a starter for 6, cut the cod into 6 pieces and use 12 oysters – 2 per person.

CHRISTMAS PUDDING

Grated suet was an essential ingredient in traditional puddings, sweet and savoury, and in lots of pies. It contributes to their unique flavour, though it makes them unsuitable for vegetarians. You can use vegetarian suet instead, or, better yet, melted butter. Victorian writers made much of the size of Christmas puddings. Dickens described Mrs. Cratchit's as a 'cannonball', and a cartoon in *The Strand* suggested that they had become distinctly bigger as the century progressed.

175g/6oz currants
12 glacé cherries, halved
280g/10oz raisins
280g/10oz golden raisins
55g/2oz candied peel
1 cup Amontillado sherry
¼ cup rum
1 tbsp lemon juice
grated zest of 1 lemon
280g/10oz breadcrumbs from day-old brown or white bread
225g/8oz brown sugar
¼ tsp each or more to taste: ginger, cinnamon, cloves and mace or nutmeg
3 eggs
$^2/_3$ cup milk
280g/10oz shredded suet or butter, melted and slightly cooled

Put the currants, cherries, raisins, golden raisins and peel in a large bowl. Pour on the Amontillado sherry, rum and lemon juice and stir in the lemon zest. Cover and leave overnight. In a large bowl, mix the breadcrumbs with the sugar. Stir in the fruit and any unabsorbed liquid. Stir in all the spices. Mix the eggs and milk and stir in. Finally stir in the cooled but still liquid melted butter or suet. Turn a 2-quart basin upside down on a doubled sheet of parchment. Draw around then remove and cut out the circle thus made. Grease the basin with butter. Put in the pudding mixture, patting it down so there are no air pockets in it. Put the parchment circles on top. Place the basin in the middle of a long length of foil and bring the foil up from both sides and fold over the ends on top. Repeat this with another sheet of foil making the second fold at right angles to the first. Spread another sheet of foil over the top and the sides so the folds on top are sealed in. Put an old saucer upside down in the middle of a pasta pan. Put the pudding on top. Fill with water to come three quarters of the way up the basin. Cover and simmer for 6 hours, adding more boiling water as the first lot evaporates. Let cool. Take off foil and cover with fresh foil as the first time around. On Christmas Day repeat the boiling for 1½ hours.

FRANCATELLI'S SWEET PUDDING SAUCE

Born in England to a family of Italian cooks, Charles Elmé Francatelli became Maître d'Hotel and Chef to Queen Victoria. He wrote many cookery books including *Plain Cooking for the Working Class*, which includes this sauce after the recipe for Christmas Plum Pudding. 'If you can afford it, pour over the following sauce,' he writes. This version is made with brown sugar, which gives it a butterscotchy flavour that is delicious with Christmas pudding – or indeed with fruit pies.

    55g/2oz butter at room temperature
    55g/2oz brown sugar
    55g/2oz plain flour
    350ml/12 fl oz water
    freshly grated zest of 1 lemon
    1 tbsp lemon juice
    100ml/3½ fl oz dark rum

In a saucepan, cream the butter with the sugar, then mix in the flour a little at a time until you have a smooth paste. Add the water a little at a time, stirring to thin the paste. When half is added, put the pan on a moderate heat, add the rest of the water, the lemon zest and lemon juice and bring to simmering point, stirring all the time. Cook until you have a thick custardy sauce. Stir in the rum and serve.

BLACK BUTTER

Sugar, once a great luxury, became cheaper in the Eighteenth Century, when it was imported from British plantations in the Caribbean rather than the East. Cheap sugar inspired numerous recipes for jams, marmalades and fruit cheeses and butters. Of the latter, only lemon cheese remained in favour, though damson cheese is regaining popularity. Recipes for the black butter that Jane Austen and her family served during the Christmas season of 1808 are rare. A Scottish recipe of 1829 uses berries. In New England apple butter is made with unpeeled apples. They produce so much pectin that the resulting preserve is jellied. The following recipe combines apples with dark berries. One way of using it is to pour it into small dishes such as ramekins and then turn it out onto a plate for serving either with cheese or with toast. Jane Austen mentions that she and her mother served it with widgeon – a kind of small wild duck – and preserved ginger.

  900g/2lb apples
  450g/1lb blackberries or blackcurrants
  450g/1lb mixed berries (strawberries, raspberries, blueberries for example)
  625g/1lb 6oz white sugar
  1 tsp powdered ginger
  ½ tsp powdered cinnamon
  ½ tsp powdered allspice

Sterilise jars or dishes by immersing them in water, bringing them to the boil for 10 minutes and letting them stand in the water until ready for use. Wash the apples, and trim off the stalk and the dry bits at the blossom end. Cut each apple into 6 or 8 rough chunks. Put them in a large pan with 4 tablespoons of water. Put on the lid and cook slowly over low heat until they begin to soften. Add all the berries and let the mixture simmer (with the lid partly on the pan) until the apples are very soft. Press the mixture through the finest blade of a food mill or through a sieve. Return the strained mixture to the pan and add the sugar, ginger, cinnamon and allspice. Bring to the boil and boil rapidly with the lid off the pan until it sets. You can tell when this point has been reached by the following: the mixture should look smooth and glossy, it will fall from a spoon in a dollop rather than drops, and a spoonful of it dropped onto a plate will mound rather than run into a puddle. Dry the sterilised jars with a freshly laundered towel or paper towels and pour the black butter in. Top with discs of paper dipped in brandy if you have them. Store in a cool place. Note this butter does not keep as well as jam does because it has less sugar. Eat within 2–3 months.

ELIZA ACTON'S MULLED WINE

Spiced and sweetened hot wine was one of many kinds of wassail popular over the centuries. Elderberry wine was a country favourite for making it, as Mr. Wardle did at Dingley Dell, while port was the choice of luxury. In 1845 Eliza Acton included a mulled wine recipe in her *Modern Cookery for Private Families*, a book that Catherine, Dickens' wife, used when compiling her own book *What Shall We Have for Dinner?* Acton notes that orange peel is an optional ingredient, and that 'In France light claret takes the place of port wine in making it, and the better kinds of *vin ordinaire* are very palatable thus prepared.' The following recipe is closely based on hers.

    300ml/½ pint water
    100g/3½oz sugar
    7.5cm/3-inch chunk fresh ginger, peeled
    10cm/4-inch cinnamon stick
    10 whole cloves
    6 black peppercorns
    strips orange zest to taste
    600ml/1 pint port or claret or elderberry wine
    2–3 slices navel orange

Combine the water and sugar in a saucepan. Slice the ginger and bruise the pieces with a rolling pin. Add them to the water and sugar along with the cinnamon, cloves, and peppercorns. Using a blade-type vegetable peeler, strip some thin pieces of zest from an orange, leaving the white pith behind. Add one or two pieces, about 4cm / 1½ inches long and 2cm / ¾-inch wide, to the mixture. Bring to simmering point for 15 minutes. Then, increase the heat, and boil more rapidly until the volume is reduced by half. Stir in the port or other wine, and stir until the mixture just simmers again. Strain and serve hot with half an orange slice. Serves 4–6.

The Robin

The robin reigns supreme as Britain's bird of Christmas, a favourite on Christmas cards and wrapping paper, and one of the prettiest things to perch on the icing of a Christmas cake. We love robins because they stay with us all winter, their red breasts splashing colour into the sere gardens of the season. Yet other winter birds don't command such intense affection. Folklore and nursery rhymes suggest that the love of robins goes deep:

> *The North Wind doth blow, and we shall have snow*
> *And what will poor Robin do then?*
> *Poor thing!*
> *Sit in a barn, and keep himself warm*
> *And hide his head under his wing.*
> *Poor thing!*

Many regional rhymes pair the robin with the wren. From Warwickshire comes:

> *The robin and the wren*
> *Are God Almighty's cock and hen.*

> *The martin and the swallow*
> *Are God Almighty's*
> *Bow and arrow.*

A Cornish rhyme promises ill luck to anyone who injures the robin or a wren:

He who hurts the robin or the wren,
On sea or land will n'er do well again.

Notwithstanding this threat, an old custom in both England and Ireland was to hunt wrens on Boxing Day, killing one and distributing its feathers for good luck. Robins were immune from this abuse, perhaps because their red breasts were supposedly won when a kindly robin plucked a painful prickle from Christ's crown of thorns, and was stained with His blood. Another legend tells of Mary asking for help when she was shivering in the stable. A little brown bird flapped its wings over the fire to keep it alight. It succeeded, but only at the cost of setting its breast on fire. It has remained red ever since.

CHAPTER 7

Conclusion: The Twentieth Century and Beyond

It seems wrong and unfair that Christmas with its stressful and unmanageable financial and emotional challenges, should first be forced upon one wholly against one's will, then rudely snatched away just when one is starting to get into it.

Helen Fielding, *Bridget Jones's Diary*, 1996

THE NINETEENTH Century gave the Twentieth Century the Christmas we know today with Christmas trees, Christmas cards, Christmas crackers, and Father Christmas bringing presents to the children. The Nineteenth Century also created many favourite Christmas carols and stories. Even the iconic Christmas dinner with the big turkey or other bird followed by Christmas pudding and mince pies was codified in the Nineteenth Century. To be sure, this meal was rooted in centuries-old traditions, as was the emphasis on food and drink in general, but the family Christmas with the focus on children was a Victorian invention. It has never been cheap. The tree, the crackers, the presents, the food, the drink all cost so much that while Christmas became the family celebration *par excellence*, many early Twentieth-Century working-class families could not afford to buy the full array of Christmas commodities. Spreading the good cheer around so that the majority could enjoy it was the achievement of the Twentieth Century.

The march towards today's widely shared Christmas did not proceed uniformly. It was slower in Scotland and parts of Wales, where some churches had retained the Puritan view that there was no biblical sanction for its celebration. Both world wars, especially the second, stayed Christmas in its tracks. Nor did today's Christmas come without a social as well as a financial cost. Twentieth-Century Christmas literature captures the nostalgia already familiar in the work of Nineteenth-Century writers, but also anxieties about whether Christmas will really bring its good things, and about whether its good things are entirely worth the effort to acquire them.

Early Twentieth-Century memories

When Nineteenth-Century writers such as Washington Irving and Charles Dickens wrote nostalgically about Christmas they had to look way back beyond their own childhoods. They evoked the shared Christmas of some unidentified time ago, though rooted, at least notionally, in the medieval custom of keeping open house with feasting, drinking, dancing and games for rich and poor alike. A century later nostalgic writers could draw pictures of Christmas as they had known it themselves, usually focusing on families and friends celebrating together.

One of the best-known, Dylan Thomas' *A Child's Christmas in Wales* (1954), whirls up a snowstorm of memories: snow, cats, postmen, sweets, whistles, knitted presents, painting books and building sets – all culminating in turkey and blazing pudding. Uncles snore the afternoon away, and aunties drink port and elderberry wine and tea fortified with rum. This is an Ur-Christmas:

> *One Christmas was so much like another, in those years around the sea-town corner now and out of all sound except the distant speaking of the voices I sometimes hear a moment before sleep, then I can never remember whether it snowed for six days and six nights when I was twelve or whether it snowed for twelve days and twelve nights when I was six.*

Thomas studs his reverie on Christmas with crystal-clear images: a cold postman with a red button-nose, mistletoe dangling from a gas bracket, a packet of pink-tipped sweet cigarettes:

You stood at the corner of the street and you waited for hours, in vain, for an old lady to scold you for smoking a cigarette, and then with a smirk you ate it.

Agatha Christie also bundles several remembered Christmases together in her story *The Adventure of the Christmas Pudding*. In the Introduction she explains that the fictional Christmas party at King's Lacey comes straight from her memories of the Christmases she spent at Abney Hall, near Manchester. She loved going there, cheerily confessing that though skinny, she was perpetually hungry and brought a huge appetite to the gargantuan Christmas dinner. She and the boys of the house ate the first course of Oyster Soup and Turbot with more duty than zest, but then demolished double helpings of the beef sirloin and the two turkeys; one roast, the other boiled. They were still ready to eat Christmas pudding, mince pies, trifle and dessert. Similarly, in *The Adventure of the Christmas Pudding* three teenagers, Bridget and her two cousins, energetically tuck into a Christmas dinner. Bridget gets a red trinket in her portion of pudding. Hercule Poirot recognises it as the missing ruby he is trying to find – but how did it get there? The youngsters, especially Bridget, help set a trap that reveals all. Implicitly, their help validates them as almost adult and worthy heirs to the Christmas traditions of King's Lacey.

Harrods Meat Hall with its magnificent turkey display in 1921. (Photograph courtesy of Company Archive, Harrods Limited)

Spreading Christmas around

When Agatha Christie, daughter of a wealthy stockbroker, was enjoying Christmas at the turn of the century, and in the 1920s, when Dylan Thomas, son of a schoolmaster, was larking through Christmas in Swansea, Britain still had millions of children for whom such Christmases were only a dream. At best parents may have managed a Christmas dinner like the Cratchits', though with chicken rather than goose. Each child would have got an orange and perhaps some sweets and a small toy. Many children simply depended on the Victorian and early-Twentieth-Century charities that devoted themselves to putting on Christmas meals for the poor. Companies and businesses also put on parties for employees' children. Even the overseers of workhouses, normally hawk-eyed scrutineers of every unnecessary expense, usually relaxed at Christmas and provided not only extra food, but sometimes luxuries such as tea for the women and tobacco for the men. However, even though these efforts made Christmas cheerier for some who would otherwise have had little in the way of festivity, creating their own Christmas with their own tree and presents for young and old was the goal for poorer families.

Twentieth-Century technology fed their desire. Newspapers and magazines had long celebrated the family Christmas. The newsreels that accompanied all films until the 1950s joined in. In 1932 King George V agreed to address the nation on the radio on Christmas Day. Since then the Royal speech, which always notes the monarch's own family celebration, has been an annual Christmas event. For the last fifty years television has played the family theme so loudly that anyone spending Christmas away from their family can seem an object of pity.

By 1935 when Harrods printed this advertisement, shopping for Christmas presents had become a major middle-class preoccupation. (Photograph courtesy of Company Archive, Harrods Limited)

Conclusion: The Twentieth Century and Beyond

Wartime Christmases

The Second World War ushered in the more universal Christmas, but first it spelt curtailment to Christmas as it had been known before. Wartime rationing and shortages of food and consumer products meant that those who had previously celebrated with a laden table and bulging Christmas stockings could no longer do so. Yet the allure of Christmas was so strong that every stratagem was used to make Christmas as much like it had been before the outbreak of war in 1939. Christmas cards had doubled in price because there was a 100 per cent tax on them designed to preserve paper. Pictures from one year's cards were cut out and pasted onto salvaged card to make new cards or calendars for the next year. Dipping holly and fir in Epsom salts then letting them dry produced sparkle for Christmas. Parents snapped up second-hand toys for their children. Magazines encouraged gardeners to give Christmas presents of seed potatoes, cloches and even manure. Seed tokens exchangeable at seedsmen's shops were another possibility.

Most families had at least one gardener because the government-promoted Dig for Victory campaign encouraged everyone to increase the food supply by growing their own back-garden or allotment vegetables. This was vital because at the outbreak of the war Britain produced only 30 per cent of its own food. The Dig for Victory campaign increased land under cultivation from 12 million to 18 million acres. Nonetheless rationing was essential and stringent. Each adult got 2 ounces of butter and 2 ounces of margarine or lard a week. Sugar was limited to 8 ounces per person a week, jam to 1 pound every two months, and eggs to one per person per week. Meat was also rationed, as was bacon. Offal and sausages were not rationed, but were hard to find. Near Christmas the government gave an extra ration of sugar and fat, and stores of tinned and dried fruit were distributed so everyone got some plus the wherewithal for making Christmas cakes and trifles. Even so, making the traditional Christmas foods was difficult. Providing the centrepiece turkey was impossible for most people because government regulations made it unprofitable for farmers to raise them. Only one family in ten had a turkey; chicken or perhaps duck or pork took its place. At the beginning of the war farmers could not raise pigs for themselves. When this ruling was relaxed people created pig clubs: everyone contributed potato peelings and food scraps to feed the animal, and then got a share of the meat when it was slaughtered at Christmas. Pig clubs reputedly produced over 4 million pounds of extra meat.

Such stratagems were common. Food writer Marguerite Patten, who worked as a demonstrator and teacher for the Ministry of Food, wrote that everybody acted like 'a zealous squirrel'. Week by week, they routinely hoarded small amounts of sugar, flour and butter from the rations so that they could accumulate enough to make Christmas cakes and mince pies. They picked blackberries for puddings and jam in autumn, elderberries for the wine that was a rural favourite at Christmas, mushrooms for breakfast and rosehips because they had fifteen times as much vitamin C as oranges and they could be made into syrup for children. Popular food writer Ambrose Heath advised his readers to make old-fashioned fruit butters and cheeses – like Jane Austen's black butter (recipe p. 181) – because they require less sugar than jam. Sloe gin, he pointed out, was the best of all home-made liqueurs, and sloes with which to make it were available in the hedgerows. He also suggested making nasturtium seeds into capers and apples into vinegar. He listed all the birds that were edible, and went so far as to give a recipe for cooking grey squirrels. Their rarity in the 1950s suggests that many people popped them in the pot. Mallards were also far less common then, and may have met the same fate.

The government helped households make the most of their rationed food by running a non-stop advertising campaign to teach basic nutrition, printing numerous recipe pamphlets, and hiring demonstrators to show how to use unfamiliar ingredients like soya flour, Spam, and dried eggs. Vegetables remained unrationed. At Christmas they appeared in odd places. Carrots were a mainstay of every Christmas cake and Christmas pudding recipe. Mashed potatoes replaced some of the fat in frugal pastry recipes. Apples took over Christmas mincemeat. One recipe suggested improvising with grated apples flavoured with 'plenty of spices' and mixed with either chopped cooked prunes or chopped raw dates. Apples appear again in Mock Goose, made from alternate layers of potatoes and apples flavoured with dried sage and sprinkled with grated cheese. This is no substitute for a goose, but not without appeal on a cold winter night. Similarly, a newspaper article *Good Things for Xmas* (quoted in Jennifer Davis' *The Wartime Kitchen and Garden*) suggested substituting powdered gelatine mixed with fruit juice for a hard-to-find table jelly – a stratagem that would produce a much more pleasant confection. The same writer also suggested making a trifle of home-made sponge cake, plums that the wise housewife had bottled in autumn, and a custard of dried eggs, supplemented, if possible, with either a table jelly or dabs of jam. Other wartime recipes cut trifle down more severely: one recommended using four small tea buns soaked with juice from bottled fruit, and topped with custard made from potato flour.

As for the Christmas cake, marzipan could be made with 2 ounces of melted margarine, 4 ounces of sugar or golden syrup, 4 ounces of soya flour plus some almond essence for flavour and enough water to make it into a paste. Icing could be contrived with 6 tablespoons of powdered milk, 4 dessertspoons of sugar, water and colouring. Even with these stratagems making or buying a Christmas cake was often to be hoped for rather than achieved. In *The Wartime Kitchen and Garden* Jennifer Davis tells of a Rotherham woman who bought a cellophane-wrapped McVitie's Christmas cake in 1939. It was never unwrapped, but sat in state on each Christmas table, and did guest appearances at birthday and homecoming parties throughout the war.

Writers at war

Socially, wartime food shortages had a levelling effect because in general everyone was equally deprived. Novelists who wrote about the war often evoke its drabness by focusing on some especially hated food: for example, dried egg or snoek – a canned fish that no-one seems to have liked. Conversely, finding something pleasant was an achievement. In *The Valley of Bones* Anthony Powell suggests the excitement of two soldiers who spotted stale but 'still beautiful' sausage rolls in a station buffet. In *Brideshead Revisited* Evelyn Waugh described the pre-war years at Oxford and Brideshead with their gorgeous buildings, lavish meals and luscious wines. Looking back several years after its publication in 1945 he speculated that wartime rationing had provoked such a longing for sumptuous food in himself and his readers that writing and reading about it was an imaginative substitute for meals that were no longer obtainable.

Those who were abroad could fare better than people in Britain. Travelling in a convoy to West Africa in 1941, Graham Greene recorded the officers' Christmas dinner:

Christmas Day started in the morning with a bottle of champagne to cure the hangover. Round-the-Empire broadcast and the King's rather lugubrious speech at lunch. Dinner was a huge menu. Hors d'oeuvres, soup, fried whiting, tinned asparagus, roast turkey and chipolatas, plum pudding, grapefruit ice. It was like peace.

Noting the details of meals in diaries and fiction was common because for good or ill, all meals were special when food was scarce and people had to make do with whatever was put before them. As Greene notes, a Christmas meal complete with turkey, plum pudding and plenty of accompanying delicacies was so unlikely that it recalled peacetime.

In *The Balkan Trilogy* and *The Levant Trilogy*, Olivia Manning traces the course of the war by the presence or absence of food, with Christmas dinners as emblems of the current situation. Her heroine Harriet Pringle arrives in Bucharest just before Britain declares war on Germany. There she finds a café society where food is cheap, and where the affluent entertain at loaded tables. Traditionally, wealthy Romanian men shopped for meat and imported luxuries at Dragomir's. At Christmas a wild boar and a deer flank the doors. Inside are cheeses from all over Europe, luxuries such as Oxford marmalade and tinned fruit for the English community, and in the centre an unsorted mountain of birds and animals: rabbits and hares with grouse, snipe, pigeons, geese and turkeys. Harriet gets a turkey for Christmas. The down-at-heel Prince Yakimov is a guest. He's always avid for food, especially luxurious food, and he wolfs down much of the soup, virtually all the turkey breast, and more than his share of the large mince pie. Harriet is furious. Yet this simple Christmas dinner, though scarcely sufficient because of Yakimov's greed, soon seems bountiful. During the next few months, food stocks diminish as Germany demands more of Romania's harvests, and the Romanians, anxious to appease them, comply. Yakimov is an analogue of the never-sated Germany, and Harriet's Christmas dinner now seems less of a make-do and more like a sign of what is happening in Europe.

A year later Harriet is in Athens, having fled Romania just as the Germans marched in. Christmas Day arrives and she is walking on a deserted beach with friends. They have little prospect of dinner. Fortune shines on them when a fisherman shows up with some red mullet. He looks kindly on the British because they are helping to defend Greece, and so he cooks them a few of his fish at his beach shack. Having watched food disappear like water out of a drain as the Nazis set their sights on Romania, Harriet now hopes the Greek resistance to the Italian invasion means that the country will withstand the Nazis. However, the lack of food, which is mostly reserved for the army, suggests a repeat performance of the German invasion.

Eventually, Harriet and her husband must flee again, this time to Cairo. The battle for North Africa is raging nearby, with Rommel apparently winning. Harriet reluctantly agrees to be evacuated back to England. A couple of days before her departure, her Christmas dinner is no different from an ordinary luncheon, which in Egypt was always adequate, but a squabble ruins it. Harriet takes herself off to the zoo, where she gazes in sympathy at a lone polar bear. Like Harriet and so many of her compatriots, including the army, he is marooned in the unforgiving Egyptian sun. However, though Harriet identifies with him, at least she has a choice about whether to leave or not. This had not been the case in Bucharest and Athens. In retrospect her Egyptian Christmas, comfortless but not foodless, is the still point before the tide turns. Harriet resolves some of her problems in a fortuitous way, and improbable as it seemed, the British begin to push the Germans out of North Africa.

The post-war years

Rationing continued until 1953, and even though the war was over, it was more stringent than during the war itself. The food in George Orwell's *1984*, written in 1948, suggests a post-war world in which little had changed: pinkish stew, bread, a cube of cheese and coffee sweetened with saccharine are the regulation lunch. A morsel of real chocolate is a luxury reserved only for the élite. In a December 1945 article called *In Defence of English Cooking* Orwell had looked ahead to the day when good things, including Christmas pudding, would return, and, he hoped, attract tourists to the country. Yet even when rationing ended, food in Britain was often less than stellar because the generation of people who had married at the beginning of the war had only learned wartime stratagems for making do; they had had no chance to play with food, or to use ingredients lavishly. Too often they continued these ways long after rationing and its stringencies had passed. However, while the war stretched a long shadow over life, it also brought changes. A combination of the welfare state and full employment meant that even the working class had enough money to celebrate Christmas with the decorations, foods and presents that had become its essentials. Indeed, the Victorian Christmas has become so entrenched as the 'old-fashioned' or 'proper' Christmas that the Christmases of preceding eras, including both the low-key Eighteenth-Century family Christmas and the long medieval Christmas with its adult games and dances and hunts have been forgotten by almost everyone except historians.

Christmas in children's books

The establishment of the modern Christmas as a holiday that is widely shared means that late-Twentieth-Century writers have not had to campaign for it like Dickens did, nor nowadays strike the more sentimental attitudes toward it that appeared as late as the 1960s in tales such as Agatha Christie's *The Adventure of the Christmas Pudding*. Christmas as the central topic of fiction has migrated to children's books. One typical theme is the reassertion of the magic of Christmas, as Raymond Briggs achieves in his popular *The Snowman* (1978), in which the Snowman comes to life and plays with little James Brighton before whisking him off to the North Pole on a motorbike. There they join Father Christmas and his helpers making toys. James gets a new scarf, and when he wakes next morning he still has it, though the Snowman has melted, leaving only his hat and muffler behind. On the other hand, children's books sometimes suggest that Christmas can disappear – or at least its goodies can – as they do in Dr. Seuss' *How the Grinch Stole Christmas*. When the Scrooge-like Grinch hears the Whos of Whoville getting ready for Christmas, he decides to thwart them by stealing the Who-pudding, the roast beast, and even the Christmas tree. However, on Christmas morning the wise Whos are singing happily because they know that Christmas things are nothing; the Christmas spirit is what counts. Like Scrooge, the Grinch realises what he's been missing, and returns all the stolen stuff.

J.K. Rowling braids together the twin themes of Christmas under attack and Christmas as magic in her *Harry Potter and the Philosopher's Stone*. Harry has never really had a Christmas because the uncle and aunt he lives with hate him. When he stays at Hogwarts School for Christmas he gets presents for the first time: a measly 50p coin from his uncle and aunt, but a whistle from Hagrid, a hand-knitted sweater from Ron's mum, and an amazing invisibility cloak. Then comes Christmas dinner:

> *Harry had never in all his life had such a Christmas dinner. A hundred fat roast turkeys; mountains of roast and boiled potatoes; platters of chipolatas; tureens of buttered peas; silver boats of thick rich gravy and cranberry sauce – and stacks of wizard crackers.*

There's snow and snowballs, and lots of fun with his friend Ron, but the real source of Harry's pleasure is the release from the sorrow of the miserable stolen Christmases he had known at his uncle and aunt's house. At Hogwarts he is entering both the world of magic with its wizard crackers and cloaks of invisibility, and also the everyday world where children expect Christmas presents and Christmas dinners as of right.

Clearly, these stories and the many others like them mine the childhood worry about whether Father Christmas will remember to come, and as time goes by, whether he even exists. When Christmas dawns and the presents are where they ought to be, children's anxieties are released in a flood of joy. Their previous concerns, now assuaged, actually make the day all the better.

Christmas for adults

In Agatha Christie's *The Adventure of the Christmas Pudding* the black-jeaned long-haired Desmond Lee-Wortley scorns Christmas. He suggests that he and his girlfriend Sarah, the granddaughter of his hosts, skip off to Scarborough for the day. Like him, she is an ultra-modern 1960s denizen of Chelsea. She doesn't want to admit to liking anything old-fashioned, but actually she loves Christmas at King's Lacey, just as the young Agatha Christie had loved it at Abney Hall. Agatha Christie cites no source or cause for Desmond's anti-Christmas attitude, though she implies that the rejection of tradition is a symptom of the times, and suggests there's something fishy about him. When her book was published in 1961, Britain was still close enough to wartime austerities and post-war rationing to remember them clearly; the full-scale Christmas with plenty of food was still new to many people, so Desmond's dislike of it raises serious questions about him, especially as a potential husband for Sarah.

However, even as the modern Christmas was taking shape in the Nineteenth Century, there had been a few nay-sayers. In Anthony Trollope's *Orley Farm*, Felix Graham whines: 'I cannot help thinking that this Christmas of ours is a mistake.' He explains:

It is not a mistake in as far as it is in any degree made sacred. But the peculiar conviviality of the day is so ponderous! Its roast-beefiness oppresses one so thoroughly from the first moment of one's waking, to the last intellectual effort at a bit of fried pudding for supper!

His complaint is that the fixedness of Christmas customs makes them a bore. Thackeray, always slightly sceptical about Christmas, agreed. He wrote in his 1862 *Roundabout Papers* essay *On Lett's Diary*:

How stale it has become that printed jollity about Christmas! Carols, and wassail bowls, and holly, and mistletoe, and yule logs de commande. Well, year after year the season comes. Come frost, come snow, come rain, year after year my neighbour the parson has to make his sermons. They are getting together the bonbons, iced cakes, Christmas trees at Fortnum and Mason's now.

Desmond would agree with Thackeray's attack on tediousness here, and today, fifty years after *The Adventure of the Christmas Pudding*, such reservations about Christmas have become quite routine. Every year most magazines and newspapers publish at least one contrarian article criticising Christmas for being too expensive, or too much work, or too commercialised – just too same-old. Set in the context of the dozens of articles that encourage more buying, more decorating, more cooking they suggest ambivalence rather than anything as drastic as serious change.

The mixed attitudes about Christmas show up in Helen Fielding's *Bridget Jones's Diary*. Bridget loves Christmas parties and is terribly upset when she thinks Rebecca hasn't invited her to one. On the other hand, Christmas makes her feel browbeaten by her mother. She gets going early, phoning Bridget at 8.30 a.m. on August Bank Holiday to talk about Christmas plans: notionally about presents, in reality to insist that Bridget come to Una Alconbury's annual New Year's Day Turkey Curry Buffet, where she will meet the marriageable Mark Darcy. In the event, Bridget is late and Mark seems dorkish in bumblebee socks and a diamond-patterned sweater. Nonetheless, she's upset at her apparent failure to appeal to him, and has to console herself with the giant bar of Cadbury's milk chocolate and a gin-and-tonic miniature waiting for such emergencies on her dressing table. Back in London a couple of days later, depressed with going back to work, she buys a bag of cut-price chocolate tree decorations and a cheap bottle of sparkling wine and scoffs the lot plus some leftover Christmas cake, a couple of mince pies and a lump of Stilton – this despite now being on a diet.

Christmas being what it is, the next one is a repeat performance, though with several complications in everyone's relationships. Bridget still feels she is being treated like a child because she is unmarried; she doesn't send cards until the last minute, and has days of doubt about appropriate Christmas presents for friends. She wonders what's the point of everyone running round trying to sort out who would like what, and ending up with a pile of things that have to be carted back to the store. In a solution that suggests Christmas is coming full circle she notes:

If gifts and cards were completely eradicated, then Christmas as a pagan-style twinkly festival to distract from lengthy winter gloom would be lovely.

Another of her ideas is that the government could legislate that we all go out and spend £500 on ourselves, then distribute our purchases to family and friends to wrap up and give to us at Christmas.

Bridget's problems with Christmas suggest that its ideals have been pushed to such an extreme that they have been turned on their head. Family togetherness at Christmas becomes the infantilisation of grown children by parents who insist they return 'home' for the holiday. Gift-giving has become an exercise in either aggression or in fine-tuned calculation as Bridget's mother insists on buying her an unnecessary wheelie suitcase, and she and her friends try to sort out what they should spend on each other. Getting presents is as stressful as buying them. Mark was wearing the ridiculous bumblebee socks and a diamond-patterned jumper only because they had been bought for him. Bridget gets a slow cooker – entirely useless in her case, as following her mother's advice to put in meat and veg before leaving for work is not remotely a possibility, given her habitual morning lateness.

Bridget compares Christmas to war: battles flare between parents and children, between women and their boyfriends, between customers and shops. Yet despite all her suggestions for dealing with the gift problem, she feels the world has become bleaker when her mother announces that she and her brother are old enough to do without presents. Of course, she is delighted when she finds the usual well-packed pillowcase on the end of her bed on Christmas morning. She sums up her ambivalence one early January when, rather than get off to work, she would prefer to stay at home eating chocolate and watching Christmas specials:

It seems wrong and unfair that Christmas with its stressful and unmanageable financial and emotional challenges, should first be forced upon one wholly against one's will, then rudely snatched away just when one is starting to get into it.

Twentieth-Century additions and deletions

While Bridget Jones's mother and Una Alconbury are working together in the kitchen putting crosses on the end of sprouts, Bridget overhears her mother complain that smoked salmon repeats on her, especially when she's had a lot of chocolate brazils. Perhaps surprisingly in a holiday whose foods seem to have been handed down from the mists of time, sprouts, smoked salmon and chocolate brazils are all relatively new foods.

Brazil nuts didn't arrive in England until 1824, and couverture chocolate to cover them was a late Nineteenth-Century development. Delicious as they can be, chocolate brazils do not marry with smoked salmon. However, Bridget's mother would probably not have run into the problem of eating them one after the other earlier in her life, because smoked salmon has only become a widespread Christmas favourite in the last thirty years or so. It originated in fishing communities, especially in Scotland, as a fisherman's way of preserving some of his summer catch for winter use. In the early Nineteenth Century smoked fish could have been rather scorned as poor fishermen's fare, especially as the smoking techniques were less than sophisticated. By the time smoked salmon became more widely known, it was a luxury because wild salmon were scarcer. Until the development of large-scale salmon farming in the last few decades of the Twentieth Century, salmon was prohibitively expensive for all except the very occasional treat. Now, salmon farms produce fish year round and smoking it is a way to use the surplus. This has made it affordable. Its popularity at Christmas may come partly from those days when it was so extraordinarily expensive that it was a Christmas treat. Plus busy cooks like Bridget's mum also value it at Christmas because it is ready to eat straight from the package, so it makes almost instant hors d'oeuvres and starters – though best not served with chocolate brazils.

Brussels sprouts seem to have been known in medieval Europe, but they dropped out of view and the first recipe for them did not appear in an English cookery book until 1845 when Eliza Acton included directions for buttered sprouts to be served on sippets of toasted or fried bread in her *Modern Cookery for Private Families*. Since they grow so well in England, and are at their best around Christmas, they have become an essential Christmas dinner vegetable – so much so that advertisers now have to come up with reminders that they are not just for Christmas, luring customers with details such as a single sprout has more vitamin C than an orange. Since the arrival of sprouts in Britain many other new vegetables have come along: sweetcorn, sweet potatoes, butternut squash, peppers. Any of these might appear in Christmas meals, but none rivals sprouts as essential, though some vegetables keep long-established places as the accompaniment to other dishes. Red cabbage accompanies goose, for example, and chestnuts enrich stuffing (and nowadays also Brussels sprouts). And of course, there must be roast potatoes.

Supermarkets also have a bright array of fruit at Christmas. This, too, is fairly new. Until the middle of the Twentieth Century, apples, pears and citrus fruits from Spain were the only fruits widely available in December. Bananas disappeared during the war and were welcomed back after it, along with pineapples. A few leathery-looking pomegranates were a greengrocer's staple, once used for little except to give to children along with a pin to pick out the seeds. Now their glistening seeds and dark tangy juice are popular ingredients in winter dishes. Being red makes the seeds a natural at Christmas. Strawberries, raspberries, and even cherries are also popular. New technology in agriculture and transport means that they are available for most of the year rather than just a brief two or three weeks of summer. They don't taste as good in December, yet their colour has such a powerful appeal in Christmas trifles and puddings that they have become Christmassy as well as summery.

Farming technology has also ensured that there are many kinds of meat and poultry at Christmas. While turkey and goose remain favourites, with roast beef and duck also common choices, game such as venison, pheasant and other birds are now much more widely available. Families who add a venison pasty or a game pie to the Christmas fare, or pick partridge, widgeon or pheasant for a holiday meal are innovative in the context of most of the Twentieth Century, but if considered in the long view are simply eating foods that have been traditional Christmas fare since the Middle Ages.

Conversely, chocolate and many of the other sweets we now eat would have been either impossible or very rare at earlier times.

Chocolate was brought back to Europe by Sixteenth-Century Spanish conquistadores, and arrived in England in the 1650s. It was served only as a drink. In the Eighteenth Century several cooks published recipes for using chocolate to make creams or a kind of small cake called puffs. However, eating a piece of chocolate straight out of a package or using it as a coating was impossible until the end of the Nineteenth Century because its high cocoa butter content made it sickly and unappetising. When Dutch and Swiss manufacturers solved this problem, chocolate as a sweet took off. By the first half of the Twentieth Century boxes of chocolates were becoming an essential for Christmas as well as other special occasions. As early as 1897 Cadbury's had a product called Christmas Tree Chocolates, and for Christmas 1926 the company produced its first selection box of chocolate bars. In 1938 they began making Cadbury's Roses. They were not intended specifically for Christmas, but they were marketed as what the company calls 'a gifting assortment', and they quickly established themselves as a Christmas treat. The company now notes that Cadbury's Roses outsell frozen turkeys by 50 per cent during the Christmas period.

Roses' rival, Mackintosh's Quality Street, is slightly older. Created by Rowntree in 1936 and named after the popular play of the same name by Sir James Barrie, they used as their logo a picture of Barrie's characters Major Quality and Miss Sweetly to suggest elegance and luxury as well as the salient characteristics of the mixture of chocolates and toffees. A tin of Quality Street quickly became a favourite Christmas purchase, almost as essential as the Christmas pudding – more so to many people. One early advertisement shows Major Quality and Miss Sweetly walking arm in arm with Santa, who is telling them that Quality Street has simplified his job. He explains that he has appointed every confectioner his 'special agent' whose task is to make sure he has a good stock of Mackintosh's on hand for presents. 'How sweet!' says Miss Sweetly. The Christmas gift inspiration is tapped home by an illustration of 'just a few of the many delightful boxes, caskets and fancy tins' used for Quality Street at Christmas.

Luxury has always been important at Christmas. Fresh meat and pies and meat dishes with spices and dried fruit were delicacies in the Middle Ages and beyond. The giant Twelfth cakes and then the cannonball Christmas puddings fed the Victorian enthusiasm for bigger and better. Today anything that is a traditional luxury – a venison pasty, for example, or buttery shortbread or a beautifully iced cake – is welcome at Christmas, and so is anything else that's luxurious. This often includes foreign foods, rediscovered when large numbers of people began to travel to the Mediterranean for holidays in the 1960s and 70s. Some of the things they found have now become commonplace. Packaged panettone from Italy now vies with packaged mince pies in supermarkets in December for example. Also all sorts of European foods including cheeses, jams, sausages, hams, and confections such as nougat and marrons glacés are welcomed at Christmas. Domestic food producers compete with Christmas jam, Christmas chutney, Christmas mustard, Christmas coffee and innumerable other everyday products prefaced with the word 'Christmas'. Apparently they are better than their non-Christmassy equivalents, and their attractive packages appeal to the taste for all things decorative as well as all things delicious for the holiday.

Christmas in the Twenty-First Century

In the seventeen centuries that have passed since Christmas got its start in ancient Rome, it has changed many times, sometimes evolving, sometimes surrendering to pressure. It's a chameleon. It looks different now than it did when Sir Gawain rode from Camelot hunting the Green Knight, or when Pepys entertained with a fine cake on Twelfth Night, or when Jane Austen and her mother hosted a party of friends, serving specialities of the season, but not a feast. Christmas as Dickens saw it in the slums of Nineteenth-Century London probably no longer exists, certainly not for so many. Yet his vision of happiness all round is harder to establish than it seems. One of the rites of passage of children is growing from that excited phase of life so perfectly captured in Dylan Thomas' *A Child's Christmas in Wales* to the realisation of the stresses that can string up a family Christmas. Bridget Jones makes clear how dreadful singles can feel at being swooshed into the hyped-up jollity of the family-centred Christmas, forever under the control of the host and hostess. Yet the nuclear family and child is right at the heart of the Christmas story, so the stereotyped family Christmas is a manifestation of a central fact. Equally, no-one can watch today's rambunctious alcohol-fuelled parties nor the Christmas games and matches that rivet so much attention, without being reminded that games and revelry have always been part of the season. Christmas at the beginning of the Twenty-First Century still retains the lineaments of the Roman Saturnalia and Kalends, the inspiration of the gospel story of Christ's birth, and its long history of enjoying as much as possible of everything that might help to keep winter at bay.

Mistletoe

Mistletoe as shown in the 1633 edition of Gerard's Herbal.

Like holly and ivy, mistletoe has an ancient association with Christmas. All three plants are symbols of life surviving the winter because they stay green and two of them bear fruit. The survival of mistletoe seemed especially miraculous because as a parasite of deciduous trees it has no roots in the ground. This is one source of the association of mistletoe with fertility. The other is the forking paired branches, paired leaves and white berries of the European mistletoe (*Viscum album*), which suggest sexuality. The link with fertility explains the custom of kissing under the mistletoe – a custom found only in England or countries where English immigrants have settled. Though Druids consider mistletoe sacred and particularly value that garnered from oak trees, in fact apple trees are the commonest mistletoe host, so the main mistletoe area in Britain is the apple-growing region around Herefordshire and Worcestershire. In the Nineteenth Century many towns had mistletoe auctions where it was sold to wholesalers who took it to the big cities. In 1849 Henry Mayhew noted that it was the most expensive of the traditional 'Christmasing' greens because it could not be gathered from gardens and hedgerows near London. The last surviving mistletoe auction is at Tenbury Wells on the border of Worcestershire and Shropshire. When the old cattle market where the auctions took place was sold for redevelopment, it seemed that the auctions would cease, but though mistletoe is ancient, its appeal endures in the Twenty-First Century. In 2004 a group of local mistletoe supporters created a Mistletoe Festival to promote mistletoe and keep the mistletoe auctions alive. Auctions now take place just outside Tenbury Wells, and the Festival has become an early December highlight of the town's calendar. Events include the crowning of the Mistletoe Queen and the Holly Prince, a Mistletoe Auction for charity, a Lantern and Santa Parade and a Mistletoe Ball, where mistletoe is *de rigueur* for buttonholes, and of course there are plenty of chances for kissing. Information about the Mistletoe Festival and much more about mistletoe, including how to grow your own, can be found at www.tenbury-mistletoe-festival.co.uk

TURKEY CURRY

In Helen Fielding's novels about Bridget Jones, Bridget's mother browbeats her into going to Una Alconbury's annual Turkey Curry Buffet. And a good thing too: it's where she meets Mark Darcy. Una no doubt makes her turkey curry from leftover turkey but what else she puts in goes unmentioned. Here's a version that has a tomato-onion base (relatively low-calorie at a time of year when calories count). It's an easy, adaptable recipe and one that appeals to adults and children alike. Quantities here depend on how much turkey – and how many people – you have. The following modestly-sized recipe serves 4–6 but can easily be expanded to feed a crowd around a buffet. It works with chicken, too.

5cm/2-inch piece fresh ginger, peeled
3 cloves garlic, peeled
2 tbsp vegetable oil
2 medium-large onions, peeled and chopped
2 tsp medium curry powder, or more to taste
2 425g/15oz tins diced tomatoes in sauce or puree
salt to taste
1 tsp sugar
2 bay leaves
5cm/2-inch cinnamon stick
500g/1lb 2oz cold roast turkey, cut in chunks
2 tbsp mango or other fruit chutney
2 tbsp chopped fresh coriander or parsley

Cut the peeled ginger into 5–6 pieces and put them with the garlic and 125ml/4 fluid ounces of water in a blender. Whizz until they are chopped. (Or chop both by hand and add to the water.) In a deep frying pan or saucepan with a lid, heat the oil over medium heat and cook the onions in it without letting them brown for 3–4 minutes. Stir in the curry powder for about 30 seconds, then add the ginger-garlic mix, the tomatoes, salt to taste, sugar, bay leaves and cinnamon stick. Put on the lid, lower the heat and cook for 10 minutes, stirring occasionally. Add the turkey, and simmer gently for another 10 minutes. Stir in the chutney and half the coriander or parsley, cook for just another minute, then serve with the last of the coriander or parsley sprinkled on top.

PASTA WITH SMOKED SALMON, OLIVES, CAPERS AND LEMONS

Smoking fish such as haddock and salmon was a way to preserve it and the results were not considered luxurious until the Nineteenth Century. Then for many years, smoked salmon was extremely luxurious indeed. Salmon farms now produce so much salmon that it has become an affordable treasure, especially at Christmas. You can team it with some of the olives and capers from your party supplies and toss it with pasta and a lemony sauce for an easy but enticing Christmas Eve supper – traditionally, always a fish meal. Or just serve it when you are desperate for a change from the meaty meals of Christmas or need an alternative for people who don't eat meat.

2–3 lemons
40g/1½oz butter
300ml/10 fl oz double cream
salt and pepper to taste
350g/12oz fettucine or other pasta
8–10 green or black olives, each chopped into 3–4 bits
2 tsp capers, drained
350g/12oz smoked salmon, cut in 2cm/¾-inch ribbons
2 tbsp chopped chives or parsley, or a mixture of the two

Put on a large pan with 3–4 litres/quarts water and some salt to boil for the pasta. Grate the zest from one of the lemons and squeeze 1 or 2 lemons so you have 3 tablespoons of juice. Put the butter, lemon zest and juice into a frying pan and let the butter melt and sizzle for about half a minute. Stir in the cream and let it bubble, stirring often until it has reduced by a third. Season to taste and set it aside. Boil the pasta in the salted water, following the package directions for timing (which varies from one type of pasta to another but usually between 8 and 10 minutes). When the pasta is *al dente*, that is tender but not mushy, drain it, and return it immediately to the hot pan. Reheat the lemon sauce and add it to the pasta along with the olive bits and the capers. Stir over low heat for a minute to warm the cold ingredients, then finally remove the pan from the heat and stir in the smoked salmon ribbons and the parsley or chives. Turn onto a heated platter or plates and serve garnished with more parsley and with lemon wedges. Serves 4.

CHRISTMAS FRUIT AND NUT CAKE

Making your own Christmas cake can seem a daunting task unless you love baking. Here is an easy recipe that ensures a moist cake because the ingredients are boiled. In this recipe the cake is covered with fruit and nuts, but you can omit these and cover it with marzipan and icing if you prefer. This is a big cake; it makes at least 12–16 servings.

For the cake:
280g/10oz soft brown sugar
350g/12oz butter
1 bottle Guinness or other stout
900g/2lb mixed dried fruit
85g/3oz chopped mixed candied peel
85g/3oz glacé cherries
450g/1lb self-raising flour
1 tsp ginger
½ tsp nutmeg
½ tsp cinnamon
pinch powdered cloves
4 eggs, beaten
1 tsp almond essence
115g/4oz blanched almonds or walnuts (optional)
about 175ml/6 fl oz brandy or rum

For the fruit and nuts:
6 tbsp smooth apricot jam
2 tsp brandy or rum
250g/9oz glacé fruits of mixed colours and sorts
85g/3oz glacé cherries
10 whole brazil nuts
12 pecan or walnut halves
16 blanched almonds

In a large saucepan put the sugar, butter and Guinness. Bring to the boil over medium heat then add the dried fruit and candied peel. Simmer for 10 minutes then add the cherries. Take from the heat and let cool.

While it is cooling, preheat the oven to 150°C (300°F). Grease a deep 23cm/9-inch cake tin. Line the base with a double sheet of parchment. Stand parchment paper round the sides, making snips in the bottom to make it fit.

In a large bowl, mix the flour, ginger, nutmeg, cinnamon and cloves. Make a well in the centre and pour in the fruit mixture from the pan. Also add the eggs and almond essence and mix thoroughly. If you are using walnuts stir them in at this point. Turn into the prepared tin. Put the tin onto a baking sheet and bake for 60 minutes, then lower the heat to 140°C (285°F). Lay a sheet of foil on top of the tin to prevent the cake over-browning and continue baking for about 2 more hours or until a knitting needle or skewer poked in the middle comes out clean. Cool in the pan for an hour, and then remove and continue cooling to room temperature. Invert it onto a plate. Poke holes in the top (which used to be the bottom) and pour in some of the brandy or rum. Wrap the cake in clingfilm and a clean cloth. Repeat the brandy or rum soaking at least a couple more times at 2-day intervals.

To finish the cake, warm the jam so it thins down a little. Take from the heat and stir in the brandy or rum. Brush the top of the cake with it. Cut whole glacé fruits such as oranges or pears into attractive pieces. Arrange the fruit, cherries and nuts to cover the top. (If you run out of pieces or don't have enough, either leave a border of cake uncovered or, ideally, fill in spaces with pantry staples such as candied peel or sultanas or dried apricots.) Reheat the jam and brush all over the surface. It's important to get a good cover, so if necessary use extra jam. Transfer the cake to its serving plate. Tie a wide ribbon or band around it. Keep covered with tented aluminium foil.

STREUSEL-TOPPED APPLE AND CRANBERRY MUFFINS

Raisins and currants speckle so many traditional Christmas breads and cakes, that it is a pleasure to see and eat a sunny muffin dotted with crimson cranberries and full of apple flavour. These are good for breakfast at Christmas or any time when you need something quite small to tide you over to the big meal that's on its way.

For the streusel top:
40g/1½oz plain flour
15g/½oz brown sugar
¼ tsp cinnamon
40g/1½oz unsalted butter

For the muffins:
375g/13oz plain flour
140g/5oz sugar
15g/½oz baking powder
½ tsp cinnamon
2 eggs
225ml/8 fl oz milk
70g/2½oz butter, melted
1 large eating apple, peeled, cored and diced into 1cm/½-inch pieces
115g/4oz cranberries
finely grated zest of 2 oranges

Preheat the oven to 250°C (475°F). Line a 12-cup muffin tin with paper liners or grease the cups.

To make the streusel, in a small bowl mix the flour, brown sugar and cinnamon. Cut the butter in small bits and rub it in briefly, stopping when it is mixed in but while you still have a lot of lumps. Set aside.

To make the muffins, mix the flour, sugar, baking powder and cinnamon in a large bowl. Beat the eggs with the milk and then stir in the melted butter. Make a well in the centre of the dry ingredients, and pour the milk mixture into it. Drop the apple pieces, cranberries and orange zest into the liquid, then with a fork stir everything together for no more than 30 seconds. Do not worry if the mixture looks lumpy; it will sort itself out. Divide it among the prepared muffin cups. Sprinkle the streusel on top and put into the oven. Immediately turn down the heat to 200°C (400°F). Bake for 18–22 minutes or until a skewer or wooden toothpick poked in the centre comes out clean. Cool on a wire cooling rack.

FIRST-EVER CHRISTMAS COOKIES

Ever since their invention in the Nineteenth Century we have been enjoying boxes of factory-made biscuits at Christmas. Now American-style Christmas cookies are also becoming popular. In America any cookie that lends itself to being hung on a tree, or, failing that, just tastes richly delicious, can be a Christmas cookie. The custom arrived from Holland with Seventeenth-Century Dutch immigrants, who made butter cookies in a variety of shapes to serve on New Year's Day. Fittingly, the first-ever recipe specifically identified as a Christmas cookie appeared in the first-ever cookery book to be written and published in America: Amelia Simmons' *American Cookery* of 1796. Called simply A Christmas Cookey, the recipe is a richer version of an earlier recipe for a more everyday cookie. It has more butter, more sugar, and significantly, ground coriander seed. Readers were instructed to 'Roll three quarters of an inch thick, and cut or stamp into shape and size you please.' This is a bit thicker than we would like, but of course, you can roll the dough thinner. Here is a contemporary version of Amelia Simmons' recipe. The coriander gives it a mysteriously different flavour. Few people guess what this 'secret' ingredient is.

175g/6oz all-purpose flour
½ tsp baking powder
85g/3oz granulated sugar
1 tbsp (not tsp) powdered coriander
115g/4oz unsalted butter at room temperature
⅓ cup milk or as needed
white icing or icing sugar for serving

Preheat the oven to 180°C (350°F). Grease 2 baking sheets and dust with flour or line with parchment. Mix the flour, baking powder, sugar and coriander. Cut the butter into several bits and rub into the flour mixture as if making pastry. Make a well in the centre, and pour in a little less than ⅓ cup of milk. Pull the mixture together to make a handleable dough, adding more milk if necessary to achieve this. Lightly flour a pastry board and rolling pin. Roll out the dough to ¼-inch thickness. Using cookie cutters or a sharp knife, cut into shapes. Place the cookies on the prepared sheets. If you want to hang them on a tree, take a skewer or knitting needle, poke a hole in what you deem the right spot, and wiggle it about a bit. Bake for about 18 minutes, or until golden brown. Cool on wire racks. Tie a ribbon through the hole and pipe on icing if you want to hang them. Otherwise dust with icing sugar.

SHORTBREAD

In Scotland, there must be shortbread for Hogmanay, and in the rest of Britain too, its butteriness makes it perfect for the season of rich food. Traditionally, shortbread needs no liquid of any form.

375g/13oz unsalted butter at room temperature
175g/6oz caster sugar, plus 2–3 tsp more for finishing
625g/1lb 6oz plain flour
55g/2oz rice flour

Preheat the oven to 140°C (280°F). Grease 2 loose-bottomed 9-inch cake tins or a shallow baking dish and line the base with parchment. Cream the butter for 2 minutes with an electric mixer or 4 minutes by hand. Add the sugar and continue creaming until it looks pale and smoothly creamy. Mix the flour and rice flour then add it to the mixture, stirring or mixing it in until it looks like fine crumbs. Divide this between the two cake tins or dump the whole lot into the dish. Press down with your knuckles to compact it into an even layer. With the point of a knife mark the top into wedges if using the cake tins, or oblong fingers if using the dish. Prick the surface with the tines of a fork, then sprinkle a little sugar on the surface. Bake for 50–60 minutes or until fawn-coloured and buttery-smelling. Cool before removing from the container. An alternative way to shape the shortbread is in a wooden shortbread mould or by forming into a round shape on a parchment-paper-lined baking tray.

MINCEMEAT ICE CREAM

This is the queen of mincemeat recipes. Serve it with mince pies or just on its own. And don't forget about when summer comes; it's just as nice on one of those hot days that seem so unimaginable in winter. You don't need an ice-cream maker to make it.

4 eggs
175g/6oz sugar
350ml/12 fl oz double cream
1 tsp pure vanilla essence
2 tbsp dark Jamaican or Bermuda rum
about 250g/9oz mincemeat
glacé cherries (optional)

Warm a large bowl with hot water, dry it, then beat the eggs in it with an electric mixer or whisk vigorously for 10 minutes by hand until they are bulky and primrose-coloured. Beat in 1 tablespoon of the sugar. When it has been absorbed, beat in another tablespoon. Finally, add in the remaining sugar and continue beating until a noticeable trail or ribbon remains on the surface for several seconds when you remove the beater. In another large bowl, beat the cream until it forms soft clouds. Blend in the vanilla and 1 tablespoon of the rum. With a rubber spatula, fold in a quarter of the egg mixture. Gradually fold in the remaining egg mixture, a little at a time, until it is thoroughly combined. Pour into a plastic freezer box and freeze for an hour or until frozen at the edges. Remove and beat hard, adding the remaining rum. Replace in the freezer for another hour, then stir well again. Stir in half the mincemeat. Freeze for another hour or until it is close to completely frozen. Now stir in the rest of the mincemeat. (Adding it in 2 portions prevents it all falling to the bottom.) Freeze for another 4 hours or longer as convenient. For serving, remove from the freezer about 15 minutes ahead of time to let it soften slightly. You can add Christmassy red glacé cherries, halving them and adding some with the mincemeat and using a few for garnish. Serves 6–8.

CRANBERRY CRUMB TART

Cranberries grow in chilly bogs, and ripen in late September and October. They withstand frost and even ice for several months. Their imperviousness to cold means that unlike most berries you can freeze them without affecting their texture. Keeping a bag or two in the freezer to tide over the months until their season comes round again is a good idea. Sound cranberries bounce; bad ones don't. Because they are a winter crop and, of course, because of their super crimson good looks, they are perfect for Christmas desserts. This crumb tart makes a nice presentation and will be welcomed by anyone who doesn't like mincemeat pie.

For the pastry:
175g/6oz plain flour
pinch baking powder
115g/4oz cold unsalted butter
50ml/2 fl oz single cream

For the filling:
100g/3½oz plain flour
½ tsp baking powder
150g/5½oz brown sugar
125g/4½oz cold unsalted butter
350g/12oz fresh or frozen cranberries, washed and dried
freshly grated nutmeg
100g/3½oz white sugar
1 tbsp icing sugar

Preheat the oven to 220°C (425°F) and grease a deep 23cm/9-inch diameter pie dish with butter. To make the pastry, combine the flour and baking powder in a bowl or in a food processor. Cut the butter into small cubes and rub them in or process until they look like fine crumbs. Make a well in the centre and pour in the cream. With your fingers gently pull the flour mixture into the cream and mix until everything hangs together. (It might be necessary to add a little more cream, a teaspoonful at a time to achieve this.) Roll the dough out into a large circle on a floured surface. Roll it over the rolling pin and place across the centre of the pie dish, unroll and fit it into the dish. Chill in the fridge without trimming the excess from the edge of the dish.

To make the filling, mix the flour, baking powder and brown sugar in a bowl. Cut the butter in cubes and rub them into the flour and sugar to make clumps for the topping. Remove the chilled pie shell from the fridge and trim off the edges. Pour the cranberries into the pie shell. Grate a little nutmeg over them, then sprinkle with the white sugar. Spread the topping on top of the cranberries. Bake for 35–40 minutes until the top is golden brown. Remove and cool on a rack. Serve slightly warm or at room temperature with the icing sugar sifted on top.

CHOCOLATE BROWNIE TART

Chocolate became an important part of Christmas in the Twentieth Century. This easy tart pleases most people, and it can be cut into many slices, each with its own raspberry at the wide end, making it handy when people say 'Just a little for me.'

350g/12oz dark chocolate, chopped in small bits
1 tsp vanilla essence
115g/4oz plain flour
¼ tsp bicarbonate of soda
90g/3¼oz butter
175g/6oz sugar
2 eggs, beaten
about 3 tbsp seedless raspberry or redcurrant jam
16 large perfect raspberries
16 tiny mint leaves or bits of angelica

Preheat the oven to 180°C (350°F). Grease a loose-bottomed tart tin or springform tin measuring 28–30cm/11–12 inches. Line it with parchment. In a large bowl mix the chocolate and vanilla. In another bowl mix the flour and bicarbonate of soda. Heat the butter and sugar along with 2 tablespoons of water in a small saucepan, stirring occasionally to dissolve the sugar. When it boils pour it onto the chocolate mixture. Add the eggs and mix well. Thoroughly blend in the flour. Spread it in the prepared tin and bake in the centre of the oven for 20 minutes or until the edges are set but the centre is still a bit damp. Cool. Warm the jam over low heat. Spread it over the cooled tart. For serving arrange the berries evenly around the edge and tuck a mint leaf or piece of angelica by them. Use a serrated knife to cut into 16 pieces – one berry per serving, or 8 pieces – 2 berries per serving.

TRIFLE

Trifle began life in the late Sixteenth Century as a dish of cream often combined with egg whites and wine. Over the course of the years dry biscuits or almond-tasting ratafias were added until by the Nineteenth Century trifle was recognisably the dish we know today with its layers of sponge, jam or jelly, fruit, custard, cream and a decoration of cherries and angelica or hundreds and thousands – a reminder of the comfits that would have been used in earlier times. It has become a favourite at Christmas as well as at other times of the year, probably because its creamy and fruity flavours are a relief from the heavier spicey flavours of so many traditional dishes. This recipe uses frozen raspberries or strawberries – wonderful if you froze your own in summer, but good also bought from the supermarket. In winter fresh ones are not the best-tasting, but they look attractive waving their little hands from the clouds of cream on top of the layers. The recipe includes a home-made custard, but if you prefer Bird's, as many do, substitute it.

For the base:
About 450g/1lb sponge cake, or Madeira cake or Swiss roll
125ml/4 fl oz sherry
125ml/4 fl oz white wine

For the berries:
280g/10oz frozen sliced strawberries or whole raspberries
85g/3oz sugar, or more to taste
1 tbsp cornflour (more if the berries are very juicy)

For the custard:
2 eggs plus 2 egg yolks
85g/3oz sugar
1–2 tsp vanilla extract
3½ tbsp cornflour
650ml/1 pint 2 fl oz milk

For the topping:
300ml/10 fl oz extra-thick double cream
about 12 strawberries or 24 raspberries

To make the base, roughly crumble the cake and put it in a 1½ or 2-quart bowl. (If you are using a glass bowl and Swiss roll, you can cut the cake in slices and stand them around the sides, leaving a few slices to be crumbled in the base.) Mix the sherry and wine and sprinkle it all over the cake to moisten it. If the cake is very dry, use more wine and sherry to moisten it. Put the frozen berries in a saucepan with the sugar and heat over low heat. Meanwhile stir the cornflour with enough water to make a smooth thin paste. Add some of the hot juices from the pan and then stir the cornflour mixture into the hot berries. Stir until this mixture thickens. Pour it on the cake in the bowl and let cool. To make the custard, fill a large saucepan a quarter full with water and put it on the heat to boil while you work on the custard. In a large bowl, whisk together the eggs, egg yolks, sugar and vanilla. In a small bowl, mix the cornflour to a smooth paste with 125ml/4 fluid ounces of milk, then briefly whisk it into the egg mixture. Heat the remaining milk until it is almost boiling. Pour it into the egg mixture and whisk briefly to blend it in. Take this bowl to the pan of simmering water and place it on top. (Or use a double boiler for this whole operation.) Stir until the mixture thickens, about 4–6 minutes. Gently spoon it over the layer of fruit in the bowl. Cover and chill.

To make the topping, spread the cream on the custard and chill again. You can do this a couple of hours before serving. Just before serving, garnish with the fresh berries. You can add extras such as small mint leaves, hundreds and thousands, silver balls, mini-meringues or tiny amaretti biscuits.

SLOE GIN

In September and October sloes can be found growing in most hedgerows. They look like a large dark berry, usually much smaller than their damson relatives. They are too hard and bitter to be eaten raw and not much better when cooked, but they are the heart and soul of sloe gin, which is delicious. Made in late September or early October, it's ready for Christmas, which is why it was something of a Christmas speciality. On the other hand, it keeps for as long as you can resist it. In the war people were encouraged to forage for wild food, including sloes, but now this free-for-all fruit is often neglected.

500g/1lb 2oz sloes
175g/6oz sugar or more to taste
1 litre/1 quart gin
a drop or two of almond essence

Wash the sloes. Prick each one with a darning needle. Put them into a wide jar that has a lid. Add the sugar and gin and stir. Add the almond essence and stir again. Put on the lid. Stir every day for the first week, then once a week. Store it in a dark place. You can taste to see if you would like more sugar or almond essence. After 8–10 weeks, pour off the liquid into a bottle and discard the sloes. Leave for 3–4 weeks before serving. The longer you leave it, the better it gets.

Stir-Up Sunday

Bridget Jones's mother gets too much of a head start on Christmas when she calls Bridget on August Bank Holiday to make arrangements about presents and turkey buffet that are still four months off. However, Christmas does call for cooks to get going on the work ahead of time. Christmas cake needs feeding with dribbles of brandy or rum, so it has to be made at least a month before it gets its jacket of marzipan and coat of icing. Mincemeat matured for weeks or months is better than freshly made, and Christmas puddings, too, should be made a few weeks beforehand. One reminder to get started in the Anglican collect for Advent Sunday: 'Stir up, we beseech thee O Lord, the wills of thy faithful people; that they, plenteously bringing forth the fruit of good works may of thee be plenteously rewarded.' The call to stir up and the reminder of fruit and the plenteous reward to be expected should get the congregation into their kitchens. Traditionally, everyone in the household should take a turn at stirring the pudding, wishing for something good as they do so. This can be tried when making mincemeat, too.

Bibliography

Buday, George, *The History of the Christmas Card*. London: Spring Books, 1954.

Gulevich, Tanya (2003), *Encyclopedia of Christmas and New Year's Celebrations*. 2nd ed. Detroit, Michigan: Omnigraphics.

Henisch, Bridget Ann, *Cakes and Characters: An English Christmas Tradition*. London: Prospect Books, 1984.

Hieatt, Constance B., 'An Ordinance of Pottage', an edition of *The Fifteenth Century Culinary Recipes* in Yale University Ms. Beinecke 163. London: Prospect Books.

Hieatt, Constance B. and Butler, Sharon, eds, *Curye on Inglysch: English Culinary Manuscripts of the Fourteenth and Fifteenth Century (Including The Forme of Cury)*. Oxford: Oxford University Press for the Early English Text Society, 1985.

Miller, Daniel, ed., *Unwrapping Christmas*. Oxford: Clarendon Press, 1993.

Nissenbaum, Stephen, *The Battle for Christmas*. New York: Alfred A. Knopf, 1996.

Pimlott, J.A.R., *The Englishman's Christmas: A Social History*. Hassocks: The Harvester Press, 1978.

Poston, Elizabeth, *The Penguin Book of Christmas Carols*. Harmondsworth: Penguin Books, 1965.

Spurling, Hilary, *Elinor Fettiplace's Receipt Book*. London: Salamander Press, 1986.

Weightman, Gavin and Humphries, Steven, *Christmas Past*. London: Sidgwick and Jackson, 1987.

Welsford, Enid, *The Court Masque.* Cambridge: Cambridge University Press, 1927.

Wilcox, Susan M. Rossi, *Dinner for Dickens*. Blackawton: Prospect Books, 2005.

Index